COMMUNISM AND GITA

About the Author

Dr. Himmat Singh Sinha (*b.* 1928) passed M.A. in Philosophy from the Punjab University in 1960; stood first in the whole Punjab University (Camp) College and secured second position in the University. He secured his Ph.D. degree from the Meerut University.

He has published two Books in Hindi: (1) *Jnana ki Akarika*, and (2) *Manav Prakritek Adhyayan*. Besides, he has published about 100 articles in various magazines and journals in Hindi, Urdu and English.

He knows English, Persian, Urdu, Hindi, Punjabi and Sanskrit, and is the editor of *Young Thinkers*.

He has to his credit about two decade's of teaching experience and is at present teaching Philosophy in Kurukshetra University.

COMMUNISM AND GITA

A Philosophico-Ethical Study

H.S. SINHA

CONCEPT PUBLISHING COMPANY PVT. LTD.
NEW DELHI-110059

ISBN: 978-93-5594-615-7

First Edition 1979

Published and Printed by

Concept
Since 1974

Concept Publishing Company Pvt. Ltd.
A/15-16, Commercial Block, Mohan Garden,
New Delhi-110059 (India)
T: 91-11-41101460
E: publishing@conceptpub.com, *W*: www.conceptpub.com

To

The Memory Of

My

Late Father

Revered Dr Dalip Sinha

Preface

Man sits atop a nuclear volcano. The threat of global destruction dangles before him. Existence is itself a torture.

Yet man's spiritual regeneration has to come from within himself. History has placed many an option before him. Marx who wrote the most powerful indictment against industrial civilization assured the groaning masses that a new world devoid of exploitation and suffering can be created by man in this world.

On the other side of the horizon at another critical moment of history a philosophy of crisis evolved. This is the philosophy of Gita which assures humanity that Divine will always stand by those who are fighting for justice. Can Gita which inspired Indians for thousands of years find an answer to the crucial problems of the contemporary world ?

Which of these two philosophies can be the foundation of a new social order ? At the face of it "Scientific materialism" and the doctrine of "Selfless devotion" seem to be opposed to each other. But are they really so ? There are some of the questions to which answers have been sought in this book.

This Comparative study owes much to Dr R.N. Sharma, Head of the Department of Post-Graduate Studies and Research in Philosophy, Meerut College, Meerut. Words cannot repay indebtedness to him. I express my gratitude to my close associates Prof. M.L. Gupta and Dr Prem Sagar Sharma. My thanks are also due to Dr B.L. Sharma, Head of the Department of Philosophy University College, Kurukshetra, and Dr S.P. Varma, of the same University. I also gratefully acknowledge the cooperation and help rendered by Janabe Chand Sahab, University Library, Kurukshetra and Shri M.L. Gupta, Librarian, M.L.N. College, Radaur by providing me with all possible library facilities. My cousin Rajiv Sinha have helped me in numerous ways.

Thanks are also go to Shri A.N. Sachdev, who devoted special attention in typing this manuscript.

Last, but not least a number of my students have come forward at various stages of my research to help me. My sincere thanks to them also.

Department of Philosophy,
Kurukshetra University,
KURUKSHETRA—132119 (Haryana)

H.S. SINHA

Contents

	Preface	vii
1	A New Look at Communism	1
2	Anasakti Yoga of Gita	38
3	Philosophical and Cultural Influences	80
4	The Ideal Social Order	106
5	Concept of Social Justice	136
6	Varna Vyavastha vs. Classless Society	153
7	Ideals of Human Life	178
8	Ethical Basis of Human Progress	202
9	Means and Ends	224
10	The Confluence and the Divergence	244
	Bibliography	271
	Index	285

1

A New Look at Communism

Need for Ethical Approach

In every age of crisis man pauses to reflect on his own destiny. Every such age finds its own social thinkers who find a way out. Any possible annihilation anticipated by that crisis is thus warded off. They search for the *vera causa* of the human miseries; they reflect on the factors responsible for these sufferings and how they can be removed. All significant generalizations about socio-cultural processes have indeed appeared either in the period of serious social exigency, catastrophe and transitional disintegration or as Sorokin points out,[1] immediately "before and after such periods." *Avtāras* in India and the Prophets in other lands are the products of such crises. The book of Daniel was also written at a debaculous moment in Jewish history. It was under convulsive conditions of the Roman history that St. Augustine came forward with the Christian philosophy of history. The great doctrines of Bhagavadgītā were narrated to Arjuna at the time of his despondency, specially when he was facing one of the greatest moral crisis ever faced by man. Not only that, but crisis was so deep and far-reaching that the Divine narrator entered into a covenant declaring that whenever negativistic and indifferent attitude prevails over social and moral values, the Divine forces would immediately reveal themselves to resolve the crisis generated by such decline of virtues. It was in conformity with this recurrent tradition of human history that Marx also enunciated his epoch-making philosophy of communism to resolve the crisis of early 19th century Europe.

"Philosophers have sought to interpret the world ; what matters is to change it", wrote Marx. Any question improving or restructing the society involves choice between good or bad. Hence it is primarily an ethical problem. Judged from this view, the present crisis is neither economic nor ideological, but in the last analysis it is moral and spiritual. Since western materialism has not been able to meet the challenge, humanity today stands in need of a moral regeneration.

The growing despair and tensions have made the Western thinkers realize that materialism has no answer to present-day conditions of the man's alienated existence. Unless man reflects on his essential nature and his fundamental goodness, he will continue to feel frustrated and lost in the world of objects. This sinful neglect of the man's inner life and over-emphasis on the opportunities for aggrandizement has destroyed the meaningfulness of his life. Thus haunted by the discontent of civilization, man is gradually becoming hostile against himself and his environment. In his endless quarrel with the hostile world, he has developed ever more deadly weapons of murder and destruction. In doing so, he has, unconsciously or consciously, started asking whether such social order is worth maintaining while individuals are unhappy in it. Karen Horney corroborates this fact that "the constructive possibilities stem from man's essential nature, from the core of his being, from what we call his real self. Man turns unconstructive only if he cannot fulfil himself—that it is an unfulfilled life which makes him barren or destructive."[2]

Gita and communism both take into cognizance the imperfections and miseries of the present state of affairs. Both want to change the present system in favour of a higher and better form of existence. Such desire of finding some remedies for the human miseries has been the dominant note of Indian systems. Indian philosophy starts with the practical problem and the empirical fact of human miseries. The most striking and fundamental point of agreement (of all Indian systems) is that all the systems regard philosophy as a practical necessity and cultivate it in order to understand how life can be best led. The oriental philosophic wisdom aims at not merely the satisfaction of intellectual curiosity, but its main emphasis is the enlightened life. Anāsakti Yoga of Gita represents this attitude of Indian mind. Communism too in the words of Afanasyev "sprang from profound humanist motives and their main concern was to give the people of the new society the conditions for a real human existence for developing and improving their talent."[3] Marx writes, "The main princip e which must guide us in the selection of a vocation is the welfare of humanity and our own perfection."[4] Both these philosophies agree that fundamentally philosophy must be intimately related to life.

Throughout his voluminous work *Das Capital* Marx has depicted the dehumanizing conditions of the English society where exploitation of women and children led to incredible sufferings. Consequently, communism emerged as a philosophy of the liberation of mankind. Although Anāsakti Yoga of Gita agrees on this issue with communism, that escapism is no solution, yet there is a difference of approach in making the life worth living. Consequently, they have come for ward with different value-systems with difference in the institutional means proposed to realize these values.

What is Communism

Communism is the name given to the philosophico-ethical doctrines formulated by Marx. It has meant different things to different thinkers. Volumes and volumes have been written to project the image of communism as a political system and a political theory. But rarely has the ethical dimensions of communism treated adequately. Some other writers try to read communism as a theory of economic reconstruction or a theory of economics. Few of such studies have really understood that the primary concern of Marx was ethical and his interest in political and economical fields was secondary, to the extent as to how far these can be instrumental to the realization of the ethical ideal. The goal posited by Marx was to end the corruptive and demoralizing effect of the mechanistic civilization and to liberate man from these conditions. He raised a rebellious voice against the disparities in the western civilization.

In order to understand the ethical aspect of communism, one must have a peep into the conditions into which it was born. Whitehead summed up the conditions, that 'the western world is now suffering from the limited moral outlook of the three previous generations.'[5] This narrow outlook of the West was putting an embargo on human freedom, dignity, and aspirations. Marx duly realized this state of affairs, and if the solution offered by Marx is read in this context, then the goal of redemption, put forth by Marx, would be just like the ideal of the Kingdom of God, the Paradise, the Christian salvation or *Nirvāna*. Afanasyev's following definition of communism, also corroborates this view.

> "Scientific communism is thus a science dealing with the ways and means of destroying capitalism, with the laws governing the creation of the new, communist society and with the economic, social and spiritual conditions for the all round development of man."[6]

It is obvious from the above statement of the official exponents of the doctrine that the final aim of communism is 'all round development of man' and the economico-political considerations have mere instrumental use. These do not have any intrinsic value. The destruction of capitalism as a pre-condition for the construction of the communist society has been emphasized by Marx himself. He wrote in the Preface to *Das Capital* that the ultimate aim of this work was to "lay bare the economic law of motion of modern society in order to prophesy its fate."[7] But why did he want capitalism to be destroyed? According to Marx, this is to be done as a means for the realization of higher ideal which lies beyond, far beyond the communism itself. "Communism", wrote Marx, "is for us not a stable state which is to be established, an *ideal* to which reality will have to adjust itself. We call communism the *real* movement which abolishes the present state of things."[8] Accordingly, communism cannot be taken as a static utopia. Rather, in the words of Marx himself, "Communism...is the actual phase necessary for the next stage of historical development in the process of *human emancipation and recovery*."[9] It is clear, then, that Marx had a clear conception of human individual as striving for 'emancipation' from the bonds of economic determinism and his theory was oriented to rediscover his 'original and real nature', to realize his real self. It is a picture of man as striving for his self-perfection and self-realization. Marx first of all in his early writings, laid down the basic framework of his moral theory as to how the dehumanised man is to become real 'man' and thereafter, in *Das Capital* and in *Communist Manifesto* he worked out the dynamics of world revolution to achieve this moral ideal. Let us make a detailed survey of what communism is and what it is not.

Sovietization of Communism :

To most people communism, is just the economico-political activity going on in the Soviet Union.[10] But in its deeper understanding, it will be evident that Soviet political system is not the same thing as the philosophical 'communism'. No one would deny that the doctrines of communism have played highly significant role in fashioning the destiny of the Soviet society. Showing the impact of the communism on the contemporary Soviet culture, Northrop says[11] that "Russia is what it is today, not because there was any necessity that it be that way but largely because the leaders of the Russian revolution took the speculative philosophical theory of Marx and built political action and cultural institutions in terms of it." Sorokin also holds more or less the similar views when he points out that the "Marxian-Hegelian philosophy is the key to a comprehensive explanation of total Soviet culture."[12]

But the other side of the picture can also not be denied that in passing from one culture to the other, communism changed its hue and lost most of its original features. This was probably due to the vast difference between the cultures of the origin of communism and the land of this application. "The Russian soul", according to the assessment of Spengler, "is will-less having the limitless *plane* as its prime symbol. It is not the soul and culture of 'I' the Ego, nor of individualism, but of the 'we', of collectivity. It condemns 'I' as a sin."[13] In such a transmission from one culture to the other, the teachings of communism were most likely to be distorted. This is a normal phenomenon in cultural interaction. Dynamics of cultural transmission follows the principle that if the culture of departure and culture of infiltration differ, the migrating cultural phenomenon changes and the greater the difference of two cultures, or persons, or of groups, the more it changes. This is exactly what happened when communism went to Russia.

The Sovietization of communism also rendered it into a political doctrine relegating its ethical aspect to the background. Due to this omission, the philosophical part of its theory of historical materialism was so much distorted that Wayper thus denounces. Lenin's book *Materialism and Empirio-Criticism* in which the meta physical foundations of Marxism were reinterpreted, "it is a dreadfully dull repetitive dogmatic and superficial survey, chiefly of note for its crude notion of materialism, hardly different from the materialism of Feuerbach which Marx attacked."[14] Not entering into the historical details, how the communist doctrines were modified to suit the Soviet requirement, we may conclude that despite the reverence that Lenin had towards original teachings of Marx, he was instrumental in introducing more changes in the master's doctrine than any other professional follower of his. In applying communism, he was concerned with adapting it to the peculiar socio-cultural fabric of Russia, as the conditions necessitated without caring for the theoretical consistency. Sabine has rightly said that "Lenin's formula remained the formula of Marx. The meaning of Leninism departed very widely from the meaning of Marx."[15]

Lenin, himself, however, admitted that through the Soviet experiment they were trying to go towards communism. In its existing form, it can be called communism only by courtesy. Lenin writes, "In so far as the means of production become common property, the word 'communism' is also applicable here, providing we do not forget that this is not complete communism."[16] It would, not therefore, be advisable to evaluate the Soviet System in a bid to understand the ethico-philosophical doctrines of communism.

Not Merely Economics :

It is a common belief that communism is an economic theory. *Das Capital* the title of Marx's *magnum opus*, is in itself misleading and so are his off-quoted some of pronouncements. For example, Marx wrote in *The Critique of Political Economy* that the mode of production of material life conditions the social, political and intellectual life process in general."[17] The same thing was reiterated by Engels in the Preface to the *Communist Manifesto*.[18]

But an analysis of such writings will show that they lack economic fervour. On the testimony of learned economists, Whitehead points out that *Das Capital* does not express a sound scientific doctrine which will stand comparison with the facts. The success of the book can then be accounted for by the magnitude of the evils ushered by the first phase of the industrial revolution."[19] Clarifying that Marx has used the term 'economic' in a very technical connotation in his materialism, another thinker points out that "when Marx says that history and politics depend on man's economic struggle, the term 'economic factor' is very crucial because Marx has used it in a broad variety of connotation, e.g., technological means of production, legal relations of private property or ownership of means of production, natural resources, labour, and struggle for existence in human society."[20] From this, it is obvious that Marx was not writing a book on the economics as the term is generally understood.

If a close analysis of the *Das Capital* is made, it becomes evident that this is not a book of political economy. It is rather a criticism of the political economics from a moralist point of view, probably in the same way in which Carlyle and others castigated economics as the 'Gospel of Mammon', 'a dismal science'. His disparaging attitude towards economics is also revealed from one of the letters which he wrote to Engels[21] wherein he called the economic literature that he was studying an 'economic filth'. The whole purpose of writing *Capital* was to show, in the terminology of economics, i.e., in terms of 'labour' and 'capital', that man is alienated from himself when, under the domination of egoistic needs, he externalises his productive power in the form of money.

The theory of surplus value which is often quoted as the central theme of Marxian economics, nowhere, throughout the *Capital* admits of any economic interpretation. What Marx wanted to stress through this theory was that ; (i) the motivating force of production in the capitalist process is surplus value which is the self-expansion of capital ; and (ii) the labour power spent in the quest for surplus value, which is called 'wage labour' is 'humanity in bondage' which is to be released from its fetters. Already in the essay *On the Jewish Question*, Marx touched upon this theme. He called the economic life in civil society, 'the extreme practical expression of human self-alienation.'[22] He also called it 'material' or 'political-economic alienation' and this is the dominating theme around which the whole fabric of *Capital* has been woven. The economic terminology has been used with a view to convey this idea of alienation to the common readers.

Marx wrote in the Preface to the *Capital* the famous passage, "In Hegel's writings Dialectic stands on his head. You must turn it right way up again if you want to discover the rational kernel that is hidden away within the wrappings of mystification."[23] However, realizing that Hegelian philosophy is too difficult to be grasped by a lay reader, he expressed his desire in a letter written to Engels in 1858[24] that he wanted to make accessible to the ordinary human intelligence in two or three printers sheets, what is rational in the method of Hegel but at the same time enveloped in mysticism. After the expression of this desire whatever Marx wrote, was for the 'man of ordinary intelligence' and not for the men of philosophical insight. It is natural that when high philosophical principles are rendered into the cast and moulds of common mind, they become over-simplified. This is why Karl Lowith points out that 'the talk of so-called material basis etc., is 'vulgar Marxism'.[25] If the whole literature of Marx from 1844, when Marx started writing *Philosophical and Economic Manuscr pts*, till the writing of *Das Capital* is gone through, it would become evident that Marx never became a political economist as such; he always remained a bitter critic of political economy which, in the light of the definition given by Adam Smith, was considered to be a science of earthly accumulation of capital. Even in *Das Capital*, Marx does not deal with the laws of economics, but with the mechanism as to how the forces immanent in it, work its destruction inevitably. At best if any classification is to be made this can be called 'History' and not 'Economics'.

Dehumanizing Effects of Greed :

If we read *Capital* from beginning to end, we shall come to realize that the whole drama at the heart of *Das Capital* is a representation of man being dehumanized and destroyed by a tyrannical force of acquisitiveness that has grown autonomous within humanity. This force represented by capitalist, controls the movements of society, usurps all the life-energies, torments humanity mercilessly but drives its possessor, the capitalist, relentlessly to aggrandizement for the sake of aggrandizement and ultimately ruins the social life. At the same time, the dehumanized victims of compulsive drive towards absolute enrichment, are aware of this 'dehumanization' and they rebel against the force responsible for reducing them to this state. In this acquisitive mania, Marx sees a 'will-to-power' in pecuniary disguise. Quoting Luther's lengthy study of the usurers, Marx shows that love for power is an element in the impulse to acquire wealth. Marx writes " 'Usurer' wants to be God over all men, and so does the capitalist."[26]

Marx denounces this acquisitive drive so much that sometimes it appears as if he is preaching to the people to shun all desire for wealth and to avoid the worldly pursuits of wealth. It is due to this damnatory attitude towards the acquisitiveness, which is reflected recurrently in Marx's writings, that Prof. Tucker comes to conclude that "world-denial is a theme running through the writing of his mature and later years, as well as the early years... and for all its tortuous elaboration of abstract concepts *Capital*, his supreme achievement, was in its way, a nine-hundred-page-cry of pain and outrage against the bourgeois civilization."[27]

Like the first Noble Truth of Buddhism that all is suffering, the *Capital* is also a picture of wide-spread misery and discontent The capitalist society has been depicted as a scene of the growing inequality of wealth, untold riches accumulated by minority of avaricious capitalists and masses sinking deep into miserable poverty. The whole earth, for Marx, is a scene of a process of production motivated by capitalists' boundless drive for self-expansion. The lust for more and more profits is never satisfied. It increases with the increase in surplus profits. Impelled by this ever-increasing greed, the capitalist searches for newer avenues for multiplying his production. The great bulk of all that it produces is turned into dead capital which weighs down upon its creators 'like an incubus'. To quote Marx himself, "just as in the sphere of religion, man is dominated by creature of his own brain, so in the sphere of capitalist production, he is dominated by the creatures of his own hand."[28]

This dead capital is accumulated in the form of machines. The mechanized modes of production bring a tremendous increase in the surplus value but the capitalist further invests it in increasing more machine instead of spending this surplus on the welfare of those who are the creators of this surplus profit. However, the capitalists can't help it as he is under the sway of greed. Marx tells us that "the end and aim of capitalist production is an endeavour to promote to the uttermost the self-expansion of capital, meaning thereby the production of the largest possible amount of surplus value and therefore the maximum possible exploitation of labour power by the capitalist."[29] Through his theory of 'surplus value', Marx had exposed that greed, lust, and material attachment are the sole ingredients of exploitation. He writes. "Capital, in its unbriddled passion for self-expansion develops a greed for surplus value, an impulse to suck labour dry or a vampire thirst for the living blood of labour."[30] To express his moral indignation and improbation, he uses frequently in *Capital* such vituperative terms as 'ruthless', 'insatiable' and diabolically sadistic force of greed confiscates every atom of freedom.'[31]

Marx in *Das Capital,* paints a disparaging picture that capitalism is inhuman because it wants to extract all energy of the worker for the sake of satisfaction of his own selfish desire, just as in Argentina, a whole beast is slaughtered simply in order to get its hide or its tallow. The whole system of capitalist production is vicious because it transforms the worker into a cripple, a monster, by forcing him to develop some highly specialized dexterity at the cost of a world of productive impulses and faculties.[32] From this description, it is clear that Marx is condemning capitalism because a worker is not treated as 'an end' under capitalist production. When humanity is treated as a 'means' for the pleasure of the greedy, it is a sign of moral decadence and it reflects the viciousness of the system itself. Marx laments this state of affairs and says that "a worker is a tormented man who mortifies his body and ruins his spirit in productive activity performed under compulsion of greed.[33] The moral disgust of Marx is also reflected in the frightful picture of the industrial labour that he paints in *Capital.* After quoting lengthy references from the report of various British factory inspectors and the Royal Enquiry Commission, he compares the factory life as being worse than hell and then disdainfully remarks, "Dante would have found the worst horrors of his Inferno surpassed in this manufacture."[34] There are numerous passages in this book which depict the same tale of misery.

All these pronouncements of Marx show that although the terminology used in *Das Capital* has been derived from the economist Adam Smith, the tone of crit'cism is moral and religious. At various places, Marx has taken recourse to the realm of religion explicitly for the explanation of his case and castigating the tendency of money worship. Marx himself writes :

> "To find an analogy, we must enter the nebulous world of religion. In fact the products of human mind become independent shapes, endowed with lives of their own and able to enter into relation with men and women. The products of the human hand do the same thing in the world of commodities."[35]

Marx had said the same thing in some of his other passages also. In his essay *On Jewish Question*, the same attitude, that under the spell of greed men start worshiping money, has been reflected in other words. The sum and substance of this whole essay is that money is the alienated essence of man's work and his being. This alien being rules over him and he worships it. What Marx wanted to convey through these passages, is that when capitalism prevails, humanity is purchased like a marketable commodity and money becomes the god of lustful and greedy persons. In Marx's own words, "when it becomes possible to hold-fast to a commodity as exchange value or to exchange value as a commodity, the greed for money awakens."[36]

The contention of Marx is that previously there was no exchange in terms of money. Man used to produce for the fulfilment of his biological and social needs but he never hoarded or stored his production by converting them into gold. At that time the labour power of man was not measured in terms of money and in terms of gold. But the people exchanged their products according to their requirements and their needs. However, when money-exchange system was invented, man started converting his products into gold and everything including his own labour power was measured in terms of money. The greed awakened when the 'gold-exchange-system' replaced the old system of man's needs being the sole measure of the value of things, the society became a victim of greed, of possessing more and more gold. Marx refers to this historical episode and says, "Modern society which when still in its infancy, pulled Pluto by the hair of his head out of the bowels of the earth, acclaims gold, its Holy Grail, as the glittering incarnation of its inmost vital principle."[37] Since for the capitalist money is the universal power, Marx resolved to end this degenerated and dehumanized society where people worship money and where humanity is sold as means of production, a marketable commodity.

This sort of strictures on 'money-exchange-system', a round which whole economics revolves, shows clearly that the aim of Marx was not to write a theory of economic planning, of production and distribution, but to ostracize the economic system as such and to vilify those who want to keep monetary considerations in determining the value of things as superior to the humanitarian considerations and even to human beings themselves. This moral zeal, continued till he concludes his *Das Capital* with a revolutionary denouncement : "The knell of capitalist property sounds. The expropriators are expropriated. It is negation of a negation."[38] This sounds like the pronouncement of a curse on the sinners against humanity who misappropriate the surplus production for their selfish ends.

Against Religion and Mammon :

Our contention that the approach to Marx in vituperating the economic modes of human existence was religious, is substantiated on another ground also. One of the signs of religious thinking is that the natural forces and human qualities are personified to play their role in the world-drama. Indian and Greek mythologies are full of such personifications. Marx has also used this process of 'personification' and symbolizing to narrate the story of the struggle between good and evil. In *Das Capital* the image of society has been projected as a split-personality in which the urge to self-aggrandizement is on the one side in the form of capitalist and the creative power, in the form of labour is on the other side. Marx uses personifying attribute for the collective 'Capital-personality' and calls it 'Monsieur Capital' or 'My Lord Capital.'[39] Similarly, the collective labour-personality is described as 'The Collective Worker', when Marx says, "It is the totality of the labour force of society and the "Individual Worker' is an organ of the 'Collective Worker'."[40] The way of presentation is also like Paurāṇic story telling. In *Das Capital,* the social scene has been depicted as the arena where *My Lord Capital*, the infinitely greedy, despotic, exploiting, vicious, werewolf and the *Collective Worker*, he exploited, enslaved, tormented, rebellious but productive, are fighting out the war for humanity. In this whole drama, *My Lord Capital* sows the seed of his own destruction due to his own lustful deeds.

Marx narrates the tale saying that "fanatically bent upon the expansion of value, he relentlessly drives human beings to production for production sake, thus bringing about a development of social production and the creation of those 'material conditions of production' which can alone form the real basis for a higher type of society, whose fundamental principle is the full development of every individual."[41]

What are those material condition which the capitalism creates for its own destruction and the building of a new society ? According to Marx the general law of the capitalist accumulation is that the collective worker sinks deeper and deeper into an abyss of misery. Marx himself states that "the accumulation of wealth at one pole of society involves a simultaneous accumulation of poverty, labour, torment, slavery, brutalization and moral degradation at the opposite pole where dwells the class that produces its own product in the form of capital."[42] In this whole drama when a point is reached at which the despotism of Lord Capital becomes absolutely unbearable, the 'Worker' wrests the world of alien wealth from "My Lord Capital" by destroying the monster. The gist of the whole story is that the capitalist is a personified form of a single life urge, i.e., the urge to self-expansion. He is greed incarnate, the living symbol of *Iṣaṇa* and *lobha.*

Numerous such passages can be quoted from *Das Capital* which substantiate our view that it is not a treatise on economics. This attitude of deprecating economics from moral and humanitarian point of view is continuous in him from beginning. In his early writings also Marx had consistently been expressing his indignation against the political economy. As Prof. Tucker has rightly pointed out, the main concern of Marx seems to expose that the only wheels that set political economy in motion are greed and the war between the greedy—competition.[43] Greed, according to Marx is 'lust for money', a veritable fanaticism of appropriation of the world of created things. In so defining greed Marx seems to have come very close to Gita's concept of '*lobha*', *dhanamānamada* and 'parigraha'. It is an acquisitive mania in the capitalist that sees in money, means of exercising power over everything. At another place, when Marx was writing an essay *On the Jewish Question*, he also presented the idea that 'the economic life in the state of egoism' is a practical religion of money-worship—a religion in which money is the god. Marx himself writes, "Money dethrones all the gods of man and turns them into a commodity. It has deprived the whole world of man and nature, of its own value. Money is the alienated essence of man's work and his being. This alien being rules over him and he worships it.[44]

This is an unhealthy affair that instead of worshipping humanity, instead of showering love over his own fellow-beings, man worships money and devotes all his energies in acquiring, safeguarding and further augmenting this alienated thing. This sort of things is really condemnable, because so long as the things go on as they are, the lovers of humanity will not find solace in it. Hence Marx rejects the existing state of human existence and goes on further to say that "the modern commercial world where man is universally dominated by the egoistic need, is, practically speaking, a world of those whose practical religion is money."[45] It was to this religion of money-worship that Marx later on gave the name 'capitalism'. It is obvious now that the purpose of writing *Das Capital*, was to exterminate this defiling creed of money-worship from the world of man and to enthral humanity once again. On no consideration, this can be called 'economics'.

On the basis of the above description of the contents and background of *Das Capital*, we should not hesitate to say that the Marxian approach is moralistic and sometimes like a religious man. Tucker rightly says that "Marxism is essentially a moralistic system ; that it stands or falls as ethical and that *Capital* is a moral treatise in economic disguise."[46]

As a matter of fact, while formulating the basic postulates of his philosophical system, it was in his *Economic and Philosophic Manuscript of 1844*, that Marx had described the passion of greed that holds sway over everything, as the worst enemy of mankind. This served as an *a priori* premises and *Das Capital* seems to be a bid to fill empirical evidence and factual data from the history of capitalism. The purpose of *Das Capital* seems to be to prove the hypothesis of the inhumanity of this inhuman force to the extreme. In the light of this, any search for 'economics' in this treatise is bound to result in failure.

Meaning of Economic Interpretation :

A critic at this point may draw our attention to Marx's fundamental concept of economic interpretation of history which *inter alia* says that the 'relation of production' tend to determine the consciousness of man.[47] But it is the misunderstanding of this para of the *Critique* that has given rise to many serious misconceptions about Marx's doctrine of communism. When Marx says that the economic structure of society determines the social consciousness of man, he is describing a socio-historical fact, which he regards as man's alienated condition of existence. When he is exposing the dehumanized nature and corruptive influence of the industrial and capitalist society, which he wanted to destroy, he is also expressing his indignation to the prevailing order of the society in which the relations of production have an over-riding sway in forming and deforming human relations and man as such is divested of his creative freedom to exercise his control over the economic factors. As brought out by Marcuse,[48] Marx emphasizes time and again that his materialistic starting point is forced upon him by the materialistic quality of the society he analysed. Marx had no love for the "realm of necessity", which he considered as the society in bondage to its material needs and he cherished the vision of the "realm of freedom", about which he writes "Beyond it begins that development of human power which is its own end, the true realm of freedom.[49] Engels also confirms this when he says "at this point (at the level of communism) man in a certain sense separates finally from the animal world, leaves the conditions of animal existence behind him and enters conditions which are really human......it is humanity's leap from the 'realm of necessity' in 'the realm of freedom'.[50]

It is at the level of bondage then that man's social relations are 'determined' by economic factors. The communist revolution will relieve man from the bonds of materiality meaning thereby that when man is liberated from the drive for accumulation or capital-formation, man will produce in order to realize his real nature as 'being with manifold creative capacities'. It means that so long as man does not leave the conditions of his animal existence', his behaviour and his consciousness will be determined by the economic modes of existence. But when man enters the era of communism which is the era of his freedom, the economic modes will not determine his productive behaviour. But then his consciousness will be determined by his own real nature. Engels adds : (when communism prevails) "the productive labour instead of being a means to the subjection of man, will become a means to their emanicipation by giving each individual the opportunity to develop and exercise all his faculties, physical and mental in all directions.[51] At this level the economics will not determine the course of human history which it is determining at the level of man's animal existence. It will rather be transformed into higher. Another author points out, "at the level of communism, man will realize his natural tendency to arrange things according to the laws of beauty. Economic activity will turn into artistic activity. The alienated world will give way to the aesthetic world.[52] It becomes evident, on this account, that upto the level of capitalism which is dehumanized state of human existence, man's consciousness is determined by economic factor. However, he wanted to finish this dehumanized state of affairs and with that also the economic determination which is a bane of man's pre-historic existence. Accordingly, communism is a trans-economic theory which wants man to be liberated from the bondage of economics.

In his earlier writings Marx defines communism as the transcendence of human self-alienation.[53] In other writings he has been labouring to lay down the fundamental principles which are the pre-requisites of and implied by this transcendence. To understand this concept of transcendence, we shall have to seek help from Hegelian philosophy. Transcendence in Hegel's philosophy has a technical connotation which signifies ; (i) destruction and (ii) preservation. The transcended object is destroyed *qua* object or 'other' but preserved as mental content. It is, as Prof. Tucker points out, the spirit's way of rebelling against finitude, against fetters and making a break-through for freedom.[54] Marx seems to have followed this concept in the formulation of his theory.

While laying down the material conditions of communism, Marx deviated from the classical materialism of the west and called his own theory as 'new materialism'.[55] On the basis of this new approach, he criticised all the past doctrines of materialism because they failed to grasp the external material objects as the 'mater alization' of human activity. In the Ist Thesis on Feuerbach, Marx writes : "The chief defect of all materialism upto now (including Feuerbach's) is that the object, reality, what we apprehend through our senses is understood only in the form of the 'object' or 'sense perception' but not as sensuous human activity, as practice, not subjectively. Hence in opposition to materialism, the active side was developed abstractly by idealism, which, of course, does not know the real sensuous activity as such.[56] It is evident that Marx did not enter into the arena to side with those who try to understand the external world either in terms of the sub-atomic entities or of the sense-data. Nor he entered into such metaphysical superfluities as of distinguishing the 'sensuous objects' from the 'objects of thought'. For him, the 'practical activity of man', as distinguished from the cognitive activity, was the real 'material reality', which the materialist should take into account. Obviously, this activity includes man's subjectivity as well. Marx makes his position more clear when he says that Feuerbach's error was the failure to comprehend 'the sensuous world as the total living sensuous activity of the individuals composing it.[57] The classical and the mechanical materialists would not agree to this position of Marx because here Marx is clearly asserting that the material world is the *materialization* of human activity, the externalization of 'humanity'. The idealists, if they like, can own Marx because of his emphasis on the 'subjectivity', the 'human activity', but the only thing that has turned him to the camp of materialists is his conviction that 'of course in all this, the priority of external nature remains unassailed.[58]

From the above statements of Marx, it becomes clear that the term 'materialism' in the philosophy of Marx does not have a physical, mechanical or physiological connotation. It is only indicative of an approach to the understanding of human history, in contradistinction with the idealist approach. This approach is reflected in the various writings of Marx. For example, at one place, he says, "Man who is fundamentally a *productive being*, produces mentally as well as materially. As a worker he produces non-conceptual objects in the course of 'material life-process', 'material activity', or 'material production of life'.[59] Marx wanted that this productive aspect of man which is for him the 'real life process' or 'practical developmental process of man' must be given priority in understanding the human history. He, therefore, stressed that the fundamental principle of his materialism was that 'life is not determined by consciousness, but consciousness by life'.[60] By this principle of materialism Marx wanted to emphasize that man cannot think or even cannot live without producing the material means of his existence. This position is re-asserted at another place where he says, "The mode of production of material life conditions the social, political and intellectual life process in general. It is not the consciousness of man that determines their being, but on the contrary their social being that determines their consciousness.[61] These passages are indicative of his approach to materialism that the practical aspect of life is prior to cognitive and speculative aspect and that the role of man producing his means of existence should be given priority in understanding the whole course of human history.

Dynamics of Marx's materialism consists of a new approach to the thinking about the laws operating in human history. This approach may be called 'dialectical'. Marx and Engels employed the terms 'dialectic' and 'dialectical method' in a substantive as well as methodological sense. Elaborating what this actually meant to them, Engels writes, "Thereby the dialectic of concepts itself became more conscious reflex of the 'dialectic motion of the real world' and thus the dialectic of Hegel was placed upon its head; or rather off its head, on which it was standing and placed upon its feet."[62] According to this, 'dialectical' is the mode of the movement of human history. The whole process of human history is moving according to the dialectical principle and, therefore, the correct understanding of man's practical life on this earth can come only if the laws of dialectical operation are fully grasped. It is the law of motion of human history. That is the reason that his materialism is called 'historical materialism'.

Surprisingly enough, the expression 'dialectical materialism' has nowhere been used by Marx himself for his materialism. This word was used by Engels in his book *Anti-Duhring* and his posthumous book *Dialectics of Nature*, presumably in his bid to link the movement in human history with the movements in nature. It was his bid to extend the hypothesis of the motion of man's history to whole universe but this bid did not find much favour.

Now the Soviet communist writers on communism like T. Borodulina, D. Chesnokov, G. Glezerman and G. Kursanov etc., in their writings continuously use the word 'historical materialism' to denote the philosophical theory of Marx whereas the word 'Dialectical Materialism' has become more prevalent in non-communist writers on Marxism.

Without entering into this controversy, we should have no objection in agreeing with Marx that 'dialectic' is a way of seeing and understanding the history that takes the 'practical developmental process' as the primary datum and human thought-process as its reflex. Marx claimed it to be a radically new and unprecedented way of thinking. He writes, "In the whole conception of history upto the present, this real basis of history has either been totally neglected or else considered as a minor matter quite irrelevant to the course of history."[63] Thus speaking, the material basis of the transcendence of man's alienated existence is to conceive the human history as 'the world-creating activity' of mankind or the "human activity of material production. It is in this sense only that philosophy of communism may be more appropriately called *Historical Materialism.*

Ethics of Communism

Marx came forward to attack the institutionalized preaching of morality in his *Manifesto.* He advocates that, "Law, morality, religion are to him (to labourer), so many bourgoise prejudices behind which lurk in ambush just as many bourgoise interests.[64] This statement of Marx, detached from its contextual significance has often been quoted to show that communism has no concern with morality. For example, Walter Kolarz holds "Communism does not know any morality *per se* and their morality is liable to be changed with the shift in political and sociological situation.[65] But such an assessment of communism seems to be based on superficial understanding. The indignation expressed by Marx towards the ethical thinkers seems to be directed against those who were vainly wasting their efforts in searching for the meanings of ethical predicates instead of guiding the suffering humanity out of the crisis. He expressed his firm conviction in VIII and XI Theses on Feuerbach, wherein he said that "social life is essentially practical," and "that philosophers have only interpreted the world in various ways; the point, however, is to change it."[66] This shows that Marx wants to reject all theoretical discussions about the practical problems of human conduct, as mere pedantary. Marx avoided laying down an explicit moral theory because he hated preaching. "Deeply distrustful of the moralist who usually preaches water and drinks wine, Marx was reluctant to formulate his ethical convictions explicitly. The principles of humanity and decency were for him matters that needed no discussion—matters to be taken for granted."[67]

Other Marxist thinkers also try to remove the misconception about the ethical negativism in communist doctrine. "In combating the excesses of ineffective and sentimental moralizing", says Sidney Hook "Marx leaned so far backward that soon after his death the myth became current that he had no place for any ethics in his philosophy of social activity."[68]

Marx has not given any theory of ethics in its conventional sense. Nevertheless, these writers are correct in their assessment because the earlier writings of Marx clearly show that he was less of a social scientist and more of a moral thinker. His morality passes beyond the customary level of searching for the inspiration in scriptures. He, on the other hand, had a conviction that the criticism of religion ends with the precept that the supreme being for man is man. His tone and emphasis is so much moralising that Buber saw in communism 'the socialist secularization of eschatology.'[69] Let us examine the moral doctrines of communism in details.

Dissatisfaction with the Present form of Existence :

While analysing the content of *Das Capital*, it has already been shown in great details that to Marx the present life, the life as it existed in the age of capitalism, is full of misery and pains. Poverty and exploitation are rampant in this world. Marx advocated that this dehumanizing state is to be transcended in order to enter into the realm of ideal existence, communism, which is free from all human miseries.[70] Such a despair over the hopeless disorder of earth is the starting point of almost all the ameliorative disciplines, Buddhism being foremost in them, of which the first Noble Truth is *sarvam dukham*. It has also been shown that throughout the *Das Capital*, Marx seems to be obsessed with a moral vision of reality and a vision of this world as an arena of conflict between the forces of good and evil. This attitude is typical of moral philosophies.

Nature of Evil :

Writing the *Introduction* in 1843, Marx put forth the idea that "human nature possesses no reality, that man exists in this world as 'Unmensch' (Unman)."[71] It was in this context that Marx came to conclude that 'in sum, the proletariat is a class that represents the complete *loss of man* and can only regain itself, therefore, by the complete resurrection of man.'[72] Here 'complete loss of man' signifies the 'totally alienated 'man' who does not know his real nature, does not know that he is 'man' and he 'ought' to exist as 'man'. Marx reasserted the same thing that man, the real man was deprived of the minimum that is required for calling him as human being. According to the picture of this 'unman' given by Marx, "none of his senses exist any longer and not only in his human fashion, but in an inhuman fashion and therefore, not even in an inhuman fashion."[73] Clearly Marx had an image of man as to what he 'could be' and therefore, he 'ought to be'. But he saw that in actual existence it was a far cry from that image. This dehumanization of man was a consequence of alienation.

Thus Marx reached the conclusion that alienation is the prime evil. Man is fighting to finish this debasing condition. Summarizing the efforts made by various predecessors, Marx himself pointed out that 'the philosophers have conceived the whole historical process as a process of self-alienation of man.'[74] Once this evil was apprehended, Marx tried to search for this evil in the economic and political life of man. To develop the idea of 'alienation' as a social phenomenon as related to the practical life of man was an original contribution of Marx. Even Engels has confessed this fact. He says : "What I contributed, Marx could very well have done without me. What Marx accomplished, I would not have achieved.'[75]

This great achievement was the application of the concept of 'alienation' to the field of political and economic activity of man. In political field the State and in economic field the division of labour are the expressions of the alienation. Once the evil that cause dehumanization of man was so clearly detected, it was easy to wipe it out from the practical life. Accordingly, Marx started working out the effective methods for that. Thus speaking, his ethics is the ethics of finishing the alienated existence of man and an ethics of man's return to himself as 'real man'. This is really a revolutionary novelty of Marx to have brought forth the real nature of human sufferings. Man suffers a torture of his existence when he is alienated. Marx might have taken the idea of 'alienation' from old psychiatry where it meant 'loss of personal identity'. The great psychiatrists of the day subscribe to this symptomatology of mental sickness, that pathological personality has the feeling of not being a moving force in his own life. According to Dr. Karen Horney, the patient feels as if all his activities are performed with a feeling. 'I am driven, instead of being a driver.'[76]

Marx's description of a religious man as well as of the alienated labour is the same as are the symptoms of severe alienation in neurotic persons. Therapists of Freudian/Jungian school also find their patients complaining that some unknown forces are driving their life, but in the last analysis these forces come out to be the psycho-dynamics of their own 'unconscious'. They are alienated from their own unconscious which is the ground of their own 'being'. This is the most original and humanistic contribution of Marx, highly significant in understanding the suffering of the modern man, that Marx borrowed this idea of alienated existence from psychiatry and made it a social problem of humanity. Such diagnosis of man's anxiety is corroborated by other humanistic philosophies of this age. The existentialist thinkers also confirm that 'modern man's alienation is the central problem.'[77] Heidegger lauds this contribution of Marx when he says 'because Marx through his experience of alienation of modern man, is aware of a fundamental dimension of history, the Marxist view of history is superior to all other views.'[78]

The dehumanizing effect of alienation in all walks of man's practical life, has been elaborately worked out by Marx in his philosophical communism. When the worker becomes alienated from his own nature, he starts experiencing the process of production as an oppressive activity, as a loss of freedom. According to Marx, 'he no longer feels himself to be freely active in any but his animal function—eating, drinking, procreating. And in his human functions he no longer feels himself to be anything but an animal.[79] Certainly eating, drinking, procreating etc., are also genuinely human functions. But what Marx wants to lay stress on is that these are the activities which serve man to realize his dignity. If these are performed for their own sake then in the abstraction which separates them from the sphere of all other human activity and turns them into sole and ultimate ends, these are animal activities and these make a man no better than animals. It means that alienated man as worker, becomes something less than human, for he is separated from his potential human qualities. He is deprived of his humanity and he exists as 'unman'. This happens under capitalism when man becomes increasingly alienated from himself.

After analysing the facts of the political economy, Marx raised a pertinent problem as to whom this alien activity belongs and who is the being whom the working man considers as a being *other* than himself. After a long deliberation on the issue, Marx comes to the conclusion that 'the other' is not God as the religious thinkers conceived falsely, but it can be man himself. He expressed the idea saying that, "not the god, not nature but only man himself can be this alien power over man. It can be himself apprehended as another man outside himself, i.e., and alien, hostile powerful man, independent of him, a non-worker."[80] Him he called capitalist. Accordingly, when capitalism prevails, the humanity splits into two 'warring' classes, each considering the opposite class as 'the other'. This means that under capitalist modes of existence, the whole humanity becomes a victim of mental sickness of the kind described by Karen Horney. Man wanders on this earth alienated from his own real nature. A worker, who has totally been alienated is a non-man, a dehumanization, a proleterian devoid of every human property save the essential one, viz., the productivity. To relieve humanity of this torture of alienation, the conditions under which man has been dehumanized, will have to be removed once for all. Alienation thus emerges in Marxian account as the great problem of mankind, and has to be done away with

Concept of Man :

To understand the real significance of alienation, one must also know what Marx means by 'real' human nature from which man feels alienated under capitalist society. Man, according to the description of Marx, is fundamentally a productive being, a creator, and material production is the basic form of his productivity, on which other non-material forms are produced. Mankind is endowed with a multitude of creative capacities, faculties and drives which seek outlet in productive activity. Marx verily called them his 'essential powers', his 'vital powers', 'productive powers' and 'productive forces'. Seen in this context, the whole history of industry is, as Marx says, "The exoteric unfolding of human essential powers and it is so understood, the human essence of nature and natural essence of man are also understood."[81]

Accordingly, as Marx tells us, "the 'nature' that develops in human history and in the history of industrial progress is the *real nature* of man."[82] It is clear from this explanation of human nature that man by nature is progressive and in exercising his faculties on the inert nature, he goes on expressing his real essence. It implies that 'the practical production of an *objective word*, the working up of inorganic nature, is the expression of man as a conscious species being'. Marx tells us very clearly that "It is in the working up of the objective world, therefore, that man first really proves himself as a *species being*. This production is his practical species life."[83] Here the position of Marx becomes clear. What he wants to convey is that man proves his authenticity of existence when he is 'producing'. The nature that has progressed around, is nothing but the objectified form of his own productive activity, the projection of, the externalization of his 'essence'. But this productivity required unfettered freedom. It is this fr edom, i.e., freedom to express and externalize his 'essence', which differentiates man from the animals. The animal produces only when he is dominated by his immediate physical needs. But man, as Marx holds, "can produce even when he is free from physical need and only truly produces in freedom therefrom."[84]

This process is reversed under the condition of alienated labour where man's whole conscious being and life activity, 'his essential being becomes a mere means to his existence', and he produces only to continue his existence, under the pressure of his physical needs. This is the humanity in bondage. It is not the state of existence in which only poor class is under bondage but the evil of alienation binds the whole humanity in his snares. Marx himself points out : "It is not the worker, but the non-worker as well who is subject to the conditions of alienation. Everything, which appears in the worker, as an *activity* of alienation, of estrangement, appears in the non-worker, as a *state* of alienation, of estrangement."[85] Thus, under the dehumanizing conditions of capitalism, the entire world becomes a field of alienation. It is because the capitalist system does not allow the freedom to produce for the expression of human nature, but under it, the sole motive of production remains something else. The worker produces for his subsistence only. He produces because he is to earn wages for filling his own belly and for the survival of his family.

The capitalist produces, under the sway of his profit motive. His motive is the appropriation of surplus value and the satisfaction of his acquisitive mania. No one is free to realize his real essence because the modes of capitalist economy do not allow the production for the sake of the projection of man's nature. When, therefore, the freedom of production is sacrificed for the sake of limited motives, man feels estranged and alienated from his essence. Thus, under capitalism, the whole humanity stands alienated.

Nature of Human Bondage and Release :

Why does man become victim of alienation ? Marx found the ground or cause of alienation in the aggrandizing tendency, the 'self-infinitizing movement' in man, which he named 'Capital'. Like an ardent spokesman of non-attachment, he disdained the tendency of acquisitiveness (*Iṣaṇā*). Tucker rightly brings forth the position of Marx "Man is alienated from himself when he produces under the compulsion of egoistic need."[86] So long as these egoistic tendencies are dominant in him, his productive living has been a realm of alienated labour. His activity has never been 'self-activity' by which Marx means free creativity in which a person feels thoroughly at home with himself and experiences his energies as his own. Explaining the dynamics of human bondage, Marx explains : "the material world around us is a materialisation of man's productive labour in history. The world so created confronts its creators as an alien world and a gigantic fetters upon them. Thus man's own deed becomes an alien power opposed to him, instead of being controlled by him.[87] From such pronouncements of Marx, it becomes evident that under the influence of his own egoistic needs, man becomes slave of the objects of his gratification. On this consideration, it can be inferred that the forces of selfishness, egoistic needs, and greed are the main ingredients working behind man's dehumanized and alienated existence in the world as it exists. Popper, however, cautions us here not to search for too much emphasis on greed in communism. He says that "the vulgar Marxists would say that Marx revealed hidden motives of greed and lust for material gain behind the scene of human history, but Marx interpreted 'greed' and profit motive as 'symptom' of the corruptive influence of social system."[88]

Popper's assessment about the role of the forces of greed does not appear to be correct. Marx is very clear on this point. Man can look towards the objects of his creation either as a producer or as a consumer. As producer, he can enjoy them as the 'expression of his creativity'. This sort of enjoyment does not attach him to the objects. But when he acts as consumer, he uses these objects as the 'objects of his sensuous gratification'. It is this attitude of 'gratification' that makes him dependent on the object and puts on embargo on his freedom. Had he not utilized these object with the tendency of gratification, he would not have become bound to these things. Thus speaking, the history of production or externalisation is a history of man's self-alienation.

According to Marx, "Man in history reifies himself in an objective world of material things. He becomes object to himself in this way and looks at himself in a world that he has created. In doing so, the objects, in which he has externalized himself, confront him as 'alien beings' and what he sees when he looks at himself in the vast aggregate of these objects is an 'alien and hostile' world standing over against him."[89] This is an experience of bondage. Marx prefers to call it 'object bondage'.[90]

What a lofty moral predicament Marx has placed before mankind ! In creating the economic goods for the purpose of his gratification, man creates fetters upon him. This implies that the process of production under the sway of profit takes the form of 'a loss and servitude to the object'. In fact, the more the capitalist mode of production advances, the more impoverished the real producers become. This degeneration takes place when man is treated not as a man but as an object. The main point, on which Marx wants to lay emphasis, is that in capitalism the material objects, which are produced, become treated on a par with the worker himself. Marx asserts that 'the worker becomes an ever cheaper 'commodity'. The devaluation of the human world increases in direct relation with the increase in value of the world of things."[91] No body would raise any doubt that this state, from moral point of view, is highly undesirable state when 'man' is treated just like 'a commodity' and most often his value is reckoned less than the objects that he has created. This is an evil state of existence.

Further according to Marx, the lust for accumulating money keeps man bound to this present state of existence, capitalist society, which is the dehumanized form of existence. When man becomes a slave of the objects of his own creation, he wants to reincorporate them into himself in order to finish the 'otherness'. Thus a desire to own the objects privately develops. In order to fulfil this desire, the objects are converted into money and into private property. But as soon as the money comes into market and private property comes into existence, it becomes itself a great source of human fall, his degradation and his bondage. Condemning the lust for money as something debasing, dehumanizing and the source of bondage, Marx writes, "Money is the alienated essence of man's work and his being. This alien being rules over him and he worships it."[92] When a man is under the domination of egoistic needs. he can act in a practical way and create objects practically only by subordinating these products as well as his activity to the power of this alien being, viz., money. The attitude of Marx shows that he thinks money to be the source of human misery and his bondage. The notable thing in his writings is that Marx speaks of money as the *alien being* and the worship of this 'worldly god' as an evil that alienates man from himself. It means that a man in bondage worships money as the externalised potentiality of mankind and as an *almighty being*, which, according to the belief of the greedy, confers unlimited power upon its possessor. Marx contemptuously quotes some passages from *Timons of Athens*, in which yellow glittering. precious gold is apostrophied as 'Thou visible God'.[93] This reflects his indignation for all those who make money the sole motive of their life. These are the capitalists. Unmistakably the capitalists are also under bondage of their dehumanized and degenerated mentality.

This sort of indignation of the egoistic and profit motive was the dominating note of communism in contrast to the political economy of his times. Marx reacted sharply to Adam Smith's *The Wealth of Nations*. He took economists of his day to task for believing that the drive to amass wealth *ad infinitum* was the 'ethic' implicit in political economy in which case money was the means of exercising command over all the produce of labour. Marx summed up the situation thus :

"The less you eat, drink and read books ; the less you go to the theatre, the dance hall, the public house, the less you think, love, theorize, sing, paint, fence, etc., the more you save—the greater becomes your treasure which neither moths nor dust will devour - your *capital*. The less you are, the more you *have* : the less you express your own life, the greater is your alienated life."[94]

He dubbed this sort of ideal of human life as the ethics of 'extortionate miser' and of the 'productive slave' and ridiculed it, in a highly satirical language.[95]

Thus, the all-embracing passion of greed is seen by Marx as an utterly alien power or 'inhuman force that holds sway over the whole of human existence',[96] from which man was to be liberated. It is with this premise that Marx sought to relieve humanity from the clutches of greed.

Liberation from Alienated Existence :

Consequently the aim of communist revolution is to abolish the general condition of alienated existence. If men were to elevate themselves to a truly *human* status, they will have to realize this real essence as productive beings. Although the alienated man is a creature of the very social conditions he himself has created, yet he need not remain a prisoner of those conditions. Marx is neither a pessimist nor an escapist. On the contrary, he, as a practical man, wanted the 'revolutionary transformation of this alienated world' in which man was everywhere estranged from his own nature and being. Although Marx has so much contempt for the present form of human existence, yet he does not seek flight into the imaginary world of happiness, as, according to him, the religious man used to do. He also does not want a man to seek the pleasure in neurotic fantasy. The realm where the man must seek his true reality is, of course, the existing world. Marx himself says, "The goal for man is to realize his humanity, his human nature and this carries the categorical imperative to overthrow all the relations in which man is debased, enslaved, helpless, contemptible creature."[97] It was for the realization of this ideal, the ideal of ending man's alienation from his life situation that Marx worked out the solutions throughout. Man was to replace the conditions of his enslavement by creating new conditions of his freedom. This idea has been put forth by Marx in *German Ideology*, wherein he advocated that the change of self, in the revolutionary activity coincides with change of the circumstances.[98] This means that Marx was giving a clarion call to change the circumstances completely if man wants to exist as man. The destruction of private property, which is the source of all the dehumanization, is a condition *sine qua non* for the transition to a new form of human existence. This he called communism. By positive abolition of private property, which hence-to-forth has worked as fetters, the human self-alienation will also come to an end. This would mean, in Marx's own words, "the return of man himself as a social, i.e., really human being, a complete and conscious return which assimilates all the wealth of previous development."[99] Under the capitalists productive order, the productive organs of man in society cannot operate freely. But in the communist society, men will regain their creative potentialities. As Marx says, "the appropriation of a totality of instruments of production is the development of a totality of capacities in the individuals themselves."[100]

Here Marx comes very close to maintain that the aim of human endeavour contains in the realization of all the capacities of human nature. To this theory, which emphasizes the realization of all the capacities of man, Rashdall called 'self-realization'.[101] Thus the ethical theory of Marx can be placed under the category of *self-realization*. To Marx, self-realization means completion of the process of "self-development" of species and the emergence of 'socialised humanity'. Marx reasserts this very ideal in *Das Capital* saying that only at the stage of communism, does self-activity coincide with material life, which corresponds to the development of individuals into 'complete individuals' and the casting off of all natural limitations.[102]

Seen in this perspective, the communism is a vision of mankind in a state of perfection. It combines a vision of an ideal social order in which man returns to himself fully realized and a belief in the possibility of realizing it. The sole quest of Marx seems to be to guide humanity to traverse the path from the 'world as it is' to the 'world as it ought to be'. The vision of a perfect order of the future remained integral to the communist social doctrine. The central theme of Marx's ethical teaching views history of world as a process by which man makes himself fully 'man'. The 'act of world history' is the self-developmental process of man. By 'man', Marx, however, does not mean 'this' or 'that' individual man, but following Feuerbach, he means 'mankind' or 'human species'. It means that for Marx, the act of world history is the self-realization of 'Man' in his collective or generic sense. In his opinion, the individual human life and species life of man are not different things. He writes that "the determinate individual is only a determinate species being."[103]

Marx clarifies his position further on this issue and says, "Though a man is a unique individual, he is equally the 'whole', the ideal whole, the subjective existence of society as thought and experienced."[104] Accordingly, the individual is a microcosm of life of 'Man' or humanity at generic scale. On Marxian consideration, the pre-communist history may be called the developmental process or the act of 'becoming' of the species, and communism may be described as the state of veritable 'being' which begins when the history of the capitalist exploitation, i.e., the history as it has hence-to-forth existed, comes to an end 'as such'. It will be a release from the snare of the history. The temporalised pre-history will come to an end and with that the era of man's temporalised post-history will dawn on the earth. If man has existed all through the unfolding of his history in the state of self-alienation, in a dehumanized condition, communism will be his liberation from this alienation. If this process is seen as a whole, then it may be said without reservations that for Marx, history is a process of man's realization of himself as man and man's ultimate end is simply to become fully man. It is man's gaining of self, the integration or return of man to him. Man will repossess his previously enslaved inner productive powers and thereby he will be relieved from the suffering conditions of alienated labour. He will recover his lost productive freedom in a new non-acquisitive life of self-activity where the productive activity will become a joyous creation. Elaborating the nature of liberation from the bondage, Engels writes that "the whole sphere of the conditions of life which environ man and which have hitherto ruled man, now comes under the dominion of control of man, who, for the first time, becomes the real conscious 'Lord of Nature'. The extraneous objective forces that have hitherto govern history pass under the control of man himself. It is the ascent of man from the 'Kingdom of necessity' to the 'Kingdom of freedom.'[105]

It is clear, then, that Marx had a conception of the human individual as he could be, and for this he has laid down the practical means for realization. Marx upheld that religious method of self-realization is pseudo-self-realization, because in religion, man does not realize himself. He merely dreams of it.[106] It is by breaking fetters in his real practical life that the real freedom will be achieved. The fetter in practical life is the egoistic need and the private property. Marx, therefore, advocates that it is "the transcendence of private property that would mean the annihilation of the alienated character of the objective world."[107] Man's creative powers, his capacity for self-perfection and self-realization are practically unlimited, if the fetters, which so drastically impeded this development, are abolished. In laying down the theoretical foundation of his communist revolution, i.e., revolution to finish the present conditions, he was guided by the Hegelian idea of 'negation of negation' according to which the birth of truth required the death of given state of being. Hegel believed that "all forms are seized by the dissolving movement of reason which cancels and alters them until they are adequate to their notion."[108]

Gita presents the same idea in other way saying that the outmoded manifestations are to be cast asunder in order to take on others that are new.[109] This is a matter of common agreement that truth will reveal itself by the destruction and supersession of that phase which represents only a partial truth of man's existence. Marx also wanted to elevate man from his partial existence to his fullest development. Therefore, the means, which follow from his description of the communism, were such as may be conducive to the transcendence of the world of private ownership by 'communist action'. The sum and substance of the communist action is to evolve some method by which working man may liberate himself from alienation. This may be called the act of 'reappropriation'. This will be a practical action of 'the seizure of the whole alienated world at a single huge stroke'. Marx justified the appropriation by the mass of proletarians of all the material objects that man has created through the ages, in his work *The Holy Family* wherein he wrote that "the proletarian cannot regard these product of its self-externalization as being simply some ideal phantasmagoria or mere externalization of self-consciousness and cannot seek to destroy 'material' alienation through a purely 'inward spiritual action.[110] For removing the fetters in the practical life, the very source of lust and greed, which manifests in the form of 'private property', will have to be finished, because he thought that it is the sense of private possession that has defiled man.

He writes, "Private property has made us so stupid and one sided that an object is ours only when we *have* it, when it exists for us as capital, or when we possess it directly."[111] This shows that the lust for the ownership of an object degrades man to do every sort of crime against humanity. He loses all sense of humanity. Marx tells us that "for all the physical and spiritual senses, therefore, the sense of *having*, which is the simple alienation of all these senses, has been substituted."[112] Accordingly, the transcendence of private property will bring the complete emancipation of all the human senses and attributes.[113] As a corollary to this, when the private property is finished, man will not try to appropriate every thing for himself. He will be socialized with the socialization of the property. According to the vivid picture painted by Marx, this socialist man will be man returned to himself as 'social', the 'human' man. Man, in the end of communist revolution, will be freed from the lust for wealth, in whose service he has laboured so far. It is clear that Marx is preaching the lesson that lust for money and wealth, which he names 'private property', is the source of our miseries, and our alienated existence. When this prime source of alienation is finished, man will become one with 'Man', his 'species being' and the difference created by the forces of acquisitiveness will fall asunder. It is thus evident that the moral doctrine of communism comes very close to the theories of self-realization.

Self Realization Theory

When we place the ethical doctrine of communism under the category of self-realization, it becomes necessary to reflect how other protagonists of this theory have understood it and whether or not

Marxism approximates them. About the chief characteristic of this theory, Mackenzie tells us that the 'idea that man partly is and wholly hopes to be, works underneath the theories of this type. It is what he hopes to be that determines the direction of his growth in the theories of self-realization.'[114] If the whole description of communism, as given by Marx, is evaluated in the light of this criterion provided by Mackenzie, then Marxism fits well within the framework of self-realization theory. At this point, it is relevant to note that Marx deduced his philosophical theories from the theories of Hegel, and under his impact, it was natural for him to unconsciously or consciously adopt the Hegelian standards in Ethics.

However, the Hegelian idealists have interpreted the ideal of self-realization suggested by Hegel with metaphysical moorings, and in doing so, they have made the 'self' something mysterious. Nevertheless the uniformity of views regarding the realization of man *qua* man is clearly discernible in the views of Marx and some other Hegelian idealists. For example, Prof. Green tells us that "for any truest idea of what is best for man that can guide our action is still a realization of that capacity for conceiving a better state of himself."[115] Accordingly, the expression of dissatisfaction with the present and striving for a better state of existence will bring a theory into the scope of self-realization. Marx will go hand in hand with this view because this characteristic is clearly discernible in his theory. Throughout *Das Capital*, Marx has been expressing this discontent with the present state of existence and on Green's criterion also Marxism falls within the scope of self-realization theories. Beyond this limit, Marx does not go with Green and other Hegelian idealists to enter into the abyss of metaphysical quandaries. Rashdall, however, tears off the metaphysical veil of self-realization. He confines himself to purely ethical aspect of the theory of self-realization as the end of life. He discusses the two meanings, in which this term is generally used, viz., (i) that self-realization is the realization of some potentiality or capacity of the self which is at present unrealized or (ii) that self-realization may be interpreted to mean an equal, all-round development of one's whole nature—physical, intellectual, emotional.[116] It is in this sense also that Marx's theory can fall under the category of self-realization.

What modification Marx has made in this theory? The genus being self-realization, what is the differentia which distinguishes Marx from other protagonists of this theory. Marx has simply suggested to substitute the word 'man' for 'self'. By this sort of substitution, he solves all mystery about 'self'. He would say that the self which we are to realize is not something mysterious or something metaphysical, but it is 'man' himself. The aim of communism is, that man ought to realize in practical life that he is 'man' by breaking the 'fetters' which have compelled him to exist as 'unman'. Thus speaking, his theory becomes a theory of 'man-realization', which in the light of various views put forth by the advocates of self-realization theory, has very close affinity to their approach. The central theme of the ethical doctrines of communism can be summarised, that 'man's ultimate end is simply to become fully human, which he cannot be so long as the remains alienated from himself.' Prof. Tucker has rightly pointed out that Marx does not insist on God-realization but simply upon man actualizing himself *qua* man, becoming what he essentially is.[117] By emphasizing on this point of view, Marx very well brings his theory to fall within the sphere of 'self-realization'.

This deliberation of the ethics of communism brings us to state in brief, that: (i) the communist ethics is a variety of self-realization theory; (ii) communism considers 'egoistic needs' and 'greed' as the enemy of man and a hindrance in his self-realization; these are the fetters which a man ought to break, (iii) it is advocating for a social order where attachment with the private property and the criterion of money being the measure of man's dignity will be negated, he is preaching something like *apaṛigraha* and *anāsakti*, as the pre-conditions for a man to become 'a communist man'. The moral fervour in criticising the evils of industrial civilization, the assertion of human activity as the material reality and the emphasis on a moral richness of communist man—all these elements would suffice to arrive at the conclusion that communism has placed the moral uplift of man, the dealienation of the alienated man, the liberation of humanity from the bondage of lust and greed, as its prime concerns. Accordingly, the economical and political implications of these ethical teachings are only of secondary value. They serve only as mere means and have an instrumental value in so far as they help in the realization of this goal.

REFERENCES

1. Sorokin, P.A., *Modern Historical and Social Philosophies*, p. 4.
2. Horney, Karen, in Simon Doniger (Ed.), *Nature of man*, p. 181.
3. Afanasyev, V., *Scientific Communism*, p. 26.
4. Loyd D. Easton and Kurt H. Guddat, *Writings of Young Marx on Philosophy and Society*, p. 39.
5. Whitehead, A.N., *Science and the Modern World.*, p. 243.
6. Afanasyev, V., Op. cit., p. 12.
7. Marx, K., *Capital*, p. 864.
8. Marx, K. and Engels, F., *The German Ideology*, p. 26.
9. Ibid., p. 114 (italics mine).
10. Some eminent Indian writers define communism that "it is as professed in Russia, economic determinism, plus self-sufficient humanism, plus science and technology, plus atheism (Radhakrishnan, S., and Raju, P.T., in *The Concept of Man*), p. 37.
11. Northrop, F.C.S., *The Meeting of the East and West*, p. 246 and Chap. 6.
12. Sorokin, P.A., op. cit., p. 151.
13. Sorokin, P.A., op., cit., p. 85.
14. Wayper, C.L., *Political Thought*, p. 221.
15. Sabine, F.H., *A History of Political Theory* (3rd Ed.), p. 699.
16. Lenin, V.I., *Collected Works*, Vol. 25, p. 271.
17. Marx, Engels and Lenin, *On Historical Materialism*, p. 137.
18. Marx, K. and Engels, F., *Communist Manifesto* (London Edition), p. 5.
19. Whitehead, A.N., *Adventures of Ideas*, p. 42.
20. Bronstein, Daniel J., Krikorin, Y.H., etc. (Ed.), *Basic Problems of Philosophy*, p. 146.
21. Tucker, Robert C., *Philosophy and Myth in Karl Marx*, p. 204.
22. Marx, K., *Early Writings* (Trans. and Ed. by T.B. Bottomore), pp. 25-31
23. Marx, K., *Capital*, p. 873.
24. Marx, K. and Engels, F., *Selected Correspondence*, p. 102.
25. Karl Lowith in *Social Research*, No. 2, Summer 1954, pp. 204-205.
26. Marx, K., *Capital*, p. 651.
27. Tucker, Robert C., *The Marxian Revolutionary Idea*, p. 182.
28. Marx, K., *Capital*, p. 685.
29. Marx, K., *Capital*, p. 346-347.
30. Ibid., pp. 235, 237, 239.
31. Ibid., pp. 259, 270.
32. Ibid., pp. 381, 384, 390.
33. Marx, K., *Selected Works*, p. 439.
34. Marx, K., *Capital*, p. 248.
35. Ibid., pp. 45-46, 47, 49.
36. Ibid., p. 113.
37. Ibid., p. 189.
38. Ibid., p. 846.
39. Ibid., pp. 677, 708.

40. Ibid., pp. 551-552.
41. Ibid., p. 651.
42. Ibid., p. 741.
43. Tucker, Robert C., *Philosophy and Myth in Karl Marx*, p. 138.
44. Marx, Karl, *Early Writings* (Trans. and Ed. by Bottomore, T.B.) p. 37.
45. Ibid., p. 605.
46. Tucker, Robert C., op. cit., p. 13.
47. Marx, K., *Critique of Political Economy*, p. 137.
48. Marcuse, Herbert, *Reason and Revolution*, (2nd Ed.), p. 273-74.
49. *Das Capital*, pp. 954-55.
50. Engels, F., *Anti-Duhring*, pp. 420-421.
51. Ibid., p. 438.
52. Tucker, Robert C., op. cit., pp. 158, 235.
53. Marx, K., *Early Writings*, p. 155.
54. Tucker, Robert C., op. cit., pp. 51-52.
55. Marx and Engels, *German Ideology*, p. 199.
56. Ibid., p. 197.
57. Ibid., p. 37.
58. Ibid., pp. 36-37.
59. Ibid., pp. 42, 64.
60. Ibid., p. 15.
61. Marx., K., *Critique of Political Economy*, p. 137.
62. Marx, K. and Engels, F., *Selected Works*, Vol. II, p. 350.
63. Marx, K. and Engels, F., *German Ideology*, p. 30.
64. Marx, K. and Engels, F., *Manifesto of the Communist Party*, p. 15.
65. Kolarz, Walter, *Religion in Soviet Union*, p. 26.
66. Marx, K. and Engels, F., *German Ideology*, p. 13.
67. Popper, K.R., *The Open Society and its Enemies*, Vol. II, pp. 187-88.
68. Hook, Sidney, *From Hegal to Marx*, p. 51.
69. Buber, Martin, *Paths in Utopia*, p. 10.
70. Marx, Engels, Lenin., *On Historical Materialism*, pp. 38, 112, 296.
71. Marx, K., Introduction to the Criticism of Hegelian Philosophy of Right, 1843 quoted by Robert Tucker—*Philosophy and Myth in Karl Marx*, p. 113.
72. Marx Karl., *Early Writings*, pp. 137-39.
73. Marx, K., *Economic and Philosophic Manuscripts of 1844*, p. 117.
74. Marx, K., *German Ideology*, p. 68.
75. Marx, K. and Engels, F., *Selected Works*, Vol. II, p. 349.
76. Horney, Karen, *Neuroses and Human Growth*, pp. 159-160.
77. Heinemann, F.H., *Existentialism and Modern Predicament*, pp. 10-13.
78. Heidegger, Martin, quoted in *Soviet Survey*, No. 33, July-September 1960, p. 88.
79. Marx, K., *Economic and Philosophic Manuscripts of 1844*, p. 73.
80. Marx, K., *Early Writings*, pp. 90-91.
81. Marx, K., *Early Writings*, pp. 121-122.
82. Ibid., pp. 84, 122.

83. Ibid., pp. 88-89.
84. Marx, K., *Economic and Philosophic Manuscripts of 1844*, p. 75.
85. Ibid., p. 83.
86. Tucker, Robert C., *Philosophy and Myth in Karl Marx*, p. 240.
87. Marx and Engels, *German Ideology*, pp. 22, 23, 25.
88. Popper, K.R., op. cit., p. 100
89. Marx, K., *Early Writings*, pp. 86, 89 (German Edition).
90. Ibid., p. 83.
91. Ibid., p. 121.
92. Ibid.
93. Marx, K., *Early Writings*, pp. 145, 147-148 (German Edition).
94. Marx, K., *Economic and Philosophic Manuscripts of 1844*, p. 110.
95. Marx, K., *Early Writings*, p. 145 ff.
96. Ibid., p. 136.
97. Marx, Karl, *MEGA*, p. 615.
98. Marx and Engels, *German Ideology*, p. 198.
99. Marx, K., *Early Writings*, p. 155.
100. Marx and Engels, *German Ideology*, p. 66.
101. Rashdall, H., *The Theory of Good and Evil*, Vol. II, p. 62.
102. Marx, K., *Capital*, pp. 527, 685.
103. Marx, K., *Early Writings*, p. 117 (German Edition).
104. Ibid., p. 158.
105. Marx, K., and Engels, F., *Selected Works*, Vol. II, pp. 140-141.
106. Tucker, Robert C., *Philosophy and Myth in Karl Marx*, p. 99.
107. Marx, K., *Early Writings*, p. 166.
108. Marcuse, Herbert, *Reason and Revolution* (2nd Ed.), p. 26.
109. *Bhagavadgītā*, II. 22, vāsāṁsi jīrṇāni yathā vihāya navāni gṛhṇāti naro paraṇi.
110. Marx, K., *MEGA*, p. 254.
111. Ibid., p. 118.
112. Ibid., p. 119.
113. Ibid., pp. 115, 166.
114. Mackenzie, J.S., *A Manual of Ethics*, pp. 197-198.
115. Green, T.H., *Prolegomena to Ethics*, p. 202.
116. Rashdall, H., op. cit., pp. 62-63.
117. Tucker, Robert C., *Philosophy and Myth in Karl Marx*, p. 99.

2

Anasakti Yoga of Gita

Gita has meant different things to different people. But the central theme of this great Scripture is unmistakably *Anāsakti Yoga* the discipline of non-attachment in human performance. Mahatma Gandhi has named his interpretation (Bhāṣya) of Gita Anāsakti Yoga. These two terms are co-extensive in this study too.

For centuries Bhagavadgītā has inspired the Indian Society and fashioned its destiny according to the tenets prescribed therein. It forms part of the all important, *prasthāna traya* along with Upaniṣads and Brahmasūtras. Gita has guided man to the light when his vision is darkened and blinded ; when he faces conflicts in his choosing the right course of action. It represents the crisis of moral man who encounters the temptations of life *vis-a-vis* the social call. It tries to resolve the most important ethical question which was worrying the mind of Arjuna, viz., the question of deciding *dharmasaṁmūḍhacetāḥ*, 'what I ought to do and what I ought not to do'. If the teachings of Gita are understood truly in the sense in which Arjuna understood them. It will become evident that beyond the solving of this ethical predicament, Gita does not want to puzzle man unduly. When after a great deliberation, the doubts of Arjuna were removed, he did neither renounce the world, nor he withdrew into seclusion for meditating on the glory of the Lord, but instead, he showed an ethical preparedness for doing his allotted social job. Arjuna says :

'*naṣṭo mohaḥ smṛtirlabdhā tvatprāsādānmāyacyuta* ;

sthitosmi gatasandehaḥ kariṣye vacanaṁ tava.'

My delusion is gone, I have regained my understanding (of my duty) through your kind courtesy. O Krishna I, with all my doubts dispelled stand before you and I shall act upto your calling. And, even then the preceptor did not ordain him to seek recourse to withdrawal, become a mendicant and thereby to become immune to social problems. The warrior fought valiantly to change the conditions of his existence.

There is a need to understand Gita in this very sense that it is concerned with the discharge of man's duty and desistence from inaction. In practical life-situations, the doctrine of Anāsakti Yoga as enunciated in Gita, has a great ethical significance. Explaining the connotative use of this term, Bahm has rightly pointed out that "what in modern thought has come to be called 'disinterested action', is more commonly spoken of as 'non-attachment'. Since the attitude of non-attachment is itself a good, maintaining an attitude of indifference has the effect of bringing one closer to his ultimate goal."[2] This approach of searching for the disinterested answers to the practical problems of one's duty, has kept Gita very close to Indian life. Dasgupta tells about Gita that "neither the Yoga-Vāṣiṣtha nor Gita are systematic works on philosophy, yet no treatment of Indian philosophy can legitimately ignore their claims."[3] The reason, as Dasgupta has pointed out for this, is that "starting from the ordinary frailties of attachment and desires, it tries to show how one can lead a normal life of duties and responsibilities and yet in peace and contentment in a state of equinimity and in communion with God."[4] This sort of synthesis between the instinctual and the spiritual or in Freudian terminology between the demands of libido and those of super-ego is the pre-requisite condition for balanced personality formation.

This balanced attitude towards life, has saved the Indian Society from mass neurosis that afflicts the western world today. Freud even wonders, "would not the diagnosis be justified that possibly even the whole of humanity have become neurotic under the pressure of civilizing trend ?"[5]

Gita is categorical that whenever the righteousness wanes, the exploitation of the nobles goes to the extreme and the forces of evil have their sway, the moral connoisseur manifests itself into some concrete human form and re-establishes the social equilibrium.[6] It is this moral optimism that has not allowed the importance of Gita to mitigate. Annie Besant, rightly calls Gita "a true scripture of the race, a life rather than a book. For each age it has a new message for each civilization a new record."[7] The importance of Gita is too well recognised in the Indian socio-cultural milieu to need any further assertion.

Various Interpretations of Gita

Because of its important place in the Indian thought and India's cultural life, Gita has been interpreted by various thinkers of east and west. Interpretations and perspectives vary. Still the more it is read the greater appears the possibility of fresh interpretation. The enthusiasts for action (karma), for knowledge (jñāna) and for devotion (bhakti) all find their special tenets in the Gita. Gita, like any *Śāstra* as Tilak says : can have three types of interpretations, viz., (i) *Ādhidaivika* (theological), (ii) *Ādhyātmika* (metaphysical), (iii) *Ādhibhautika* (positivistic).[8]

Both Comte, the father of modern sociology and Feuerbach, who has so much influenced the thought of Marx, considered positivistic explanation of scriptures the best. Feuerbach's book, *Essence of Christianity* and Khalil Jibran's work, *The Son of Man*, etc., are a few important attempts to present the secularised and humanistic version of Christianity. Such an orientation to Gita has been given by M.K. Gandhi in his commentary Mahatma it may be remembered based his teachings on the tenets of Gita.

Before *Śaṁkara*, Gita was considered to be a treatise of *jñānakarmasamuccayavāda*,[9] which means that with understanding, a man should do his social duties, and the moral activity of the agent is a rational activity. Tilak's own approach to Gita is also that of *karmayoga*, the Gospel of Action. The post Śaṁkara emphasis on abstract spiritualism has led to many serious misconceptions. Titus, for example, has been led to believe that "the value system of India on the whole is other worldly. "Love for life, for its own sake is a secondary consideration."[10] This is not, however, a correct approach to the understanding of the Indian thought. The very opening phrase of Gita 'dharmakṣetre kurukṣetre' denotes practical life 'Kurukṣetra' in its true connotation, is pregnant with deep sociological meanings. A.J. Bahm's view is that "Kurukṣetra is the sphere of actual affairs."[11] Taken in this sense, the phrase comes to mean kṣetre kṣetre dharmaṁkuru ; do your duties commensurate with your social station and life-situation. Seen in this light Indian thought is far from other-worldly. The Indian thinkers have always been deliberating on the practical problems of human sufferings. The removal of this evil has remained a prime concern for the ancient Indian thinkers and the concept of mokṣa (liberation) in all the systems represents a state in which it is, in one sense or another, (this evil state of existence is) supposed to have been invariably overcome.

Every age writes philosophy according to its needs says : McIver.[12] This has been done with Gita too, where the symbolism is pregnant with rich meaning. Such varied interpretations of Gita are possible because it contains a system of uninterpreted symbols. Like a good logical system, the symbolism of Gita has been left uninterpreted. A variety of interpretations are possible without exhausting its richness. Gopi tells us that a formal deductive system consists of "axioms and theorems, some of whose undefined and primitive terms are primitive symbols whose interpretation is completely extra-systematic."[13] These extra-systematic factors for interpretation of the symbols are provided by the socio-cultural needs. The process of giving meaning to symbols, according to the cultural context, has been recognised by the psychoanalytic school as a natural process of human psyche. In Jungian system, the symbols acquire their meaning in the semantical framework of a particular socio-cultural thought-structure.[14] Cassirer also suggests that 'a symbol is a part of the human world of meaning'.[15] Thus speaking, the symbols become the metaphors, which can represent the accumulated experiences of a culture and which are the symbolic representations of the cultural values of any society. That is why that whenever these cultural conditions change, the symbols acquire a new meaning and a new set of values is placed in the system of these symbols. Accordingly, the new interpretations are the expressions of the fact that Indian genius has been highly sensitive to the cultural variations.

Gita of our Times :

Gita as interpreted by Gandhi is the Gita of our times. He

visualises the whole scene of Gita as an arena in which there is an army of lustful inclinations represented by the Kauravas, who believed in the misappropriation of the rights of others. On the other side, there are the forces of righteousness in the form of Pāṇḍavas. Thus in Anāsakti Yoga, the antagonism between the forces of good and evil has been represented.[16] Gandhi, as this shows, takes into cognisance that the present crisis is a moral crisis.

Marx also comes to express the similar views. He also presents the modern conflict in same way. Summarizing the position of Marx, Prof. Tucker points out that "on the one side is the insatiable acquisitive urge, the alien power in man which transforms his productive activity into alienated labour, detached and housed in 'another man outside the worker'. He is capitalist, the embodiment of inhuman force. On the other hand are the embodiments of rebellious productive power.[17] This is the most appropriate exposition of the predicament of the modern man tortured under the evil influence of industrial civilization. Thus, the true problem of modern society has been well brought out by Anāsakti Yoga.

Symbolic Meaning of Gita

At this point, it is pertinent to point out that Gandhi does not believe in the historicity of Mahābhārata of which Gita forms a part.[18] The evidences to prove whether or not this war is a historical event are to be provided by the historians. But the question of the authenticity of the Mahābhārata war does not effect the central problem of Gita, which is a problem of man's conflict. Modern man is to be integrated with his essential nature externally and internally. This fact that man is actually feeling this type of separation from his real being in his practical life will have to be recognised, otherwise the whole work will become a useless fiction, a mythology having no practical utility. If Gita is to serve as a practical guide for human conduct, there must be existing some real persons on this earth feeling deep-rooted crisis generated by despair and despondency for whose guidance it is meant. By making it a symbolic representation, are we not reducing it to a work of fiction ? Marx has an answer. He points out that the consciousness of good and evil will only be there when good and evil forces are actually existing in actual life-situation.

"All consciousness is the consciousness of real life. Consciousness can never be any thing else than conscious being (Sein) and the being of man in their real life-process."[19] It means that the expression of the conflict in Gita must be the expression of the existence of two conflicting classes of good and evil in real world. Real life is the primary datum reflected in philosophy. As a corollary to this, whatever, a man finds in his own body, he can also search for that in the external world. Gandhi expresses this idea as *yathā piṇḍe tathā brahmāṇḍe.*[20]

This idea of man's consciousness reflecting the environmental happenings has also been expressed by various other Indian systems. For example, Tantric Śāktism conceives human body as a microcosm, reproducing in itself the features of cosmos.[21] The Visāvasāra tantra also explicitly holds that the process of 'self' is the process of nature and 'what is here is elsewhere and what is not here is not elsewhere (*yadihāsti tadanyatra, yannehāsti na tatkvacit*).[22]

Accordingly, the Arjuna of Gita's Anāsakti Yoga must be symbolic representative of a 'non-empty universe', i.e., of some 'really' existing human group. Thus speaking, it is immaterial whether or not we accept the historical authenticity of Mahābhārata. Nevertheless we can accept the existence of a morally degenerated society full of conflicts between the forces of lust, greed and egoism and the forces of righteousness. Accordingly, the Gandhi's upholding the allegorical charater of Mahābhārata does not make any difference to the moral implication of Gita. Gita remains a manifestation of the real life of a society, which is full of conflicts and it can *ipso facto* be applied to the present day situations also. What Feuerbach said of Hegel, is true of Gita that it is no more a philosopher's phantasy but a mystified reflection of the actual state of affairs in the world, and in order to understand the reality, we are to turn our gaze from the internal to the external.

Social Philosophy of Anasakti Yoga

Dr. Radhakrishnan admits that Indian culture has failed to give political expression to its ideals. He says : "The importance of wealth and power to give expression to spirit, though theoretically recognised, was not practically realized."[23] Gandhi, in this age however, took up the task of building a social philosophy based on the Indian heritage to fulfil the social need of the age. Dr. Ramesh Betai has shown in about 71 pages of his book, that Gandhian social though right from his socialism to his removal of untouchability, has been deduced from the teachings of Gita, corroborated by other ancient scriptures.[24] The fabric of the Gandhian social philosophy and even his political thought has been woven from the value-system of the indigenous culture.

The task says, Radhakrishnan "to evolve a method to finish political domination has been worked by Gandhi, in consonance with the religious traditions and mental background of this country."[25] Gandhian Anāsakti Yoga is the only available interpretation of Gita, which can serve as a philosophical foundation for a sound social system to be built on it.

Influence of Gita on Gandhi :

Gandhi has worked out his social philosophy from the doctrine of Anāsakti, which meets the growing challenge of the hour, the growing onslaught of the materialistic civilization. He has explicitly recognised the profound influence of Gita in moulding his thought. He admits that "Hinduism, as I know it entirely satisfies my whole being and I find a solace in the Bhagavadgītā that I miss even in *the Sermon on the Mount*."[26] He goes on further that "to-day, the Gita is not only my Bible or my Quran ; it is more than that—it is my mother."[27] In short, it was his practical guide in all the situations, he faced.

Anāsakti a Remedy for Modern Problems :

The idea of *niṣkāma karma* as the central theme of the ethics of Gita has been verily recognised implicitly by almost all the modern scholars. But Gandhi has gone a step forward in this direction. He has explicitly asserted that "the self-realisation is the subject of the Gita as it is of all scriptures," but "the matchless remedy is renunciation of fruits of action "[28] Therefore, his real contribution and originality lies in suggesting the means. According to new approach of Gandhi, it would be by renunciatory spirit of the individuals that a sound social order can be built. This seems to be one of the reasons that he calls his rendering as "Anāsakti Yoga and not karma-yoga." Gandhiji bases his view on the words of Krishna. Quoted in Gita, these words are :

anāśritaḥ karmaphalaṁ Kāryaṁ karma karoti yaḥ,
sa sanyāsi ca yogī ca, na niraguir na cākriyaḥ.[29]

It means he, who performs his duty without resorting to the fruits of his action, is a *sanyāsi*, a yogī and not one who does not propitiate the sacred fire or who is actionless. Accordingly, a man, who is not discharging his social duty and not contributing to the social good, cannot be a moral being. Thus, Anāsakti Yoga of Gita insists not on the renunciation of social obligation, but on the sincere and honest discharge of one's social duties. By emphasizing on the Anāsakti aspect, Gandhi's sole aim is to free the modern man from those egoistic tendencies which are the outcome of materialist civilization and which are at the root of our present day social maladies.

Communism also more or less comes to the same position. Summarizing their position, Prof. Tucker suggests that when communism dawns, "man will be liberated from the acquisitive drive, the obsession with wealth that had made him an alienated being. He will be released from the tyranny of : (*i*) need and (*ii*) of specialization."[30] It implies that freedom from the lust and greed will lead to a better social order.

The ultimate purpose of Gandhi in writing this commentary was the rediscovery and vindication of the traditional faith with a conviction that Gita is as relevant to the present predicament as it was ever before. Gandhi pre-supposes that the tragic predicament of humanity in modern civilization is an unbound lust for aggrandisement and material pursuit, and therefore, Anāsakti is the remedy.

Philosophical Doctrines of Gita

The supreme purpose of human beings, as pointed out in the Anāsakti Yoga of Gita, is self-realization or freedom and it is with this end in view that the fruit of all action is to be abandoned.[31] Nonetheless, before rising for action, the warrior Arjuna has tried to clarify many philosophical doubts. Yet the main concern of Gita remains to inspire Arjuna to face the crisis of his life-situation with courage. Gita tells the moral agent that it is not life that matters, it is the courage that you add to it. The goal of self-realization and a call to cancel the unsatisfactory state of existence made

Gita a great moral treatise. The philosophical queries of Arjuna are merely of secondary interest and the main concern of Gita is not metaphysical.

Meaning of Brahma Nirvana

Here at this point some reader may draw our attention to certain verses which refer the concept of *Brahma-nirvāṇa* as the goal of human life. For example, describing the characteristic of *Sthitapraina,* the Gita tells us that it is a man whose senses are in his control and who has established in *Brahman* : *Sthitaprajña* invariably gets *Brahma-Nirvāṇa.*[32] This word again occurs in fifth chapter where we are told that "he who finds happiness only within, rest only within that Yogī having become one with nature attains to oneness with Brahman."[33] Numerous other verses[34] refer to such terms as *brahmayoga-yuktātmā*', '*madbhāvamāgataḥ*', '*brahmaṇisthitaḥ*'. These references to 'Braham' suggest that the ideal for man is to realize something metaphysical called 'Brahman'.

The question naturally arises that if that Being is other than man, how can the goal be called self-realization ? It would become 'other-realization'. But the position would become clear when we proceed further and we are told that 'he who sees Me everywhere and everything in Me never vanishes from Me and I from him'.[35] The question, however, still remains that if man is to merge himself in some 'other' Being, it is self-annihilation and not self-realization. It is the goal of human life, according to Gita, to foster 'totalitarianism' where a man's personality is swallowed by an 'absolute' totality. But Gita does not warrant such conclusion. It points out that "one is to seek to unite himself with Ātman (*yuñjato yogam ātmanaḥ*)."[36] The problem takes a new orientation now. If becoming one with one's own Ātman, and the realization of Brahman are two different ideals, then which is superior ? If they are one and the same thing, then there should be identity of Brahman and Ātman, and by realizing the 'essence of one's own being', man will be realizing *Brahma-Nirvāṇa.* So conceived, 'Brahman' will not be 'the other', i.e., anything other than man's own essence. It is the only way of saving man from being swallowed by something 'other' or something alien. Here the puzzling terms are 'Brahman and Ātman', which need proper understanding in order to grasp fully that Gita does not emphasize anything transcendental 'the otherness', but only lays emphasis on the sincerest realization that 'man is man' and he should learn to exist as a 'human being'.

The Semantic quandries should not puzzle us. It shall be relevant to point out that the authority of śāstra lies in the spirit and not the letter and surely who goes by the letter is likely to make mistaken assessments to misinterpret and to commit blunders. In Gandhi's words : "the canon of interpretation is to scan not the letter but to examine the spirit."[37] What is then the real spirit behind these terms like '*Brahmanirvāṇa*', '*brahmayoga-yuktātmā*' etc ? To search for an answer to this question, the Mahābhārata, of which Gita forms a part, and the Upaniṣads can serve as our guide. Let us seek their help to resolve this mystery.

The Upaniṣadic seers have discussed the nature of ultimate reality from various points of view. They named it Brahman. A deeper understanding of the nature of Brahman, as described in various Upaniṣads and in Mahābhārata, makes us convinced that it is not something other than 'Man' himself. Accordingly, what is to be realized by a man in Brahmanirvāṇa is nothing except than the realization of his own essence. Bṛ-hadāraṇyaka Upaniṣad declares that "whosoever worships another divinity (than his self) thinking that he is one and (Brahman) another, he knows not.[38] Another text refers that "the wise who perceive Him as abiding in their self, to them belongs eternal happiness."[39] These Upaniṣads tacitly refer to the fact that man should not search for his essence anywhere outside him. Instead, he should try to know what he really is. This realization, in Kantian words, is tantamount to 'treating humanity in his own person, as an end'. It means, it is the realization of his own essence *qua* human being. Man is to realize that he is an epitome of humanity. This is the realization beyond which he should not try to go. That seems to be real meaning behind the assertion of the Upaniṣad that only ignorants think that Brahman is something other than their own essence and due to their ignorance, they worship some alien being. Man is inspired here to worship 'humanity', his own essence. When man realizes his essential nature, then he becomes eligible to say that he is Brahman (ahaṁ brahmāsmi). To affirm that 'I am human' is logically equivalent to the affirmation that 'I am Brahman'. It is only in this sense that man can search him (Brahman) abiding in him.

Tagore gives the same meaning to the ultimate principle when he says, "My religion is the religion of man in which infinite is defined in humanity.[40] Mahābhārata substantiates the view that Brahman cannot be anything 'other', that Brahman is nothing but 'man' himself." According to Mahābhārata, "Guhyam brahma tadidaṁ vo bravīmi, na mānuṣāt śreṣathataraṁ hi kiñcit", means 'I tell you the secret of Brahman (it is that) that nothing is higher than man'.[41] Putting these passages of Upaniṣads and Mahābhārata, together, it becomes clear that Brahman is nothing but 'human'.

In the light of this, Brahman realization would mean man's realization of his lost unity with Man (the term 'Man' to be used in the sense in which it was used by Feuerbach in generic sense). Feuerbach tells us that the 'generic man' the species is the real being and the individual is simply a particular instance of the life of the species—the humanity.[42] It is obvious that Mahābhārata in saying that '*na mānusāt śreṣṭhataram*' is using this term in the same sense in which Feuerbach has used it, viz. the generic man or in the sense in which the existentialists have used it as 'human subjectivity'.

Accordingly, the problem of the existence of Brahma (Brahma Satyam) is expressive of the intensity of man's anxiety to know and feel that he exists. This has been emphasized by modern existentialists also and if whatever Mahābhārata has said, is rendered into the words of Heidegger, it would come to mean that "there is nothing beyond himself (man) that can solve the problem of man's existence.[43] Man's quest for this knowledge is the source of all his existential anxieties. It is a quest for giving meaning to his existence, and in search of a remedy for this, he has been hunting blindly. But the Upaniṣads and Mahābhārata and Gita want to convey to him the same thing what Sartre would say that 'there is no other universe except the human universe, the universe of human subjectivity.[44] Therefore, in self-realization or Brahma Nirvāṇa, man is not supposed to go anywhere else but to realize his lost 'humanity'.

Taken this key to the understanding of the nature of Brahma-Nirvāṇa, all the mysteries about the ideal of human life become very clear. For example, when a scholar goes to Yājñavalkya and asks him to explain Brahman that is immediately present and directly perceived, then Yājñavalkya's reply is "this is your self". This implies that according to the Upaniṣad, every individual is the epitome of the 'generic humanity' and humanity, which is an abstract category, does not lie anywhere outside him. In fact, the Brahman is considered the existence of all existences. Therefore, Taittirīya Upaniṣad is categorical that he, who considers Brahman non-existent, questions his own existence.[45] What man needs is to find himself and his human essence. The Chāndogya Upaniṣad also advocates the same idea, when Uddālaka tells his son Śvetaketu : "That which is the subtle essence, this whole world has for its self. That is the true, that is the self. That art thou Svetketu."[46] This also points out that Brahman is not different from him and he himself is an specimen of that.

The realization of Brahman means the realization of man's lost unity with humanity. So long as a man is under the spell of bewilderment (māyā), he feels that he is alienated and is unable to unite with the totality of existence. To finish this sense of separateness and estrangement, Upaniṣads also suggest the remedy that it is possible by overcoming the duality of ātman and brahman. "Where there is individuality, as it were, says Yājñavalkya, there one sees another ; there one understands another.[47] This means that when a man views the reality from 'individualized' point of view, he is involved into the tight bonds of finitude and limitation. To him, my ātman appears to be different from your ātman and your from his ātman. This is the state of confrontation with 'the other'. But when one gets a universalized outlook, he sees unity, not separateness. He says : 'I am brahma ; you are brahma and all are brahman'. Because as the Upaniṣads confirm, 'he sees the universal in his own self ; he sees all as the self.[48] The ideal of brahma-nirvāṇa, read in this context, conveys the idea that a moral being is that who considers himself as well as others to be human beings and none is considered mere stock and stone or something other than man. Individual finds his solace 'in the life of the whole'. Gita thus, revolts against the alienation of man from man and wants to inspire the moral agents to return to the lost unity of mankind by shedding off the egoism and selfishness generated by the attachment with particulars. This is the ideal of humanization of social relations.

How this unity and universality of mankind, his species being, is to be re-established ? For this purpose, the man has to be made to realize that in essence he is 'human' and that he 'ought to overcome the false conflicts created by the vested interests and despisers of human race'. As Bṛhadāraṇyaka Upaniṣad puts forth this idea that "whoever knows this 'I am Brahman' becomes this all. Even the gods cannot prevent him becoming thus, for he becomes their self."[49] In this sense, when a man realizes that he is a human being, becomes conscious of his essence, he works in his practical life also to exist as 'man' on this earth. When man so realizes his dignity, he asserts his historicity and instead of showering his love on extra-terrestrial beings, he starts loving humanity. That is the reason that Upaniṣad asserted that "whoever worships another divinity (than himself) thinking that he is one and Brahman another, he knows not. He is like an animal to the gods."[50] Such a contempt as calling an individual 'animal' is highly significant. This refers to all those who worship their own externalised 'being' thinking under the spell of their ignorance, that it is something super-natural and super-human and 'other than Man'. Why are these individuals considered 'animals' ? There may be two possible explanations to that : (i) when man becomes separated from his fellow beings, he becomes devoid of all humanitarian qualities. He is motivated solely by self-interest. In the realm of such egoistic individuals where human considerations and human values are lacking, definitely there will be barbarism, which is the quality of animal world, or (ii) when a man himself is debased and dehumanized, he is reduced to the level of animality. Whatever may be the implication in calling such persons who worship another divinity, 'animal' one thing is clear that when man asserts his realized essence as a 'human being', he finds that there is no higher plane of existence than the universe of humanity.

Commenting on this passage of the Upaniṣad, Radhakrishnan writes, "The gods are not pleased that men should know the ultimate truth, for then they would know the subordinate place the gods hold and give up making them offerings."[51] Who are those gods, who do not like man to realize that he himself (ātman) is identical with the ultimate reality (brahman) and everything is subordinate to that ? These seem to be the persons who distort the life-affirming humanistic values and misinterpret the aphorisms of Upaniṣad by raising the problems of transcendental nature. For example, they may try to confuse by raising such issues as to where the 'humanity' exists and as to whether this humanity is separate or identical with man. These gods may be like the transcendental metaphysicians who are misguided by bad grammar and who raise pseudo-questions regarding the metaphysical existence of the Brahman apart from the realm of 'Man'. As Ayer has exposed the fallacy, the source of searching for a separate realm of existence, "lies in the fact that in our language, sentences which express existential propositions and sentences which express attributive propositions may be of the same grammatical form and the fact that they have the same grammatical appearance leads one to assume that they are of the same logical type."[52] On the similar mistaken assumption, the so-called gods might have created metaphysical confusion that since 'man' (particular) exists, therefore, there should also be a realm in which 'Man' (generic) exists. Or, these gods may have been misguided by a logical misconception about the calculus of classes. They did not know that in logic the class '*man*' is the set of individual members of that class, and the domain of possible classes is called the 'universe of discourse' or simply the universe.[53] Logically speaking, what we are calling 'the class' is not another individual or object, of the same type, as its members, nor a 'property' ; it is, as Stebbing upholds, a set of things that have property.[54] Now on this account, if some one says 'man exists' (singular proposition), he is asserting a logical proposition. But on that account if some other person asserts that 'humanity also exists', he is committing a confusion of this calculus of classes, 'a category mistake' or committing the fallacy of misplaced concreteness, because a class is to be regarded as the set of individuals satisfying the propositional function that defines the class.[55] Thus the statement 'humanity exists' is not a proposition, but it is a propositional function, which comes to mean that 'we exist collectively' also. Going beyond this and stating that 'humanity' is a category like 'man', and that Brahman must exist in the same sense in which 'man' exists, is based on the confusion of 'proposition' and 'propositional function'. The so-called gods who are metaphysician demagogues, seem to be creating this logical confusion so that man may not know that logic does not recognise any other 'universe', but only the universe of their *class*, viz, their species being. Thus resolving the logico-metaphysical confusion created by the despisers of humanity, if the upaniṣadic statements about the identity of ātman and brahman, are read with the aphorism *'na mānusāt śreṣṭhataram'*, then we may conclude that the brahman of Upaniṣads is non-different from the 'universal humanity'. In the light of this, there should be no objection if the key concepts 'ātman' and 'brahman' are made co-extensive with 'man' and 'humanity', for applying them in social context and for extending their use in the field of social philosophy. The ideal of brahma-nirvāṇa put forth by Gita would then come to be reinterpreted as the desire of man for merging his transient, atomized, individuality with the essence of collective humanity.

Of course, for this purpose, man will have to transcend his alienated and isolated existence, he will transcend himself and his *de facto* existence. But the word 'transcendence', in this context, has no other meaning than what Sartre understands by this term. Sartre uses this term without having any metaphysical implications. He says that "Man is all the time outside of himself and it is by pursuing the transcendent aims that he himself is able to exist. Man is himself the heart and centre of his transcendence."[56]

Identity of Man and Divine :

The reflection on the ideal of brahma-nirvāṇa brings us to repose and have a brief glimpse about the nature of the 'ultimate' Reality and its relation with man. This concept of Brahman is very helpful in understanding the relation of the individual to the ultimate Reality. The question of the identity of the individual with the Brahman has always remained central for the Upaniṣadic seers, and has gushed out of their hearts in the form of the assertions like 'I am Brahman'. This self is Brahman[57], etc. etc. Śaṁkara also finds a perfect identity between the generic 'Man' and the particularised 'man' in his assertion *'jīvobrahmaiva nāparaḥ'*. According to him the limited and imperfect empirical human self is also an epitome of humanity and therefore it is to be treated as non-different from it. Any differentiation between the two is the product of false consciousness (ajñāna). This type of approach had great moral import in two ways : (i) firstly, it implied that every man should be considered a *human being*, i.e., an exemplification of humanity. Kant also advocated in his moral imperatives, "Treat humanity, either in your own person or in the person of others, always as an end," (ii) Secondly, it disproved the charge of self-abnegation in Indian Philosophy. If the jīva is logically identical to Brahman, then negation of one would mean the negation of other also. Consequently, what is cancelled are only those limitations and finitudes of individuality, the atomicity of existence, which are alien to the inherent unity of mankind.

The idea of treating man logically identical to divine, is a unique feature of Indian thought. Western thinkers shirk to swallow this pill and fail to understand the implications of this identity between the absolute and the individual. On the contrary, in the western tradition, this type of identity between man and divine has not been considered desirable. Kierkegaard, for example, tells us in true Christian spirit that "God and man are two qualities, between which there is an infinite qualitative difference. Every doctrine which overlooks this difference is humanly speaking crazy; understood in godly sense, it is blasphemy."[58] Karen Horney also does not approve this approach and, therefore, castigatingly remarks, "Self-deifying pride is the nucleus of the neurotic type of personality. When a man develops a set of coercive inner dictates by which he seeks to mould himself into the absolute self, he regards the actual or empirical self as an alien and starts to despise it."[59]

This type of pronouncement is based on the gross misunderstanding because in asserting that 'I am Brahman' an individual is shedding his dehumanized condition and coming to realize that he is a 'man'. This is an assertion of 'de-alienation'. However, the idea of the unity of the human and divine was present in German traditions and it was derived by the Young Hegelians from Hegel, as Prof. Tucker shows.[60] These Hegelians took up the task of the realization of this great philosophy in practical life-situation as to how man can become divine. This idea has never been absent from Gita. Gita has, at various places, recognised this essential identity of Ātman and Brahman,[61] which implies that divinity is nothing but 'idealised humanity'. Gita points out to this logical identity in another way. It says that jīva is the part of the Lord.[62] Does it mean that the Lord can be cut into parts ? If not, what does this statement signify ? Commenting on this verse, Radhakrishnan explains that "this does not mean that the Supreme is capable of division or partition into fragments."[63] Therefore, the individual is considered by him a movement of the Supreme, a nucleus. Explaining the aṁśa, Gandhi also upholds in his commentary, Anāsakti Yoga, that "integral portion of the Supreme is the individual soul manifesting himself in every one."[64] This shows that the word 'aṁśa' should not be taken here literally, otherwise the logical fallacy of false composition will be committed. When we say that Brahman is the generic 'man' and jīva is individual, then the collection of jīva will not make a separate man, 'Brahman'. Mill has cautioned us against such fallacious conclusions. He quotes numerous examples, to point out that 'men are not, when brought together, converted into another kind of substance.[65]

Gita clarifies its stand further and holds that 'he is undivided and yet seems to be divided among beings.[66] When the Supreme is incapable of division, how it is inhering in the particular jīva. If I am brahma, you are brahman and others are brahma, then either there are as many 'Supremes' as the individuals are, or the Supreme has been divided into parts to inhere in each. Gita rules out this type of division. Describing the Sāttvika knowledge. Gita advocates that 'One Imperishable Being is seen undivided in the divided.[67] According to Gita, the Supreme is present, as a whole, wherever it is. How is it possible ? This is possible only if we accept that 'aṁśa' refers to logical division of *summum genus*. It is in logical division only, and not in metaphysical or physical division, that the predicate of class can be applied to each and every member of that class.[68] Gita upholds this view also when it says that the 'Lord abides in the hearts of all.[69] For this purpose, the Supreme will have to be taken as 'class' because logical division is possible in case of a 'class' only and not of an 'individual'. In the light of these assertions, we may conclude that Gita recognised that the relation of 'man' and 'brahman' is a relation of 'class-membership' and every member of the class 'humanity' is capable of carrying the predicate 'human' with it. There is no other way of resolving the various problems of relating the 'whole' and the 'part' except that by treating this division as 'logical division'. Thus speaking, the *Jīva* and *Brahman* are only two levels, viz., the level of 'factual individuality' and that of the 'ideational humanity'. All individuals are the existential manifestations of the universal principle behind them. 'I am Brahman' and 'you are Brahman' refer to this fact that behind the false individuality, there is some common uniting principle at work. The scientists also uphold this position that facts are not mere facts but manifestation of some general principle and to discover that principle is the main problem of induction.[70] This unity behind the particulars or the particulrised facts is, therefore, inferential. It cannot be 'perceptual'. It is only when the facts are transcended that this unity can be rationally apprehended. Only in this sense the Brahman can be called transcendental. Therefore. Gita, along with the Upaniṣadic tradition, upholds that the identity between self and Brahman is only 'essential', not 'existential'. It is the empirical, the particularised individual, that is humanity in bondage, the alienated existence.

Nature of Jiva (Empirical Soul) :

In Gita, the essential soul has been regarded as eternal, imperishable, unborn and immortal.[71] This reminds one of Spinoza, who holds that individual modes perish, but the system, as a whole, remains uneffected. This view echoes the voice of Kaṭhopniṣad, which categorically asserts that "The knowing self is never born; nor does he die at any time. He is unborn, eternal, abiding and primeval.[72] But this essential Self is actionless and a mere *Sākṣin* (witness) as recognised by the Kaṭha, Muṇḍaka and Śvetāśvatara Upaniṣads.[73] Such quotations can be multiplied indefinitely. But they all refer to a distinction made between *Ātman* and *Jīva*. Gita also asserts the same truth as advocated by the Upaniṣads. According to Gita, "the Puruṣa, residing in Prakṛti, experiences the guṇas born of Prakṛti; attachment to these guṇas is the cause of his birth in good or evil wombs."[74] This implies that according to Gita, materiality in its three manifestations, as guṇas, is the cause of human bondage. It points out that "sattva, rajas, and tamas are the guṇas sprung from prakṛti, which keep the imperishable dweller bound to the body."[75] Here a question arises that when Ātman is unattached to the guṇas of material prakṛti, how it becomes bound to the body by the three guṇas. In this context Gita brings in the principle of Māyā. Māyā creates finitude and limitations, which keeps a man in bondage. In the fourteenth verse of seventh chapter, Gita declares : "For this My divine delusive mystery (māyā) made up of the three gunas is hard to pierce; but those who make Me their sole refuge pierce the veil.[76] It is under the spell of bewilderment that a man is involved in the materiality and he fails to know his real essence. According to Gita, "veiled by the delusive mystery created by My unique power (*yogamāyāsamāvṛtaḥ*) I am not revealed to all; this bewilderment world does not recognise Me birthless and changeless."[77] From this type of the description of the Māyā, it may be inferred that the empirical ego, the isolated individuality, is the product of bewilderment and ignorance, which is produced due to the attachment with the material modes. Gita makes it clear that when a man identifies himself with the material modes of existence, he forgets his greatness, dignity and uses all his faculties for fostering his egoistic satisfaction. He comes down to the level of a gross psychological hedonist. To rise above the bondage, to realize his lost dignity, one must, therefore, rise above the attachment to material mode of his existence and to become guṇātīte.[78] Gita inspires the moral man to pierce this veil of false individuality. These ego centric enclosures of the individual selfhood must be broken in order to seek liberation.

It has already been pointed out that the striving of a man for the realization of his own universality is said to be Brahma-nirvāṇa, the self-realization. He wants to make his true being identical with the universal being by finishing the apparent separation created by ignorance. Those who make their separate ego-consciousness as the centre of their activity, and those who work with baser or inferior motives are condemned as the depraved persons by Gita.[79]

Sartre holds more or less the same view about the degenerative influence of material attachment. He points out that "all kinds of materialism lead one to treat every man including oneself as an object, that is, as a set of predetermined reactions, in no way different from the patterns of qualities which constitute a table, a chair, or a stone."[80] When man is dominated by egoistic hedonism, which is the only ethical theory consistent with mechanistic materialism, he becomes victim of *mine-thine* duality and the real unity is lost sight of. So long as this sense of *otherness* remains the individual remains in bondage. This level of his existence is the realm of conflicts which is governed by the law of dialects. At this level, man faces the opposite, 'the other'.

Such duality of the empirical ego and the transcendental ego is also found in Kant's idealism where man is assumed to be a divided personality, a 'homo-noumenon' (Man-as-in-itself) and 'homo-phenomenon' (Man-as-it-appears).[81] Kant left the realm of noumenon as something mysterious, which appeared quite impregnable and, therefore, he could not establish any relation between these two aspects of human personality. His ethics of categorical imperative, however, would imply that the phenomenal self, the sensuous self is to be moulded according to the dictates of the noumenal self in order to seek moral perfection. Nevertheless, he could not say anything about the relation between them. The explanation furnished by Gita, therefore, seems to be more cogent. When under the delusion of māyā, an individual feels that he is different from the rest of the humanity, he is bound to feel unhappy. This feeling of isolation by creating false sense of duality negates the re lity of man as a Universal Self. The feeling of 'otherness' is something negative. It is negative because it confronts the man. It is negative because it negates the absoluteness of Ātman, and therefore, this *negative* must be destroyed if man is to realize his real nature.

Śaṁkara, therefore, calls the process of the liberation (mokṣa) as negation of the negation (*parihṛtaparihāra*). In order to realize one's true nature, i.e., the subjectivity, the bonds of materiality (prakṛti) are to be broken. The experience of being bounded by an object has also been portrayed by Hegel as "an experience of finitude. which is an experience of *alienation*."[82]

In Gita also, the Jīva, which is under the sway of Prakṛti, feels estranged and separated from his real essence Brahman, as has already been shown. For Indian thinkers, 'alienation' is same as the finitude created under the delusion of māyā. This is felt as bondage, because it is not content with the limitations imposed on his existence by nature or by history. The 'apprehension of finitude is an unhappy consciousness of self-estrangement', which Hegel calls the "sorrow of finitude".[83] This unhappy state of existence can be overcome by finishing all sense of mine-thine, and of the personal possession, which creates the sense of 'otherness'. Gita lays down the maxim that "the wise, who have united their intelligence (with the Divine) renouncing the fruits, which their action yields, reach the sorrowless state."[84] Here the writer of Gita is very correct in saying that an individual is not to abnegate himself in reaching the highest state, but he is to free himself from the attachment (saṅgavarjitaḥ) in order to overcome the estrangement. He is to transform himself into a socialized man by transcending his psychological egoism. The ultimate ideal before the individual here is the negation of all the discriminative tendencies and the apparent egoism The illusion that Gita wanted a moral man to pierce is the illusion of 'otherness'. (*īkṣate yogayuktātmā sarvatra samadarśanaḥ*) (VI. 29). Hegel also advocated for the piercing of the illusion of otherness. He said, "The aim of knowledge is to divest the objective world that stands opposed to us of its strangeness, and to find ourselves at home in it, which means no more than to trace the objective world back to the notion—to our inner most self."[85] Needless to say that this innermost self is 'Ātman' in Indian systems, which is the principle of universality behind the particularized, sensuous, psycho-biological individuality. Sartre rightly points out that "there is no human nature, but a 'human universality'."[86] In the context of these pronouncements, the realization that jīva is Ātman gives real meaning to man's existence. Man exists only in so far as he asserts that he is man. Sartre would also substantiate this view that 'man exists only in so far as he realizes himself'.[87] Kierkegaard also corroborates the doctrine of Gita. He says that "the reality of every one's existence proceeds thus from the 'inwardness' of man."[88] This inwardness, according to the existentialist thinkers, is subjectivity. Verily, which is the principle of subjectivity, universality and humanity, has been referred to as Ātman throughout the text of Gita.

After this brief discussion about the philosophical problems raised in Gita and the nature of the ideal suggested, we can summarise our conclusions that : (i) Gita believes in the unity of human existence. Whosoever exists on the human plane, is an exemplification of and an epitome of the same humanity; (ii) the individualism is a product of bewilderment and that in order to cancel this bewilderment, a man is to pass from the narrow ego to the real humanity by transcending the false limitations of material attachment and thereby removing the embargo imposed by the degenerated socio-economic conditions; and (iii) the ideal state of human existence (*paramavāsthā*), the par excellent mode of living (paramagati) is state of man's realization of his lost unity with the mankind.

Ethical Doctrines of Gita's Anasaki Yoga

The verses of Gita barring some narrative ones are full of moral teachings and these can be interpreted to serve as a guide for practical conduct. The very opening phrase of Gita 'dharmakṣetre kurukṣetre' may serve as a maxim of morality for the honest and sincere discharge of one's duty. Kurukṣetra is the actual life situation in which man is engaged in fighting the battle for dharma. Virtue lies not in mere cognition of good and evil but in its practice. The starting emphasis is that the field of dharma (dharmakṣetra) is the field of actual practice. Marx also emphasized this fact in VIII Theses on Feuerbach that "Social life is essentially practical."[89] Following this criterion, the discussion about the meanings of moral predicates may be an intellectual luxury but it is not a sign of moral excellence. Since all mysteries about 'dharma' find their solution in the field of human practice, the field should be a real field of action. Gita, therefore, comes to establish the reality of this world. It condemns those who deny the reality of world ; they are called depraved souls (*naṣṭatmā*), oligophrenics (*alpabuddhayaḥ*), hypocrates (*dambhamānamadānvitaḥ*) etc.[90] Only evil doers (*ugrakarmaṇaḥ*) and devilish persons (*asurāḥ*) say that the world is unreal and without a base (*asatyam apratiṣṭhaṁ te jagad āhur anīśvaram*).[91]

Accordingly, the world-denial is the outcome of the mental perversity. In this way, Gita, at the very outset, lays stress that the moral ideal cannot be realized by world-negation or bv renunciation, but man is to seek his self-realization through praxis. Gita also starts with a denunciatory note against the sense of personal possession. The use of word 'māmakāḥ' in the opening verse (*māmakāḥ paṇḍavāś cai va*) is the expression of the egoism and sense of personal possessiveness. Commenting on the use of this word, Radhakrishnan writes, "This sense of mineness is the result of *ahaṁkāra* which is the source of evil.[92] Here the Mamakāra or selfishness on the part of the Kauravas which leads to the love of power and domination has been exposed. It is worth noting that the persons having such sense of egoism, have been deplored as the persons whose wits have been warped by greed (*lobhopahata cetasaḥ*) (I.38). Accordingly, the opening scene of Gita is that the forces of greed and egoism are to be fought in actual life-situation and they are to be finished from this world, if man is to live with dignity and authenticity. Needless to emphasize again that communism is also pitted against the forces of greed, responsible for dehumanization.

The whole discourse of Gita starts with the crisis faced by Arjuna. This is not his personal problem, but, as Gandhi points out, "every seeker has one time or another to pass through a conflict of duties, a heart churning."[93] This refers to the universality of the problem. Arjuna, the fighter, represents any man in the society, who feels this moral crisis and wants to solve it. Similarly, the whole dialogue between Arjuna and Kṛṣṇa in Ist Chapter ends with despair '*viṣāda*' (*Śrikṛṣṇārjuna samvāde arjunaviṣāda yoga nāma prathamodhyāya*). This sort of distress, as Arjuna felt, is a dramatization of the recurring predicament of mankind. Radhakrishnan rightly points out that "Man, on the threshold of higher life feels disappointed with the glamour of world and yet illusions cling to him and he cherishes them."[94] The feeling of such crisis, however, has a great significance for the amelio rative disciplines. The expression of this type of existential anxiety and moral despair is considered to be a pre-requisite of moral regeneration. "The modern existentialism", says Sartre "also confronts man with a possibility of choice."[95] Such a crisis also appears, as Prof. Tucker points out in the moral theory of Kant in the form of an inner conflict or 'natural dialect' of duty versus inclination.[96] It appears from the pronouncements of various moral thinkers that such dissatisfaction with one's present state is necessary for his moral and social regeneration. Those who are engaged in improving the lot of the people, first of all make the people aware of the miserable condition of their existence. Unless this misery and wretchedness of their life situation is reflected in their consciousness, they cannot prepare themselves to negate frustrating and dehumanizing conditions. This is what Buddha and Marx also did. Moral striving cannot be expected from those who feel a 'piggish satisfaction' with the present. It is for the Socrates dissatisfied to traverse the higher path. In expressing his despair, Arjuna, the representative moral man has expressed the anxiety that his whole being needs regeneration. Arjuna of Gita is a symbol (nimitta), who refers allegorically to the widespread dejection, disgust and despondency. In this way, Gita wants to make us realize that there prevails in social life a deep rooted crisis and the whole humanity stands in the need of moral regeneration.

That the crisis of Arjuna was the expression of man's alienation, and his atomized thinking, as separated from the social situation, is evident from several pronouncements of Gita. In the battle field of life, Arjuna is confronted with the forces of evil and the lustful tendencies (*lobhopahatacetasaḥ*) (I.38), which have taken humanity to ransom Radhakrishnan makes it evident that in his depression, Arjuna faces the world as a stranger thrown into a threatening chaos.[97] This is the state of man's alienation. In Hegelian philosophy, when the spirit as conscious subject (man) is confronted with spirit as external object (the world), it is called the state of 'self-alienation' or 'self-estrangement'.[98] However, communism finds this alienation when one is to confront the forces of acquisitiveness.

Separated and alienated from this social obligation, Arjuna was expressing his concern more for his personal gain or loss. When a man is under the spell of narrow egoism and is dominated by the sense of attachment (āsakti), he leaves behind his 'socialized self' and measures everything in terms of his personal considerations. Accordingly, Arjuna's straightforward question was "what pleasure can there be in slaying these sons of Dhrtarāṣṭra ?"[99] It appears that Arjuna was measuring his social duty in terms of material comforts and discomforts. He was concerned with material happiness, as the standard of one's duty, when he said, "These I would not kill, not even for the kingship of three worlds much less for an earthly kingdom."[100] This shows that his whole thinking was polluted by hedonistic considerations. In the jargon of communism, he was motivated by a 'capitalist mentality', as the capitalists of Marxian concept are always guided by the monetary and pecuniary motives. Arjuna was totally disregardful for the 'ideals of human life', the ideals of dharma and his social responsibilities. It was due to this 'āsakti', the desire of measuring his worth in material terms, that made him forgetful of his obligation to the society and generated despair in him. He was feeling himself alone, isolated and atomisized, as if his soul was circumscribed into an aweful singleness. This was symptomatological of alienation.

Thus, we can conclude that the problem of Gita is the problem of man's alienation from his social context, under the sway of the forces of greed and attachment (āsakti), and Anāsakti Yoga finds a solution for cancelling this.

Dynamics of Human Fall :

Searching for the sources of dehumanization, Gita comes in the ultimate analysis to the conclusion that the attachment to the material objects is the cause of human miseries. Explaining the whole dynamics, Gita points out : "In a man, brooding on objects of the senses, attachment to them springs up ; attachment begets craving and craving begets 'wrath'. Wrath (in turn) breeds stupefaction, stupefaction leads to loss of memory, loss of memory ruins the reason and the ruin of reason spells utter destruction."[101] When the question is once again raised as to what are the things that impel a man to commit sin, Gita tells that it is "lust, it is wrath, born out of the guṇa-rajas. It is the arch devourer, the arch sinner. Know this to be man's enemy here.

Kāma eṣa krodha eṣa rajoguṇasamudbhavaḥ ;
Mahāśano mahāpāpma viddhyenam iha vairiṇam."[102]

It reminds one of the communist ethics which also says that the real illusion of man is the pursuit of 'accumulating private property', which has made him foolish. Gita is fore-running communism in proclaiming the sense of possession as degrading and dehumanizing. The attachment to the objects of sensuous gratification is seen as the source of the fall of man. Once he becomes victim of this, he can degrade himself to any degree. He may be prepared to do any thing debasing. He may sell his own honour and may bargain the honour of others to satisfy his material-lust. When a greedy man, a man who is under the sway of lust and greed, comes to fall, the depth of his fall cannot be measured. He can make the whole society as hell for his own selfish ends. Gita has, therefore, called them the *gate of hell*. According to the description given in Gita, 'kāma' (lust), wrath (krodha) and 'lobha' (greed) are the three gates which drag man to hell or hellish torment :

trividhaṁ narakasye' daṁ dvāraṁ nāśanam ātmanaḥ;
kāmaḥ krodhas tathā lobhas tasmād etat trayam tyajet.[103]

In so saying, Gita is asserting a psychological truth well recognised by the psycho-therapists that it is the desire of seeking pleasure that generates frustration and the resultant destructive tendencies if it is thwarted. This 'Kāma' (libidinal tendency) is the source of all frustration, which creates a hellish torment and pathogenic traits in the personality of man. Therefore, from the point of a mentally healthy behaviour in society, this is an undesirable tendency. Gita has vehemently condemned those who follow the path of lust and greed calling them the men of devilish heritage. Gita says : "Given to insatiable lust, arrogance, pride and conceit etc., these cruel scorner, lowest of mankind and vile, I hurl down again and again into devilish womb and they sink lower and lower in birth after birth."[104] The contemptuous tone of Gita shows that such persons are enemies of humanity, as they can put the whole humanity to ransom for the satisfaction of their lust and greed. Even those persons, who do good actions but do so under the sway of some hedonistic and profit motive, are not held in good esteem by Gita and they are despised as 'kāmātmanaḥ' (the carnally-minded).[105] Commenting on this pronouncement of Gita, Dr. Radhakrishnan tells that "even the vedic sacrifices are directed to the acquisition of material rewards, but the Gita asks us to renounce all selfish desire and work."[106] Without multiplying such contemptuous and denunciatory verses, the evidence provided here leads one to believe that according to Gita the actions done with lust and greed are the source of human misery and those who do work with profit motive are pitiable persons (*kṛpaṇāḥ phalahetavaḥ*).[107] The avoidance of '*kāmya karma*' is therefore, the necessary corollary of this doctrine. Accordingly, Gita has repeatedly emphasized in various verses that actions with the motive of personal profit and with attachment, should be verily avoided.[108] These actions lead to bondage, to conflicts and to neurogenic frustrations. Describing the nature of kāmya karma, Prābhākara points out that kāmya duties have sensuous import or an extraneous pleasure as their end. In either case there is a kāmanā or desire for a consequence, i.e., for a consequence other than the act itself.[109] According to this definition, some material motive and hedonistic end is always involved in kāmya karma. In such actions, the consciousness for material advantage (*iṣṭasādhanatā*) is always present. It follows from this that according to Gita, the desire for hedonistic pleasures cannot be the end of any moral action. On the contrary, the actions which have such goods as their end, are not considered moral actions at all.

Criticism of Hedonism :

The quest for pleasure, as an end, is considered as a psychological fact by the advocates of hedonism. As Freud tells us "the entire activity of man is bent upon procuring pleasure and avoiding pain. This activity is controlled by 'pleasure principle'.[110] But such descriptive statements of facts cannot serve as a normative principle. Accordingly, a moral theorist will find it hard to justify the tenet of psychological hedonism. That is why, Gita, as a moral treatise rejects this theory of '*kāmya karma*'. Denouncing the 'kāmya karma' or the actions done with hedonistic ends in view, is not restricted to Gita alone, but in west also many ethical thinkers have realized that when we limit ourselves to pleasure, we become limited to sensuous individuality, because pleasure is some such notion that one can seek only his own pleasure. That is why, psychological hedonism has met with battering attacks by the moral theorists. In general, psychological hedonism is the view that every person does, as a matter of fact, seek his own pleasure in life. The only motive that is effective in conduct is the desire to get pleasure. This approach to the problems of human conduct has not been found tenable ethically. For example, Broad has rejected this theory after a lengthy discussion saying that "I conclude then, that the arguments for this doctrine are certainly fallacious and the doctrine is almost certainly false."[111] The theory of psychological hedonism has also been rejected by Mackenzie on the ground of its not being a *sound theory*.[112]

When the hedonists are so cornered, they try to seek refuge in the rising materialism today. But the adherents of psychological hedonism will be shocked to learn that the communism also lends support to Gita in deprecating the actions done with hedonistic motives and the desire of surplus value. Surprisingly enough, the philosophical materialism of Marx is equally opposed to the theory of psychological hedonism. Communism advocates in general that passion of greed is inhuman because it deprives man of freedom and thereby dehumanizes him. But in very specific terms also, Marx has criticised the theory of Bentham and Mill, who are considered to be the best defenders of '*kāmya karma*'. According to him, the utilitarian ethics of Bentham is a monetary moral philosophy. In *Das Capital*, Marx refers to Bentham as "the insipid, pedantic, leather-tongued oracle of the commonplace bourgeoise intelligence of the 19th century." He goes on to condemn Mill that "at no time and in no century has the most trivial commonplace ever before strutted about with such appalling self-satisfaction."[113] Like Gita's rejections of Kāmya Kārma, Marx rejects the principle of utility as quite useless principle. It was the standpoint of Marx in *German Ideology* also that the philosophy of pleasure cannot serve as a sound theory. There he writes against hedonism that "the philosophy of pleasure has never been anything but the 'clever phraseology' of certain social circles that have enjoyed the privilege of pleasure...More recently the philosophy of pleasure has been elaborated in a new form by the bourgeoise utilitarian ethics."[114] Continuing his attack further, Marx has despised this approach as 'a flat and hypocritical doctrine'. It is on these moral considerations that Gita has outrightly rejected the theory of 'Kāmya Kārma', i.e., the actions having hedonistic ends. Thus, we may conclude that the attachment to the hedonistic pleasures, sense of personal possession, greed are considered by Gita as the main ingredients of human degradation, dehumanization and despair.

Way to Release :

If the attachment, greed and lust are the cause of fall, then naturally a man can rise high by following the path of non-attachment. Gandhi considers it to be the panacea for our troubles. According to him, Gita advocates that 'matchless remedy is renunciation of fruits of action'.[115] Commenting on verse 47 of discourse XVIII, Gandhi also emphasizes that 'the central teaching of Gita is Anāsakti—abandonment of the fruit of action'.[116] Released are those who have given up attachment (*gatasaṅgasya muktasya*).[117] According to Gita, he is happy on this earth, who holds out against the flood tide of lust and wrath.[118] This doctrine is also called the doctrine of 'niṣkāma karma yoga', because it emphasizes that the action should be done without the lust of pleasure or the greed of material reward. Accordingly, it brings forth a sense of disinterestedness to bear upon the accomplishment of the duties of life. The stress is that duty should be done with the sense of discharging the assigned obligation (svadharma). The call to do one's duty without attachment has been given by Gita at various places. In second chapter, Arjuna is told to act without attachment.[119] The calculations of the consequences in advance in the very discharge of the duty and weighing them in terms of personal gain is a harmful tendency. The difficulty may arise as to how one can foresee all the pleasurable and painful consequences of his actions or decisions, which need be guided by principles. How can we become fully certain of the future ? But on the other hand, as a social being, we cannot dissociate our individual performances from our relation to our fellow beings. How can, then we calculate pleasures of others as well as ours in arriving at a social policy ? These interactions of pleasures and pains are so complicated that man cannot work out all the possibilities of his action or his non-action. When anticipated gains are not achieved, there is a lag between the level of aspiration and level of actual achievement. This gap puts premium on personality by creating frustrations. The best way, therefore, is to act "without making fruits as their motive."

Pointing out that anāsakti leads to liberation from the snares of materiality, Gita lays down the maxim of morality ; which says : "Thou ever perform without attachment the work that you must do ; for performing action without attachment man attains to Supreme."[120] According to this assertion, the highest state of human existence (*parama*) will be that when the selfish motives and egoistic interests will not regulate the human conduct. For the realization of this end, the sources of greed, i.e., the acquisitive mania will have to be finished. This is the remedy of all the ills of society. Gita is very clear in specifying this remedial measure. In unequivocal terms, it tells that "the wise men, gifted with the attitude of detachment, who renounce the fruit of action, are released from the bondage of birth and attain to the state, which is free from all ills."[121] Verily, the highest state of human existence, will be achieved when humanity is got rid of the forces of the greed and a lust for the material gains. This transformed state of man's future existence appears to like that conceived by the founder of communism also where man will finish the capitalist mode of running after acquisition of private possessions and private property which is the source of all attachment. In present-day crisis, when every one is after material pursuits, this doctrine of anāsakti is the true way to get the miseries of our society mitigated and then to liberate the whole society from the bondage and vagaries of growing materialism. Radhakrishnan emphasizes this point, thus "if man rises above his egoism and acts without selfish attachment only then he is truly free."[122] According to this doctrine, what man ought to renounce, is only his narrow limitations and his selfish interest, if he wants to liberate himself from his alienation, and from the bonds of competitive goods. Thus speaking, the real liberation is the release from the 'constitutive conditions of actuality' and from the 'illusion of psychological hedonism'.

Is the ideal of performance of disinterested action a practicable one ? If an ideal is utopian, it cannot inspire the moral agent to act accordingly. Gita has nowhere doubted its practicability. In verse No. III. 20, testimony of Janaka is quoted to prove its authenticity.

But other thinkers have also recognised that this ideal is practicable. For example, Sidgwick is one of such thinkers, who uphold that "a certain degree of disinterestedness seems to be necessary in order to obtain full enjoyment."[123] Accordingly, a man, who maintains throughout an Epicurean mood and fixes his aim on his own pleasure, is liable to miss the full spirit of the chase. Here comes into view what he called the fundamental paradox of hedonism. Rashdall also corroborates this view that the existence of 'disinterested affections' is not a myth but a psychological fact. He says : "Reasonable man, contemplating the world as an impartial spectator, uninfluenced by private desires or passions, would necessarily recognise benevolence as that affection, which ought to be gratified in preference to merely self-regarding desires."[124] These thinkers rightly uphold that the scepticism about the practicability of the non-attached actions is unwarranted. Kant, in his doctrine of categorical imperative, had been emphasizing that man can act with a sense of respect for the 'Moral Law'. But his conviction that the duty is a 'universal command' and that the genuine ultimate rule of conduct must fulfil the conditions of (i) 'universality' and (ii) consistency within itself, is not correct.

Gita would not subscribe to this approach, because according to Gita, the actions done for lokasaṁgraha are also non-attached actions. Gita points out, "Just as, with attachment, the unenlightened perform all action, O Bhārata, even so, but unattached, should the enlightened man act, with a desire for the welfare of humanity (lokasaṁgraham)."[125] By emphasizing on the moral excellence of the duties done for the lokasaṁgraha, Gita has done a great service in removing many misconceptions. It has countered the charge of blind asceticism on one hand and also of mechanical performance of one's duty. Sacrifice for the sake of sacrifice is not the tone of Gita. One should sacrifice his personal interests and egoistic tendencies for some higher goal. Rashdall has correctly pointed out that "self-sacrifice for its own sake is always irrational and immoral. It is the object for which the sacrifice is made that gives it its moral value."[126] By sacrificing one's personal interests for some social good, the sacrifice becomes valuable. It is, thus, the welfare of humanity that gives moral value to an action and not mere Kantian formalism.

Bradley also comes forward to defend the theory 'anāsakti' from another point of view. His approach is that hedonistic pleasures are momentary and their pursuit is a wastage of moral endeavours, because in this endless pursuit, as Bradley says : "We have not found ourselves and we are not satisfied."[127] What is then the use of pursuing them ? Therefore, action ought to be done with the sense of discharging one's social obligation. Realizing that only a man with disciplined sense can perform action without the lust of material pleasures, Gita devotes full sixth chapter to the discourse as to how the senses can be trained to act without attachment. But surprisingly enough, Marx also, reiterates the same idea as that of Gita. Marx advocates that all that can be achieved in the direction of making us more free is to *conduct* this (human) metabolism rationally,[128] and by rational control, he means "with a minimum expenditure of energy and conditions, most dignified and adequate to human nature so that it may help a man to reach the kingdom of freedom which lies beyond the sphere of proper material production."[129] Thus speaking, Marx agrees with Gita that control on senses (*indriya nigraha*) is essential for the realization of the lofty ends of human life. In the light of this discussion, it would not be justified to doubt the practicability of the non-attached actions (anāsakti) and their moral efficacy to lead to the release from miserable and wretched conditions of existence.

Doctrine of Karma :

The most significant pronouncement in context of the performance of niṣkāma karma, has been laid down in second chapter of Gita. It is considered to be the 'essential principle of disinterestedness'. Laying down the imperative, Kṛṣṇa tells Arjuna, "Action alone is thy province, never the fruits thereof."[130] This is really a key principle which puts embargo on the level of human ambitions and aspirations. The success and failure of a man's efforts does not depend on the individual but there are many other variables which cannot be controlled. Man should act with this truth in mind if he wants to avoid frustrations of life. This is neither determinism nor a bid to reduce man to utter helpless puppet in the hands of the circumstances. The implication of this assertion is that man cannot change the laws of nature according to his own convenience. Even God cannot change the natural laws at His discretion. Putting embargo on the arbitrary powers of God also, Gita specifically points out that "the Lord creates neither the agency nor action for the world ; neither does he connect action with its fruits. It is nature that is at work."[131] If the laws are so immutable, objective and inexorable, it is merely a day-dream to think that nature will change its course according to the convenience of a man. On the contrary, man should limit his province only upto the rational exercise of his choice, taking into consideration the operation of these laws, as far as known to him. No one can work out all the possible permutations and combinations of natural events. The physico-chemical and bio-physiological laws of nature will not care for the wishful thinking of an individual. Therefore, man will have to be prepared to suffer for his wrongful choices.

Man suffers for his own ignorance and his own wrong choices. Lewis also points out that at least half of the world's avoidable troubles are created by those who do not know what they want, and pursue what would not satisfy them if they had it.[132] Similarly, the social laws cannot be subjected to the whims and idiosyncracies of any individual. In short, the questions of ultimate ends cannot be proved in any final sense. Under such circumstances, the suspension of action is neither practicable nor desirable. Therefore, the individual should adjust the domain of his legitimate freedom upto the exercise of his own choice without worrying for the problem of causal determinism or indeterminism in the events of nature. Sidgwick has taken great pain to show that the question of determinism is much less important to ethics than it has been thought to be.[133] We can, therefore, very well agree with this maxim of morality as advocated in Gita. Whatever, a man sows, he should be ready to reap. But in sowing, he can exercise his choice fully.

Through this lofty principle of karma, Gita also wants to say that social responsibilities must be discharged irrespective of one's personal ambitions, fears or temptations. In today's context, when people are becoming more and more prone to calculating the consequental gains, the moral implication of this principle becomes all the more relevant. It counteracts the all round craze of seeking more and more profit. Communism also considered that such tendency is the outcome of a degenerated state of society. Accordingly, profit motive should be avoided in social obligations. The growing trend of money-making is harmful. It is so because those, who work simply in order to make more money, will not be primarily interested in their jobs, and the quality of their work is liable to deteriorate. A morally disciplined and socially enlightened man will regard his work as a source of intellectual and moral excellence and a source of genuine happiness. Therefore, for gaining real happiness, there should be no selfish purpose behind our actions. It does not mean that man should become blind and immune to the social consequences of his evil deeds. The principle implies that consequences will follow according to the operative laws of nature. Gandhiji rightly puts forth his views on this issue, when he says : "To be detached from the fruits of action is not to be ignorant of them or to disregard or disown them. To be detached is never to abandon action, because the contemplated result may not follow. On the contrary, it is proof of the immovable faith in the certainty of the contemplated result following in due course."[134] This interpretation seems to be truly expressive of the spirit of the law of karma.

Concept of Moral Freedom :

The restriction on the domain of the moral agent to the exercise of his choice has another great implication of moral import. The freedom is exercising his choice has been guaranteed in this maxim to the moral agent without any interference. Such freedom is an essential postulate of morality. This gives immense liberty to man to decide his fate and build his fortune. The law of karma implies that every thing, happiness and misery, heaven and hell depend on one's own action and a man need not to beg the gods for boon or gift.

Sartre is more assertive on this issue when he says that "man is nothing else but what he makes of himself."[135] This is the first principle of Sartre's existentialism and this is the real meaning of law of karma also.

Another important point on which this law lays emphasis, is that it imbibes the sense of responsibility in the individual. The courage to bear the failures and to take responsibility of the consequences of one's deed is a moral courage—a courage of conviction. When a man has been granted freedom to build his fate, why to transfer the blame to others ? It is a symptom of pathological disorder. It is the patient of Paranoia, who suffers from the delusions of persecutions and with a fairly constant pattern of symptoms, he feels that the whole world is hostile to him. He generally has the complaint that "they are the cause of all his failures and frustrations."[136] Such maladjusted, pathological and abnormal persons find themselves incapable of leading tension-free life. In modern times, the psycho-analytical therapy aims to lay bare before this individual that it is no other external force but his own subconscious that is troubling him. On knowing that the source of trouble was lying in his own libidinous tendencies, the patient becomes cured and rehabilitated. Similar therapeutic role, this law of niṣkāma karma plays in the moral life. When an individual comes to realize that he himself is the cause of his own degeneration, he becomes prepared for remedying the situation by his own efforts and it is in the realization of this fact that he becomes the maker of his own destiny. Arjuna is made to realize that even God cannot improve the lot of those people who are not themselves prepared to alter their life-situation. Man may seek inspiration from here or there, but in the end, he himself will have to work out the remedy. This requires the regaining of faith in one's own freedom and his own potentialities. By realizing his self-confidence, a man realizes his lost dignity, and thereby he proves that he is really existing on human plane. Sartre also expresses the same opinion that "man will attain existence when he is what he proposes to be."[137] This is what follows from his dictum 'man is condemned to be free' and this is what this law of niṣkāma karma would also lead to, in its last logical consequence.

A life-affirming Philosophy :

The theory of non-attached action does not preach anywhere the renunciation of world. The despair of Arjuna tells us that it is only in the moments of acute dejection that a man seeks flight from this world. This is symptomatic of abnormality that the patient uses the mental mechanisms of withdrawal, and of denying the reality, etc., as a means to avoid the neurogenic tensions. This is an unhealthy symptom. Gita tells Arjuna in very clear terms that those, who are unable to face their life-situation are 'unmanly' (*Hṛdayadaurbalyam*) (II.3). An evasive attitude of running away from the field of one's duty is considered by Gita to be 'unworthy of the nobles' (*anāryajuṣṭam*) (II.2). Gita warns such persons that if they leave their allotted task, they will be morally depraved. Addressing the moral agent, Gita says : "If you will not fight this righteous fight, then failing in your duty and losing your honour you will incur sin. The world will for-ever recount the story of your disgrace ; and for a man of honour, disgrace is worse than death."[138] It is unbehoving a man of integrity and moral courage to run away from adversities. The point, in the words of Marx, should be to change it. Gita exhorts the individual to transform the life-situation by valiantly fighting against them to finish and secure ultimate victory (kṣudraṁ hṛdayadaurbalyaṁ tyaktvottiṣṭha paraṁtapa).[139] Marx also held the same position that in order to transform the 'unman' into 'man', the speculative flight into the imaginary world created by religion, will not be desirable. For this purpose, the life-situation will have to be changed.[140] 'Revolutionizing the world to finish alienation' is also the sum and substance of the Fourth Theses on Feuerbach written by Marx.[141] The aim of Gita also is the same, that is to persuade Arjuna, the moral agent to revolutionize his life-situation and finish the conditions which are the source of his confrontation.[142] This life-affirming purpose is working from beginning to end in Gita. This refutes those, who call Indian philosophy a philosophy of withdrawal or of life-negation. On the contrary, the Indian wisdom has been very clear in condemning those, who despise their mundane responsibilities. Gita pointedly tells that it is not right for a moral man to renounce one's allotted task.[143]

The real renunciation is not the renunciation of obligations (Karma Saṅyāsa) but the renunciation of the fruits thereof (Karma phalasanyāsa). According to the Gita, a sanyāsin is a man, who performs all obligatory actions without depending on the fruits thereof (VI. 1). The parasites, who live on unearned income and neglect their contribution to society, cannot be called sanyāsin. According to the words of Gita, sanyāsin is not the man, who neglects the sacrificial fire nor he who neglects action. Working out its sociological implication. Gandhi opines that fire may be taken to mean all possible instruments of action.[144] Thus speaking, Gita wants to convey that those, who are not participating in the productive process of the society are not the social persons. Similarly a yogī is not conceived as a man who withdrawing from the 'collective modes of production' goes to forests, or a man who plays physical acrobats. But, according to Gita, yogī is a man who is not attached either to the objects of senses or to actions and who sheds all selfish purposes (*Sarvasaṁkalpasaṁyāsī*) (VI. 4). For this purpose, a man needs to discipline himself to resist the allurements and baits. Man is not instigated to seek refuge in forests but he is inspired to live in this very world, but in such a way that he does not downgrade himself, when temptations are presented. A disciplined man, as Gita tells us, moves among the sense objects with the senses weaned from likes and dislikes.[145] This attitude shows that a man does not leave the world of objects, but simply leaves the desire to misappropriate them. This is the prime requirement in communism also. In the opinion of present author, no social order can function well unless the people acquire this attitude. Thus, it is not a life-negating but a life-affirming requirement.

On the basis of all this discussion, we can uphold that the ethics of Gita is not a life-denying ethics, but it is a call to transform this world in order to make it fit for dignified living

Concept of Dharma

Dharma, a Key concept of Gita has great ethical significance. Gita opens with the very word 'dharmakṣetre'. But greater still is the significance of it when Gita affirms that the need of establishing dharma remains the supreme need in every age (*dharmasaṁsthāpa-nārthāya saṁbhavāmi yuge-yuge*).[146] What is this dharma, for the establishment of which the Divine forces manifest themselves? This seems to be very important question. Apart from the concept of dharma, Gita refers to '*svadharma*' also.[147] Is *svadharma* a subjective principle or has it some socio-ethical connotation? These are the natur l questions that may trouble every enquiring mind. The question of dharma will be discussed in details in a later chapter.

But the general formula laid by Gita about *svadharma* is that each should discharge his obligations in the context of his social situation. The moral data is provided by the society, which cannot be ignored. Human beings do not live in vacuum nor they can derive the rules of conduct from '*nothingness*'. Durkheim has rightly suggested that "we should concern ourselves (in deriving our duties) with moral facts instead of abstract formulae.[148] In Gita also, the field of deciding the questions of righteousness (dharma-kṣetra) is the practical field of action (kurukṣetra), and therefore, meaning of the moral imperatives should be understood only in context of life-situation. Radhakrishnan has rightly said that "whether we look at the metaphysical truth or the social duty, our part is clear. It is possible to rise higher through the performance of one's duty in right spirit."[149] The futility of searching for the meanings of moral predicates apart from the human situation has been well brought out by all the positivist thinkers of today. In this light, 'svadharma' has a great moral efficacy as a rule of social obligation.

So far as the question of re-establishing 'dharma' in every age is concerned, this is required in order to save the morality from sinking into something static and dogmatic. Every age adjusts the moral codes and practical rules of conduct according to the requirement of that age, although the ultimate ideal to be realized progressively is not lost sight of. In communist theory also, the feudal institutions become degenerative in capitalist stage and therefore must be discarded as 'reactionary' but the ultimate ideal of communism is not lost sight of. Thus by emphasizing on the re-establishment of a new social code in consonance with the necessities of history and human life-situation, Gita advocates a progressive morality. Although the idea of a completed system remains an ideal, yet we are to bring our moral efforts to the approximation of that. Milne also expresses the similar views. He says : "On a teleological interpretation of human history, the various social moralities of different times and places appear as successive approximations in the gradual development of a universal human morality, which will be achieved when different societies are united together into the harmonious life on one universal human society."[150] Nevertheless, the progressive realization of this ideal goes on from age to age. Gita advocates that the decayed and out-moded institutional manifestations should yield place to new. When some old institutions die, we should not lament over the slow dying of the old order,[151] because it is the firm conviction of Gita that new life comes only by death of the old[152] and that the essences, which are impregnable, imperishable, do not die.[153] This attitude saves the morality from becoming reactionary, customary and ritualistic.

This brief survey of the ethical doctrines of the Anāsakti Yoga of Gita leads us to the conclusion that its emphasis is on practical life. Such a practical guide to raise the humanity to the higher plane of dignified living by piercing the bonds of egoism and attachment is most needed today when man stands bewildered, confused and oppressed by the doubts of annihilation. The emptiness and profaneness of present-day life cannot be cured by abstract sermonizing. Gita repudiates the separation of theory from practice and *vice-versa*. It holds that "only fools speak of *Sāṁkhya* (knowledge) and *yoga* (practical discipline) as separate from each other.[154] In moral life, theory cannot be divorced from practice nor practical morality can function without rational apprehension of the situation and one's obligation. In order to get success in moral endeavours and sociological transformation, Kṛṣṇa, the guide and Arjuna, the practical executer, 'the human sensuous activity' should join together (*yatra yogeśvraḥ kṛṣṇo yatra pārtho dhanurdharaḥ*) and where they join together, as Gita assures the mankind, there are fortune, victory, prosperity.[155] In the light of this, the criticism of Marx that ' the philosophers have only *interpreted* the world in various ways, the point, however, is to *change* it, does not apply to the philosophy of Gita. In Gita, no demarcation line has been drawn between salvation and the worldly life. The present writer agrees with the conclusions drawn by Gandhiji that 'Gita is not a theoretical treatise. It is a living but silent guide whose directions one has to understand.[156]

References

1. *Bhagavadgītā*, XVIII. 73.
2. Bahm, A.J., *The Bhagavadgītā or the Wisdom of Krishna*, p. 10.
3. Dasgupta, S.N., *History of Indian Philosophy*, Vol. II, p. vii.

4. Ibid., p. 501.
5. Freud, S., *Civilization and its Discontents*, p. 141.
6. *Bhagavadgītā*, IV. 7.
7. Quoted in *The Gospel of Life* by Brooks, F.T., p. v.
8. Tilak, B.G., *Gita Rahasya* (Hindi 13th Ed.), p. 63.
9. Ibid., p. 11.
10. Titus, H.H., Ethics for Today, p. 510.
11. Bahm, A.J., op. cit., pp. 17-18.
12. McIver, R.M. and Page, C.H., *Society*, p. 506.
13. Copi, I.M., *Symbolic Logic* (3rd Ed.), p. 185.
14. Jacobi, Jolande, *Psychology of C.G. Jung*, p. 127 ff.
15. Cassirer, E., *An Essay on Man*, p. 32.
16. Desai, Mahadeva, *The Gita According to Gandhi*, p. 135.
17. Tucker, Robert C., *Philosophy and Myth in Karl Marx*, p. 146.
18. Desai, Mahadeva, op. cit., p. 127.
19. Marx, K., and Engels, F., *German Ideology*, p. 14.
20. Desai, Mahadeva, *The Gita According to Gandhi*, p. 209.
21. Renou, L., *Religions of Ancient India*, p. 60.
22. Woodroffe, Sir John, *Introduction to Tantra śāstra*, p. 34.
23. Radhakrishnan, S., *Eastern Religion and Wastern Thought*, p. 55.
24. Betai (Dr) Ramesh, *Gita and Gandhiji*, pp. 165-183, 204-256.
25. Radhakrishnan, S., *Eastern Religion and Western Thought*, p. 56.
26. Gandhi, M.K., *Young India*, 6-8-1925.
27. Gandhi, M.K., *Harijan*, 24-8-1934.
28. Desai, Mahadeva, op. cit., p. 129.
29. *Bhagavatgītā*, VI. I.
30. Tucker, Robert C., *Marxian Revolutionary Idea*, p. 220.
31. *The Gita According to Gandhi*, p. 161.
32. *Gita*, II.72
33. *Gita*, V. 24, 25, 26.
34. *Gita*, IV. 6; V. 19, 20, 21; VI. 10.
35. *Gita*, VI. 30.
36. *Gita*, VI. 19
37. *Young India*, 12-11-1925.
38. *Bṛhadāraṇyaka Up.* (Trans. by Radhakrishnan, S.), 1.4.10.
39. *Śvetāśvatara Up.* (Trans. by Radhakrishnan, S.), 6.12.
40. Tagore, Rabindranath, *Religion of Man*, p. 91.
41. *Mahābhārata* (quoted) Radhakrishnan, S. and Raju, P.T., *The Concept of Man*, p. 9.
42. Feuerbach, Ludwig, *The Essence of Christianity*, p. xvi.
43. Sartre, Jean Paul, *Existentialism and Humanism*, p. 12.
44. Ibid., p. 55.
45. *Taittirīya Upaiṣnād*, VI. 1 : Asanneva sa bhavati asad brahmeti veda cet.
46. *Chāndogya Upaniṣad*, XVII.vi.7.
47. *Bṛhad. Up.*, II. iv. 14.
48. *Bṛhad. Up.*, IV. iv. 23.

49. *Bṛhad, Up.* II. 1. 4.
50. *Bṛhad Up.*, II.1.4. : Atha yo'nyāṁ devatāmupāste'nyo sāvanyo hāmasmitina sa veda yathā paṣurevaṁ sa devānām.
51. Radhakrishnan, S., *The Principal Upaniṣads*, pp. 168-69.
52. Ayer, A.J., *Language Truth and Logic*, (2nd Ed.) 1960, p. 42.
53. Cohen, M.R. and Nagel Ernest, *An Introduction to Logic and Scientific Method*, p. 122.
54. Stebbing, L.S., *A Modern Introduction to Logic*, p. 455.
55. Ibid., Thus the quantified general statement 'humanity exists' is logically equivalent to saying that all the members of the class 'humanity' have the property of existence. It may be formulated as 'given any x in the universe, if x is human, then x has the property of existence.'
56. Sartre, J.P., op. cit., p. 55.
57. *Bṛhad Up.*, I. iv. 10 and II, v. 19 (ayamātmā brāhma).
58. Kierkegaard, Soren, *The Sickness Unto Death*, p. 207.
59. Karen, Horney, *Neuroses and Human Growth*, p. 112.
60. Tucker, Robert C., *Philosophy and Myth in Karl Marx*, pp. 31, 80.
61. *Gita*, IV. 35.
62. *Gita*, XV. 7 (mamaivāṁśo jīvaloke jīvabhūtaḥ sanātanaḥ).
63. Radhakrishnan, S., *Bhagavadgītā*, p. 328.
64. Desai, Mahadeva, (Trans.) *The Gita According to Gandhi*, p. 341.
65. Mill, J.S., *A System of Logic*, Chap. VI, VII.
66. *Gita*, XIII. 16 avibhaktaṁ ca bhūteṣu vibhaktam iva ca sthitam.
67. *Gita*, XVIII. 20 : sarvabhūteṣu yenaikaṁ bhāvamavyaym īkṣate avibhaktaṁ vibhakteṣu taj jñānaṁ viddhi rājasam.
68. Cohen, M.R. and Nagel, E., *An Introduction to Logic and Scientific Method*, pp. 241-43.
69. *Gita*, XVIII. 61, Īśvaraḥ sarvabhūtānāṁ hṛddeśe'rjuna tiṣṭhati.
70. Stebbing, L.S., op. cit., p. 243 ff.
71. Gita, II. 20 and 21. (nityaḥ śāśvato' yaṁ pūrano)
72. *Kaṭhopaniṣad* (Trans. by Radhakrishnan) 1.2.18.
73. *Kaṭha*. 1.3.1. and 1.3.4 ; *Muṇḍaka* III.I.2, and *Śvetā*, IV. 6
74. *Gita*, XIII. 21.
75. *Gita*, XIV. 5 : sattvaṁ rajas tama iti guṇāḥ prakṛti saṁbhavāh nibadhnanti mahābāho dehe dehinam avyayam
76. *Gita*, VIII. 14 : daivi hy eṣā guṇamayī mama māyā duratyaya.
77. *Gita*, VII. 25.
78. *Gitā*, XIV. 20 (guṇān etān atītya trīn dehī dehasamudbhavān)
79. *Gita*, XVI. 10-13; 18-19.
80. Sartre, J.P., op. cit., p. 45.
81. Kant, Immanuel, *Fundamental Principles of the Metaphysics of Ethics*, pp. 77-78.
82. Hegel, G.W.F., *Phenomenology of Mind* (Trans. by Baillie), p. 97.
83. Hegel, G.W.F., *Science of Logic*, Vol. I, p. 143.
84. Desai, Mahadeva, *The Gita According to Gandhi*, p. 252. (*Gita*, II, 51)
85. Hegel, G.W.F., *Logic of Hegel* (Trans. by W. Wallace), p. 335.

86. Sartre, J.P., op. cit., p. 46.
87. Ibid., p. 41.
88. Ibid., p. 6.
89. Marx, Engels, Lenin, *On Historical Materialism*, p. 13.
90. *Gita*, XVI. 9-10
91. *Gita*, XVI. 8.
92. Radhakrishnan, S., *Bhagavadgītā*, p. 81.
93. Desai, Mahadeva, *The Gita According to Gandhi*, p. 135.
94. Radhakrishnan, S., *Bhagavadgītā*, p. 96.
95. Sartre, J.P., op. cit. p. 25.
96. Tucker, Robert C., *Philosophy and Myth in Karl Marx*, p. 57.
97. Radhakrishnan, S., *Bhagavadgītā*, p. 97.
98. Tucker, Robert C., *Philosophy and Myth in Karl Marx*, p. 49.
99. *Gita*, I. 36, (*Anāsakti Yoga* bhāṣya).
100. *Gita*, I. 35 (*Anāsakti Yoga* bhāṣya).
101. *Gita*, II. 62 : saṅgāt saṁjāyate kāmaḥ kāmāt krodho bhi jāyate
   II. 63 : krodhād bhavati sammohaḥ sammohāt smṛtivibhramaḥ ; smṛtibhraṁśād buddhināso buddhināśāt praṇaṣyati.
102. *Gita*, III. 37.
103. *Gita*, XVI. 21.
104. *Gita*, XVI. 10, 11, 12, 19, and 20 (*Anāsakti Yoga* bhāṣya).
105. *Gita*, II. 43, kāmātmanaḥ svargaparāḥ janmakarmaphalapradām.
106. Radhakrishnan, S., *Bhagavadgītā*, p. 117.
107. *Gita*, II. 49 (*Anāsakti Yoga* bhāṣya).
108. *Gita*, II. 51 (phalaṁ tyaktvā manī ṣinaḥ); II. 38; III. 9; III. 19; III. 25; V. 10-11.
109. Maitra, S.K., *The Ethics of the Hindus*, p. 33.
110. Freud, S., *General Introduction to Psycho-analysis*, p. 311.
111. Broad, C.D., *Five Types of Ethical Theories*, p. 237.
112. Mackenzie, J.S., *A Manual of Ethics*, p. 168.
113. Marx, K., *Capital*, p. 671.
114. Marx, K., *German Ideology*, pp. 396-397.
115. Desai, Mahadeva, *The Gita According to Gandhi*, p. 129.
116. Ibid., p. 377.
117. *Gita*, IV. 23.
118. *Gita*, V. 23 (Kāmakrodhodbhavaṁ vegaṁ sa yuktaḥ sa sukhī n arah).
119. *Gita*, II. 48 (yogasthah kuru karmāṇi sangaṁ tyaktvā dhanañjaya).
120. *Gita*, III. 19 : (*tasmād asaktaḥ satatem kāryaṁkarma samācara ; asak to hyācaran karma paramāpnoti puruṣaḥ*).
121. *Gita*, II. 51 : (Karmajaṁ buddhiyuktā hi phalaṁ tyaktvā maniṣināh; janmabandha vinirmuktāḥ padam gacchanty anāmayam).
122. Radhakrishnan, S., *Eastern Religion and Western Thought*, p. 95.
123. Mackenzie, J.S., *A Manual of Ethics*, pp. 56-57.
124. Rashdall, H., op. cit., Vol. I, p. 51.
125. Desai, Mahadeva, *The Gita According to Gandhi*, p. 184. (*Gita*, III. 25).
126. Rashdall, H., op. cit., Vol. II, p. 70.
127. Bradley, F.H., *Ethical Studies* (2nd Ed., 1927), p. 96.

128. It is significant to note that in Indian and Buddhists traditions, this human body has been verily compared with chariot to be guided by Reason. In Gita also, this analogy has been presented.
129. Marx, K., *Das Capital*, Vol. III, p. 355 (Bracketed mine).
130. *Gita*, II. 47 (Karmaṇyevā' dhikāras te mā phaleṣu kadācana).
131. *Gita*, V. 14 : (na kartṛtvaṁ na karmāṇi lokasya sṛjati prabhuḥ; na karmaphalasaṁyogaṁ svabhāvastu pravartate).
132. Titus, H., op. cit., p. 159.
133. Broad, C.D., *Five Types of Ethical Theories*, pp. 192-205.
134. Gandhi, M.K., *Young India*, 15.3.1928.
135. Sartre, Jean Paul, op. cit., p. 28.
136. Page, James D., *Abnormal Psychology*, pp. 287-288.
137. Sartre, J.P., op. cit., p. 28.
138. *Gita*, II. 34. (*Anāsakti Yoga*).
139. *Gita*, II. 3.
140. Marx, K. and Engels, F., *German Ideology*, pp. 33, 34, 37
141. Marx, Engels, Lenin, *On Historical Materialism*, p. 12.
142. *Gita*, IV. 42 ; XI. 34.
143. *Gita*, XVIII. 7 ; II. 36.
144. Desai, Mahadeva, *The Gita According to Gandhi*, p. 228.
145. *Gita*, II. 64 : (rāgadveṣaviyuk taistu viṣayān indriyaiś-caran ; ātmavaśyair vidheyātmā prasādamadhigacchati).
146. *Gita*, IV. 8.
147. *Gita*, II. 31, 32 ; III. 35 ; XVIII. 47.
148. Durkheim, Emile, *The Division of Labour in Society* (1933), p. 411.
149. Radhakrishnan, S., *Bhagavadgītā*, p. 114.
150. Milne, A.J.M., *The Social Philosophy of English Idealism*, p. 65.
151. *Gita*, II. 11 (aśocyān anvasocas tvam).
152. *Gita*, II. 22. (vāsāṁsi jīrṇāni yathā vihāya, navāni gṛhṇāti naro' parāṇi).
153. *Gita*, II. 17 (vināsaṁ avyayasya' sya na kascit kartum arhati)
154. *Gita*, V. 4 (Sāṁkhya yogau pṛthak bālāḥ pravadante na paṇditāḥ).
155. *Gita*, XVIII. 78.
156. Gandhi, M.K. *Harijan*, 3-9-1931.

3

Philosophical and Cultural Influences

The search for the removal of human bondage and making man free from his limitations has been going on since the dawn of civilization, and in every age and in every society, seers, thinkers, prophets and philosophers have made their contribution to the efforts to raise man from his frailities to perfection. Kṛṣṇa, the narrator of the Gita, has pointed out that the teaching that he was delivering there, was not something new, but it has been handed down to the posterity through a successive lineage for the welfare of humanity. Gita says : "Thus handed down in succession, the royal sages learnt it ; with long lapse of time it dwindled away in this world."

Evaṁ paramparāprāptam imaṁ rājarṣayo vidhuḥ ;
sa kaleneha mahatā yogo naṣṭaḥ paraṁtapa (*IV.* 2).

"the doctrine is not new one, occasioned by the crisis in front of Arjuna, but (the restatement of) the law of universal application followed from the time immemorial for the welfare of the people."[1] The teaching is a rediscovery and the restoration of ancient wisdom.

A man obviously cannot cut himself off the intellectual and socio-cultural heritage of the past. Neither Engels, nor Marx did. They were both proud of the German tradition, the philosophical heritage of Kant and Hegal.

Accordingly, it becomes essential to have a brief survey of the formative influences on Marxism. A brief survey of the cultural conditions is also essential which exercised their influence in moulding the Gandhian thought in so far as it has led to the additing of new interpretations to the old wisdom of Gita, in the form of Anāsakti Yoga.

Philosophical and Cultural Influences on Marx

Orthodox communists support the tenets of Marxism with a tenacity of the religious zeal. They observe a sanctifying attitude towards the basic teachings of Marxism and treat them like the 'Commandments'. The result is, that to an orthodox Marxist, an opponent is not merely in error, but in 'sin'. Such dogmatic attitude has sometimes made it difficult to discern correctly the various sources which inspired the founders of communism in formulating their doctrine.

Arnold Toynbee, a distinguished historian of modern times has tried to show the distinctive Jewish inspiration of Marxism.[2] Marx, he says, has given an apocalyptic vision of the violent revolution which is inevitable. This 'inevitability' compares well with the 'inevitable decree of God' as enunciated in Jewish traditions. Petersen traces origin of Marxism to sociological grounds. According to him "their doctrine is not something mysterious but is derived in all its parts from the empirical study of society and the universe."[3] In his bid to give a philosophy of history which predicts the inevitable downfall of capitalism and the advent of socialism Marx has tried to propound a full-fledged system covering almost all the aspects of man's practical life. Schumpeter, a great economist of 20th century substantiates this fact and says : "Economics, sociology, political theory, history and philosophy are all mixed in his sweeping analysis."[4] James Bonar points out "that the theory of surplus value was already present in the English predecessors of Marx...Similarly the vivid description of the economic view of history at all the stages of development approximating Marx was already given by "Lassalie", who was not Hegelian."[5]

There are thinkers, who find nothing original but a "jumble of various ideas infiltrating in the doctrine of Marx. For example, Beard shows with great elaboration that the idea of economic interpretation of politics, linkage of the state with class interests and property system has come to Marx through a long line of heritage from Aristotle to Machiavelli, Locke and James Madis."[6] Cohen also feels that "Marx freely borrowed his ideas from bourgoise historians as well as St. Simon, Fourier etc. whom he, with the characteristic human failings of borrowers, belittled as utopians.[7] During the period from October 1842 to March 1843, Marx worked as an editor of a radical paper known as 'Rheinische Zeitung'. Marx then had to write prolific editorials on all the important problems. Due to his wide reflection in these editorials, Marx had to cover various fields. Consequently, it becomes a difficult job to analyse and sift out all the influences that were being projected into these writings. That is why, the total complex of Marxism appears to Sorokin a "dumping ground for numberless atomistic socio-cultural phenomena, which represent the different systems—in fact a congeries or conglemeration of German, French and English heritage."[8] These three sources of Marxism have been well recognized by V.I. Lenin also.[9]

Influences of Classical Materialism :

Historical materialism of Marx is widely different from the classical mechanistic materialism. Marx enriched western materialistic philosophy with the achievements of German classical philosophy, especially of Hegel's system, which, in its turn, has led to the materialism of Feuerbach.[10] According to Lenin, the main achievement of Germans was dialectics. Apart from the use of dialectical method, Marx deepened and developed philosophical materialism to its all sociological implications. Epistemologically he extended 'the cognition of nature' to include the 'cognition of human society'. Distinguishing the stand-point of new materialism of Marx from that of the classical materialists, Lenin pointed out that, "just as man's knowledge reflects nature which exists independently of him, so man's *social knowledge* (his various views and doctrines—philosophical religious political and so forth) reflects the *economic system* of society."[11] Communism is not an outgrowth of the classical materialism. But an application of Hegel's dialect on the French Materialism. Marx has exposed the defects of the mechanical materialism particularly its French version in his Eleventh Theses on Feuerbach. His main objective is that in classical materialism, nature swallows man.

Marxism accepts the fundamental priority of nature but in contradistinction with old materialists it thinks that nature is a dialectically developing entity which undergoes qualitative changes also. Marx comes close to the Sāṁkhya systems of Indian Philosophy where the *mahābhūta*, the objects grow only in proportion with the reflection of puruṣa into prakṛti and despite all its binding character, it does not swallow puruṣa. Such a categorical assertion of the role of 'man', who for Marx, is fundamentally a productive being, makes his materialism fit to be called 'anthropomorphistic idealism'.

But Marx was allergic to the use of term idealism for his philosophy, because the German idealism over-estimated the role of ideas in human affairs. It generated a consequent tendency to assume that the concepts which emerge in various periods of history, inherently evolve from one another in a logical continuum. Marx bitterly condemned this attitude of idealism which despised the productive activity of mankind. He was so much embittered with the metaphysics of idealism that he joined hands with his colleague Engels and jointly belaboured "to settle account with their former philosophic conscience."[12] Accordingly, despite so much similarity with the idealist approach, it would not be justified to put him under the roof of 'Idealist Camp'. Marx might have sought help from the French materialism in his bid to settle scores with Absolute Idealists. But he could not reconcile him-self with the pure mechanistic modes of the materialism.

Marx puts 'man' in the centre of his philosophical endeavours, and not the ontological status or the problem of the analysis of the external world. He himself says : "The immediate task of philosophy, which is in the service of history, is to unmask human self-alienation in its secular form now that it has been unmasked in the sacred form.[13] The difference from the classical materialist doctrines which reduce everything to physico-chemical and bio-physiological laws and thereby undermine the importance and dignity of man 'as a living producer of his material modes of existence', becomes quite obvious. What Marx wanted to assert in his materialism is that man cannot think, and cannot live at all, without producing the material means of life and that the material modes of his existence should be given priority in understanding his other activities, viz., his thinking and philosophising. In short the crux of Marxian materialism is the 'assertion of human factor' and it may very well be called the 'humanised materialism.'

The French Working Class :

Summarizing the three sources of Marxism, which were duly recognised by Lenin as well, Eric Roll states that "English utilitarianism, French socialist thought and the beginning of German radicalism were the inspiration of Marx's youth."[14] Marx took his philosophical ideas from German soil and synthesized other influences into that basic frame-work. The great synthesis came when he found the proletarian of France as the practical executors of his philosophical communism. Marx jubilantly proclaimed 'just as philosophy finds in the proletariat its material weapon, the proletariat finds in philosophy its spiritual weapon.'[15] The revolutionary fervour of the French working class came to the knowledge of Marx after his intellectual contact with French writers.

Hegel and Feuerbach

The formulative influence of Communism came from German philosophy itself, and the basic frame-work of his philosophical communism, which served as 'spiritual weapon' for working class remained Hegelian in its origin. The Hegelian origin of the philosophical doctrines of Marx is reflected from the prolific writings of various contemporary thinkers. Prominent among them are Sidney Hook, who has worked out the Hegelian influence in great details in his book *From Hegel to Marx*, and R. Cooper, in his work *The Logical Influence of Hegel on Marx*. These writers have endeavoured to show that the germs of socialism were already contained in Hegel's philosophy. Not only this but Hegelian idealists like Hartshorn, etc., have also conceived the 'Reality, as 'Social Process'. This is indicative of the fact that the socialist eggs have already been hatched in German idealism by the 'Imperial Professor' Hegel. It is now a well recognized historical fact that the straitest sect of scientific socialism represented by Marx and Engels sprang from the philosophy of Hegel. What Marx did was that he converted the Hegelian philosophy of History into a social theory. Marx borrowed the 'Dialectical Method', and the concept of historical necessity from Hegel and made them the fundamental principles of his theory to reach the goal of 'socialism inevitable'.

Working out the Hegelian influence more elaborately, Prof. Tucker shows that "Marx translated the Hegelian *phenomenology* into scientific terms, following a lead given by Feuerbach."[16]

A comparative study of the Marxian and Hegelian Schemes shows that dialectical method of Marx arose as a metamorphoses of Hegel, i.e., turning Hegel back upon his feet. Marx himself has claimed : "My dialectical method is fundamentally different from Hegel's own and is even its opposite. For Hegel it is the process of thought, which he even converts into an independent subject. For me, on the contrary, ideas are only the material facts turned up side down in the human head. The mystified look of the Hegelian dialectic was criticised by me nearly thirty years ago."[17] This shows that Marxian system is a demystified version of Hegelianism. Engels also recognised the fundamental Hegelian influence on Marx. Reviewing Marx's *Critique of Political Economy*, Engels makes a reverential reference to Hegel and says : "This epoch-making conception of history was the direct theoretical premise for the new materialist outcome."[18] Recognising that Communism is the secularised version of Hegel's philosophy, Engels goes on to say, "So powerful a work as the Hegel's philosophy, could not be disposed of by simply being ignored. It had to be 'sublated' in its own sense, that is the sense that while its form had to be annihilated through criticism, the new content which had been won through it had to be saved."[19] Accordingly, 'annihilating its idealist form and filling into it the economic contents', was the historic accomplishment of Marx.

It was a firm conviction of Engels that scientific socialism was essentially a German product, and that it could only have come into being in the nation whose classical philosophy had kept alive the tradition of conscious dialectic, i.e., Germany.[20] This much indebtedness to German classical philosophy, which culminated in Hegel is a clear indication that Marx and Engels both were eager to search for the real inspiration in Hegelian philosophy itself. They, however, wanted to discover as to what was the secret of its greatness. It may be inferred from it that in formulating his theory, Hegelian philosophy influenced him most.

Hegel's *Phenomenology of Mind* was the work that deeply impressed Marx. About this work, Marx maintained, "The *phenomenology* is a criticism in a concealed, unself-clarified and mystifying form.

However, in so far as it firmly grasps the alienation of man, even if man appears only in the form of spirit, all the elements of criticism are hidden in it."[21] Marx fascinated by the charm of this book, undertook to invert *phenomenology* in order to find out its concealed meaning and to tear off its mystifying form. This task was accomplished by Marx in his philosophic communism. A deep reflection into his theory clearly shows that Marxism was indeed born as a metamorphosis of Hegelianism. The key to this demystification and metamorphoses comes from Feuerbach. The 'inverted Hegelianism' was the teaching of Feuerbach and therefrom it has slipped into Marxism and became a basic part of it.[22] When Marx was writing his "Theses on Feuerbach", he was fascinated by bold attempt of Feuerbach to invert Hegel, and unravel the secrets of that. Marx saw in Feuerbach the 'anti-Hegel' who accomplished single handedly the revolutionary over-throw of the 'great system' of Hegel. This sort of penetration into the secrets of Hegel could not be achieved by any of the disciples of Hegel. They saw it with awe and sanctifying attitude. That is why, in his doctoral thesis, Marx had referred to Hegel's disciples as 'captives of the system, and 'minds held fast in its fetters.'

In Feuerbach's method of 'transformational criticism,'[23] Marx found the key to liberation from that captivity. This method came to Marx as a great revelation. Marx became so much enchanted with this revelation that he advocated this methodology as the real road to truth. About this new discovery, Marx wrote : "I advise you speculative theologians and philosophers to rid yourselves of the notions and preconceptions of the old speculative philosophy, if you want to get to things as they are in reality, i.e., to the truth. And there is no other road to truth than the road through the 'brook of fire' (Feuerbach). Feuerbach is the purgatory of our time."[24] Engels also admitted that Feuerbach's book *Essence of Christianity* had a liberating effect, as it placed materialism on the throne again. About the influence of that book of Feuerbach, he writes : "Its main theme seems to be that "nothing exists outside nature and man, and the higher beings our religious fantasies have created, are only the fantastic reflection of our own essence."[25] This great discovery into the real meaning of Hegel's system was hailed as a great intellectual achievement. Engels hailed this victory saying, "The spell was broken ; the 'system' was exploded and cast aside. . . Enthusiasm was general ; we all became at once Feuerbachians."[26]

What was Feuerbach's revolutionary achievement which made Engels so jubilant ? It was his search for the latent meaning of Hegelianism. Feuerbach brought into light the 'latent', the underlying or symbolic meaning which Hegelian philosophy indirectly reveals. To arrive at the truth, according to Feuerbachian discovery, one has only to turn Hegel's key propositions upside down or right way up. Like logical law of conversion, the method of transformational criticism also requires to put the predicate in place of the subject every where.[27] Thus speaking, the method of transposition of subject and predicate is sufficient to turn speculative philosophy upside down and to arrive at the truth in its unconcealed pure, manifest form. Accordingly, the Hegel's proposition 'man is the revealed God' can be transformed into Feuerbach's proposition 'God is the revealed man' and so on. Feuerbach, in this way, turned Hegel upside down. Marx followed him in this pivotal operation by extending the application of this method to all the spheres of Hegelianism. On the basis of this wide application of Feuerbach's method, many eminent Marxists have recognized that "Marx in the decisive years between 1841 and 1844 was a Feuerbachian."[28]

Out of many other things that influenced Marx in formulation of his communism, the most important was the Feuerbachian idea that not God but man is essentially a creative being, who derives joy from productive activity voluntarily performed. Elaborating his idea about man, Feuerbach wrote :

> "In activity man feels himself free, unlimited, happy ; in passivity limited, oppressed, unhappy. Activity is the positive sense of one's personality...and the happiest the most blissful activity is that which is productive. Hence this attribute of the species—productive activity—is assigned to God, that is realized and made objective as divine activity. Man realizes his creativity in the imagination by projecting God as the supreme creative being without knowing that God is his own externalised humanity."[29]

This idea is the central theme of communism, pervading almost all the writings of Marx. However, Marx carried this idea to other fields of Hegelianism. After learning from Feuerbach the method of transformational criticism, Marx made the philosophy of history as developed by Hegel, his model,[30] and constructed his own system of communism by converting Hegel. Through this method, Hegel's *Phenomenology of Mind* became a kind of the 'phenomenology' of man. This was the original achievement of Marx that he transformed the philosophy of history, as the history of man, not of Absolute. When Hegel was so inverted, then Marx realized that "in its esoteric form, it is a 'revolutionary' gospel of the apotheosis of man."[31] Accordingly, Marx discovered with the help of Feuerbachian method that Hegel's philosophical religion, in essence, was the religion of man. In the form of Absolute, it was found to contain 'theme of man's soaring into the unlimited'. This is the theme which is working behind the concept of man in the philosophy of communism. Accordingly, in his desire to become Absolute, man wants to break his finitude, his limitations. Marx found that this secret was also contained in Hegel's own writings if Hegelianism is read through Feuerbach. Hegel once wrote : "By pride he fell ; by pride he shall rise again. The hand that inflicts the wound is also the hand that heals it."[32] After removing the mystifying element from it, the real hidden meaning of this Hegelian statement becomes clear that Hegelianism is a religion of self-worship. Its fundamental theme is given in Hegel's image of man that 'man' aspires to be God himself, and history is a process of man's attaining to full self-consciousness as 'Man'. Thus the inverted Hegelianism becomes the communism of Marx.

From this deep rooted impact of Feuerbach on his thought, it may not be inferred that Marx crossed the floor of his intellectual heritage. Although Marx learnt so much from Feuerbach, yet he never shook off his Hegelian frame-work. For the depth of thought, he always turned back to Hegel. Comparing the relative position of both, he writes in one of his letters in 1865 : "Compared with Hegel, Feuerbach is very poor. All the same, he was epoch-making after Hegel because he laid stress on certain points which were disagreeable to the Christian consciousness but important for the progress of criticism and which Hegel had left in mystic semi-obscurity."[33] Here Marx is applauding in effect that Hegel was a giant of thought who had penetrated into the truth and that Feuerbach is only instrumental in the clarification of Hegel's latent meaning.

It becomes evident from this survey of the historical development of the philosophical communism that Marx in his philosophical communism has restated in a clear and scientific form, what Hegel had already said before him in a confused and mystified form.

Influence of English Political Economy :

After having resolved the mystery of the Hegelian philosophical concepts like 'Dialectic', 'Necessity', etc. under the influence of French genius embodied in Feuerbach, it became easy to apply the method of inverted Hegelianism to other fields of man's practical life, the most important being the field of Political Economy. When Marx read Adam Smith's *Wealth of Nation*, he realized that Hegelianism was also fundamentally a doctrine about economics. In Marx own words : "Hegel has the point of view of modern political economy."[31] It means that what Marx found in Adam Smith's economics was already contained in a mystified form in Hegel's philosophy. In so saying, Marx went a step further than Feuerbach. Feuerbach had said that Hegelianism was esoteric psychology. Marx said, 'it is esoteric economics—man's life is an economic producer."[35] This revelation also led him to search for man's alienation in his practical life, i.e., in his life as a material producer.

Hegel stopped at religious alienation but Marx applied his mind in search for economic alienation as well. He started searching as to where existed that dehumanised man, the 'unman' in real practical life, who stands in need of regeneration. This he found in the industrial society and capitalist economy of England, of which a highly disparaging account he presented in his *Das Capital*. We have already seen under his theory of communism that the *Capital* of Marx presents a distressing image that the economic life of a capitalist society is the prime locus of human self-alienation, where man lives in a state of egoism. Instead of producing cooperatively and for the welfare of the species, as a whole, egoistic men appropriate the productive power of the species in the form of money. This appropriation from the productive process, which is called private property, was the main or the sole cause of human misery. Accordingly, his concern to finish these conditions was the practical and applied aspect of his theory of man which he had already formulated after tearing off the veil of mystery from Hegelianism.

In his magnum opus *Das Capital,* Marx criticized the system of liberal production on the basis of his Hegelian influences. It is in this sense that we may say that his socialism became mature when he applied Hegelianism to the English economy. Thus speaking, it was the influence by criticism that Marx received from the English economy. It requires a little more reflection to work out precisely what factors of English economy helped in the formulation of communism. This will lead us to the domain of the history of economic thought.

A survey of the basic maxims of communism gives a glimpse that his theory was the out-come of protest and a reaction against the gross individualism of the 19th century, which was based on (i) free competition and (ii) private property. The sharpest attack that Marx made, was on the pessimist school of economists, which discovered the antagonism between the capitals and workmen."[36] With the help of their hypothetical 'Law of Diminishing Return', the protagonists of pessimist school drew a dismal conclusion that there was a definite limit to the production of the necessities of life beyond which it cannot be increased and therefore, mankind had no prospects of bettering its lot.

To substantiate these gloomy conclusions, there appeared the revised Edition of Malthus book *An Essay on the Principles of Population* which showed a tendency of sex to over-come the means of subsistence. In nut-shell Malthus concluded that hunger will always remain the basic problem of humanity unless some restraints were imposed to check the vagaries of the blind instinct of sexuality. Malthus held, that "the people must comprehend that they are themselves the cause of their poverty, due to their own incorrigible habits."[37] This attitude of Malthusians was duly substantiated by the views of economists like Adam Smith and Ricardo. who also utilized the inexorable laws of economics to justify the pessimistic view of society. These pronouncements provided the rich classes with a good pretext for dissociating themselves from the fate of the working class and let them always remain in drudgery. The demoralizing influence of Malthus aroused a wide spread indignation and gave rise to a spate of furies against it.[38] When Marx came to read Malthus, he could not bear the endless horror of the capitalist society. Considering Malthus to be a confirmed ideological weapon used by the bourgeois to fight against the social revolution and to demoralise the workers, Marx and Engels anathematized him and cursed his populat on theory with great gusto. They vehemently condemned him as 'the vulgar economist', 'Sycophant of the bourgeois', 'the contemptible Malthus', 'the fundamental meanness of his outlook', 'a libel on the human race', 'this repulsive blasphemy against man and nature' etc.[39] The whole gamut of Malthusian theory was woven around the assumption that man is living with unlimited wants in the world of limited resources. No solution to this problem was available with English economists of that day. Disgusted with this Malthusian horror, Marx invoked the German wizard Hegel and in order to check the vagaries of Malthusian theory, he suggested a perfect control over the allocation of resources and over the distribution of economic goods till a society of abundance is created. Thus speaking, the idea of the collapse of this corrupt system and its replacement by dictatorship of the Proletariat in the transitory period, was the conclusion of his applying Hegel to the liberal economy. The Dialectic of 'Hegel's Historical March', was potent enough to pronounce that the forces of production will 'inevitably' work for the self-destruction of capitalism.[40]

Engels also supported Marx in his predicting the end of this dehumanising system. He proclaimed that "under the guidance of the blind invisible hands, the humanity will take a leap from the 'realm of necessity' into the 'realm of freedom'.[41] Such optimistic vision of the future, was obviously necessary to raise the morales of the alienated worker, the 'unman', who wanted to become 'man'. But the English economy was incompetent to provide this elevating encouragement to worker. Thus, through Marx, Hegelianism came to the rescue of the alienated man and dehumanized worker of the Industrial society. On the basis of this, it may be said that *Das Capital* pronouncing the knell of capitalist system of competitive production and private property, is the application of Hegel's concept of 'historical necessity' to remedy the evil consequences of the doctrines of the 'Pessimist School of Economists'.

The rise of the English 'Laissez faire' system, which produced unbearable dismal conditions in the economic life of society and which gave impetus to powerful currents of individual economic competition, was driving its strength from the Darwinian doctrine. The laissez faire man was the business class that wanted to be free under the guise of the slogan of consumers sovereignty. In effect they wanted freedom to make money as they saw fit. Titus admits that "their demand for freedom (they used the phrase 'laissez faire—let alone), led to a new individualism. They said 'men must be free to express his *self-interest*."[42] It is evident that behind the 'laissez faire' slogan, i.e., under the guise of the slogan of individual's freedom, the vested interests wanted to enjoy unbriddled freedom to exploit people and to earn profit. The laissez faire economists including Mill and Bentham argued in favour of their theory from the Darwinian Law of Natural selection and of the 'survival of the fittest'. The application of Darwin's law in Economics led them to discourage all the collective efforts in favour of the distressed, as all such efforts tended to perpetuate the weakness by protecting the inferiors. Thus, the Laws of Darwin put a scientist's seal of confirmation on the Malthusian horror. When Darwin's book *The Origin of Species* was first published, it was appreciated by Marx, because as Marx pointed out,[43] the idea of 'struggle among the contending species served, as a support in the natural science, for his theory of class struggle in history. Engels also applauded this theory of Darwin and said, "Darwin transferred the socio-economic struggle to nature whence it was transferred back again to society (by Marx) to prove the 'eternal laws of society'."[44]

But when the drastic implications of Darwinian law were realized in the economic field, both of them were greatly dismayed. Darwin's principle of 'prolific reproduction' and 'individual variation', substantiated the conclusions of Malthusian *Essay on Demography* that the natural state of common masses is of extreme poverty and insecurity. It become essential for these pioneers of communism to save the suffering humanity from further dehumanization. Engels, therefore, drew a line of defence against the operation of Darwinian curse and criticising the Darwinian approach, he cautioned his followers "to avoid, in the interest of communism itself, the confusion of physics (physical modes) with economics."[45] What he wanted to avoid was that the laws of natural and physical sciences should not be used in interpreting the 'productive behaviour of man'. This was the stand-point of Marx also in criticising the mechanical materialism. Lenin also cautioned the thinkers that "biological ideas should not be transferred to the domain of social sciences."[46] The way in which the Darwin's law of 'prolific reproduction' operates, leads to the natural corollary that nature was producing the species in abundance and out of that enormous production she was selecting only a few by eliminating many. This enormous waste of the natural resources, which was a consequence of the laissez faire economy, was due to the fact that nature was behaving in a very chaotic manner. Neither Darwin's law nor the liberal economy of the Utilitarians were in a position to provide any plan to nature. Such plan was, however, available in the Hegel's theory of 'Planned March of History', which always fascinated Marx. Therefore, to counteract the dehumanizing effects of laissez faire and of the blind operation of the laws of nature, Marx threw the aura of Hegelianism to arrest the unwarranted wastage of resources in the liberal competitive society. In a planned society, the resources will not be wasted like this. This is the final phase of communism. Thus the final theory of communism grew by negative criticism of the English economy.

To conclude, the basic framework of communism is the secularized re-reading of Hegelian Philosophy. The other influences of French socialism, Feuerbach's materialism, and 19th century English liberalism have been synthesized into basic thought structure. The postulates and axioms of the philosophical communism have been worked out 'apriori' by the method of transformational criticism of Hegel and the empirical facts of the British economy were adjusted into that system. In this way, communism is the repository of Hegelian philosophy and thereby it carries with it the whole intellectual and cultural traditions of Germany in its background.

Socio-Cultural Influences on the Modern Commentaries of Gita

Various Commentaries on Gita

Gita has guided the path of Indian people at various critical moments of the cultural history of India. It has been a source of perennial inspiration and whenever darkness has engulfed the social and cultural life of India, Gita has shown the light from a new perspective. Since every crisis has its own unique features, it calls for a unique approach to resolve it. Accordingly, Gita has been interpreted by the intelligentia according to the need of the society from age to age. Still it has not exhausted the richness of the symbolism of this great treatise.

Radhakrishnan has rightly said that "if the hold which a work has on the mind of man is any clue to its importance, then the *Gita* is the most influential work in Indian thought.[47] It is due to this wide spread influence of this philosophico-ethical treatise that it occupies a place among *prasthānatraya.* It is one of the three pillars of Hindu culture. Actually every great teacher, who wanted to inspire the people when visions were darkened, put forth the teaching of Gita in consonance with the demand of his age and according to his perspective as to how he diagnosed the crisis.

Thus, every commentary on Gita represents a new perspective corresponding to the socio-cultural exigencies. The survey of the varied interpretations becomes, therefore, interesting, because every study reveals the depth and charm of the Gita as well as of the interpretor as to how he apprehended the socio-cultural crisis and remedied it. Every interpretation has its own unique significance in the socio-cultural context. To understand their relative importance is to understand the fact that social and cultural problems cannot be reduced to one single formula but the complexity of social situation demands a variety of approaches for its equilibrity. We, therefore, start with a synoptic survey of the interpretations of the ancients and moderns before reckoning the social and cultural influences which worked on the present commentary by Gandhiji.

Among the ancient commentators, the names of Śaṁkara, Rāmānuja, Madhusūdana Sarswatī, and Vallabha are very important. All these thinkers have interpreted the teachings of Gita in the contextual scheme of their general philosophical thought. Śaṁkara's *Gītābhāṣya* echoes the same metaphysical and spiritual doctrines which are contained in his commentaries on the ten Principal Upaniṣads. In Śaṁkara's commentary, mokṣa, the summum bonum of human life, has been conceived as an experience of the re-union of Ātman with Brahman, which seems separate only due to ignorance.

The *Gītābhāṣya* of Rāmānuja is an interpretation of Gita in accordance with his general doctrine of viśiṣṭādvaita. It is more a work on bhakti and theism, as compared to the work of Śaṁkara, which lays exclusive emphasis on jñāna.

Ācārya Madhusūdana Sarsvatī's commentary on Gita is named as *Gūḍhārthadīpikā.* He divides Gita into *Karma Kāṇḍa, Upāsanākāṇḍa* and *jñānkāṇḍa* and places bhakti (*bhagvadbhaktiniṣṭhā*) in the middle and considers it to be the dispeller of all calamities. The Vallabhite interpretation is contained in *Gītātātparya grantha* and *Amritatarangiṇi Tīkā.* This school also lays stress on bhakti as the supreme method for self-realization. This apart, the commentaries of Yamunācārya and Mādhavācārya have also presented an account of Gita in theistic manner. All these commentaries point out that the concern of the ancient thinkers was more spiritual. They kept the spiritual traditions very high and saved the society from the onslaught of the barbaric forces which threatened the culture of this land. This bhakti tradition is also continued in the mediaval commentaries of which *Jñāneśvari* is widely influential.

In modern period, various scholars have given new dimensions to the teachings of Gita. The new commentaries have not taken away the glory of the ancient interpretations but have added a new cultural dimension to make the cultural panorma more comprehensive. Among the eminent commentaries of our age, the commentaries written by Tilak, Sri Aurobindo, Dr Radhakrishnan and Mahatma Gandhi occupy very important place. In his epoch making work *Gita Rahasya,* Tilak looks upon Gita as science of Karma-Yoga. Very clearly, he shows that Karma-Yoga fused with spiritual knowledge and devotion, is the true purpose of Gita.[48] According to Tilak, Gita preaches that "all world-affairs should be carried on,"[49] and it is in this emphasis that lies the originality of Tilak's bhāṣya. This contribution of Tilak will be lauded because of its impact on the practical life of Indians whom he aroused from the dogmatic slumber of social indolence and political inertia.

Radhakrishnan's views on Gita are contained in his *Indian Philosophy*[50] and an Introduction to his book *Bhagavadgītā.* When the western scholars were spreading great prejudices against the cultural values of India and a frontal attack was being made on our traditions by distorting their meanings, India needed a Sanskrit scholar, who may be Indian by culture and inheritance but who may be able to interpret our cultural values according to the western methods of interpretation. Radhakrishnan's commentary fulfils this socio-cultural requirement. With a view to dispelling all the misconceptions spread about Indian culture in the western scholars, Dr. Radhakrishnan points out that "the context in which the Gita is said to be delivered points out how its central purpose is to solve the problem of life and stimulate right conduct.[51]

Another most important interpretations of Gita comes from Sri Aurobindo, the prophet of the gnostic society. In his magnificient commentary *Essays of the Gita*, he emphasizes an integral approach towards the problems concerning the personality of man and the progress of civilization towards superman. He points out clearly that in leading a 'divine life,' "the first-step is Karma-Yoga. the selfless sacrifice of works, the second is jñāna-yoga, the self-realization...The last step is Bhakti-yoga."[52] This integrated approach saves personality from disintegration and tight compartmentalisation and lays emphasis that for a balanced growth an integral approach towards the intellectual, the socio-ethical, and psycho-biological progress of mankind is needed. It is evident from this very brief account of various commentaries on Gita that its fundamental tenets have eternal, values which can be used for the solution of intellectual, spiritual, emotional and cultural crisis with equal effectiveness. This brings us to evaluate the fourth commentary of our age as to what were the problems of society which inspired Mahatma Gandhi to write his own commentary, viz. *Anāsakti Yoga*.

Cultural Influences on Gandhi's Commentary

Apart from the various commentaries, which have their own value in the socio-cultural and spiritual unlift of our society, Gita has been given a new sociological orientation in *Anāsakti Yoga* by M.K. Gandhi. What factors led him to give this new interpretation to Gita's lofty teachings ? In order to understand these influences we shall have to understand the general cultural conditions and the factors, which were responsible for moulding the ideas of the interpretor, M.K. Gandhi.

At the outset, it may be recalled that while interpreting Gita, Gandhi did not recognize that it was a historical work. He is of the opinion that under the guise of the physical warfare, it described the dual that perpetually went on in the hearts of mankind.[53] Whether the characters of Gita are historical entities or not, is not much relevant, but the fact remains that the symbolic representation of the characters also reflects the conflict in the life situation. Marx would say that 'it is the real historical movement which is turning the world upside down that is reflected into the consciousness of man'.[54] This is true in case of Gita, because it has always been considered a practical guide. In the light of this, by calling it allegorical in the new interpretation Anāsakti Yoga, the interpreter has not projected his subjective fantasies, but has tried to reflect the same historical movement going on under our very eyes. Thus Anāsakti Yoga reflects the problems of the common masses of this age. Gandhi never said that he was projecting his own repressed tendencies and idiosyncracies in this new bhāṣya but he has incorporated various social and cultural influences in giving new dimensions to the old values. A brief survey of these factors will make the matter more elaborate and may help in correct assessment of these influences.

No Communist Influence :

Sometimes the impact of Marxism and of the Russian ideology is worked out on Gandhi's thought because Gandhi gave a theory of socialism. Such conclusion is drawn on many other sporadic evidences. Gandhi lived in an era when the success of the October Revolution, 1917 was widely felt. He was also waging a relentless fight against the imperialist manoeuvres. On this basis, Lenin believed that as the inspirer and leader of a mass movement, Gandhi was a revolutionary.[55] Similarly, S.A. Dange, the leader of Indian Communist movement also advocated that Gandhism was needed for this country. Dange said, "it is necessary to revive his militant defiance of the octopus of the State power and wealth, his defence of the dignity of man especially the poor, the daridranārāyaṇa and the oppressed.[56] On such grounds, some persons might be misled to think that Gandhian thought is the product of communist doctrines with something minus and something plus. But the actual fact is quite contrary to this. Gandhi continued to detest the ideology of communism as a creed of āsakti and atheism, and of violence. A great pioneer of communist movement in India,

Sardesai has rightly assessed the situation. He concludes that "those who say that Gandhism is Communism minus violence, forget that Gandhi fully reciprocated to the basic antipathy of communists towards him by a similar antipathy towards Marxism."[57] Thus, it cannot be said that Gandhi tried to inject the communist influences in his commentary.

Indian Renaissance :

At the time when Gandhi wrote his commentary on Gita, the country was under the political servitude of the imperialists. The genius of this ancient land was challenged. The masses were not only groaning under the yoke of political slavery, but were also facing economic exploitation of the resources which is a necessary accompaniment of imperialism and colonialism. This apart, an onslaught was also going on in the sphere of religion and culture. The fact that this alien rule was bent upon to finish the ancient religion of this land is evident from the declaration of Mangles, Chairman of the Board of Directors of the East India Company, who stated in the British Parliament in 1857, "Providence has entrusted the extensive empire of Hindustan to England, that the banner of Christ should wave triumphant from one end of India to the other. Every one must exert all his strength that there may be no dilatoriness on any account in continuing, in the country the work of making all India Christian."[58]

With a view to obliterate the culture of this land,the foreigners were intentionally trying to misrepresent the traditions of this land and deliberate attempts were being made to magnify the dark spots of Indian ethos. Histories like *The Cambridge History of India* are a distorted version of Indian chronicles, the sole aim of which seems to be to show that India was a nation historically determined to be conquered and ruled by the aliens. Similar other histories were also used to demoralise the forces of the insurgent freedom movement. The enemies of Indian culture thought that the new system of English education imparting academic instructions in the humanities and sciences would help to foster a feeling of inferiority among the people and a contempt for their own culture and tradition which was necessary to glorify British rule. Lord Macaulay's 'Minute on Education' written in 1834, reflected the contemptuous manner in which the new ruling class treated the age old traditions and culture and the various Indian languages.[59] The grave danger to the Indian culture from the western onslaught has also been recognised by a great historian like Toynbee. He pointed out that "Hindu civilization is one of the ten living civilizations of world, although it is under threat of either annihilation or assimilation by West."[60] This situation of the cultural onslaught was greatly challenging for the Indian genius. Indian intelligentsia was proud of its great cultural heritage, which was lying in hibernation and which wanted to re-assert itself. The soul of India had not died.

Radhakrishnan rightly says that "her political subjection has not completely deprived her of her soul."[61] When the crisis came, she rose with a great gusto to reassert her greatness. It rose in the form of many social and cultural reformers. The Indian Renaissance gave birth to a galaxy of such persons as Swami Daya Nand, Vivekanand, Aurobindo, Rabindra Nath Tagore, etc. Gandhi was also a product of this Renaissance. All these pioneer thinkers came forward to reinterpret and thereby to re establish the lost glory of the ancient wisdom of this land.

In this new cultural uprise, the imperialist rule also played its historical role, i.e., the role of producing its own grave diggers. Bringing out how the British rule in India contained its own germs of destruction, Marx wrote in 1853 in very clear terms, "The ruling classes of Great Britain have had, till now, but an accidental, transitory, and exceptional interest in the progress of India. The aristocracy wanted to conquer it, the moneycracy to plunder it and the millocracy to undersell it."[62] This is a historical fact that in their bid to satisfy their lust for money and power, the alien rule plundered the economic resources of India. They destroyed the native industry. According to Marx, who was watching the political currents in England itself, "the historic pages of their rule in India report hardly anything beyond that destruction. The work of regeneration hardly transpires through a heap of ruins."[63] But soon the tables were turned against the imperialist rulers. When the rulers discovered that the transformation of India into a productive country was of vital importance to them, they established large scale modern industry resulting from the railway system. The industrial progress and the faster means of communication fostered a political unity. It brought together the masses of India and also exercised a blow on those factors upon which rested the Indian caste system, which was a decisive impediment to Indian progress and Indian power. The industrial progress of India proved more conducive to the Renaissance and to the intensification of revolt against colonialism.

On cultural front also, Indians strengthened their position. The religious and cultural forces of Indian society expressed great concern over the growing influence of westernism. The so-called welfare activities of the foreign missionaries were also viewed with suspicion as having some ulterior motive behind them. Expressing his indignation against the exploitors under the garb of religion, Gandhi wrote, "Poverty has not been misused and exploited more by anyone else than the Christian proselytisers."[64] However, despite this vexation and resentment it remained a fact that zeal with which the missionaries conducted their campaign against various evil customs like untouchability, child marriage, etc. roused the social consciousness of the people of India. They helped in the formulation of new patterns of social thinking and activity in India. Rightly observed Dr. Sarma when he said that "it must be confessed that the emphasis, which our religious leaders, have laid on social service, is due to 'the object-lesson provided by Christian missions."[65] India rediscovered her soul with new vitality.

The Indian culture is a powerful armoury whence from weapons can be drawn to counteract any threat to its survival. The sociological history of India would reveal that the counter-force against the alien rulers has risen in every period of history in the shape of a movement, which is based on the old values of the people. Accordingly, the Indian thinkers started reinterpreting their own ancient values in the light of the new demands. They linked, whatever they found progressive, with the cultural heritage of this land, and rejected every such thing, which was found detrimental to the national spirit and which strangulated the cultural values blossomed from the very life of the people. Such an attitude of assimilation of the new values into the basic framework of Indian heritage has been considered of great cultural significance by Sorokin. He says : "Any mental production is conditioned, moulded, and patterned by each civilisation or super-system in its own way. Each basically different super-system of culture has its own system of truth.[66] Accordingly, if any ideology wants to prevail, it must either be the product of the cultural conditions of India herself or must be linked with the value system rooted in the soil of this country. Gandhi realized this necessity and thought that no society can detach itself from its historical background in living continuity. Thus, the Indian soul found its new expression in the field of social thought that Gandhi presents in Anāsakti Yoga. It may be concluded that Gandhian commentary on Gita carries the impact of Indian Renaissance on it.

Other Influences on Gandhi :

As we study the new interpretation given to Gita by Gandhi in his *Anāsakti Yoga*, we find that apart from the general conditions of Indian Renaissance, Gandhi's other experiences have influenced this interpretation. In reciprocation, Gita has also deeply shaped and influenced Gandhi's philosophy of action. It is under the influence of these factors that Gandhiji claims that "he ascribes to the *Gita*, a totally new meaning from that ordinarily given."[67] By the time the *Anāsakti Yoga* was published (12-3-1930), Gandhi incorporated various influences in his thought-scheme. The vaishnava influence was inherited by him from his family.[68] When Gandhi went to England, he was deeply influenced by *New Testament*. He writes in his autobiography, "*The New Testament* produced a different impression, especially the 'Sermon on the Mount' which went straight to my heart. I compared it with Gita."[69] This shows that the basic foundations of Gandhi were laid in Indian culture and he compared, with a spirit of assimilation and synthesis, the other great traditions of world. Thereafter, Gandhi read the books of Tolstoy, specially *The Gospel in Brief*, *What to Do*, which made a deep impression on him. Gandhi says : "I began to realize more and more the infinite possibilities of universal love."[70] But while receptive to these influences, Gita remained his prime guide. He admits this explicitly and says : "I already had faith in the Gita, which had a fascination for me. Now I realized the necessity of diving deeper into it."[71]

Taking Gita as an 'infallible guide of conduct', Gandhi read many other treatises and scriptures. But he points out that it was Ruskin's *Unto This Last*, that left lasting impression on him. According to Gandhi's own confession, "the book was impossible to lay aside. I determined to change my life in accordance with the ideals of the book."[72] But even after such a profound influence, the foundational inspiration of his convictions came from his Hindu heritage. It was only a rediscovery of his ideals that he traced in this book. Gandhi writes: "I believe that I discovered some of my 'deepest convictions' reflected in this great book of Ruskin and that is why it so captured me and made me transform my life."[73] The main teachings of Ruskin, which had laudable influence on Gandhji, were (i) that the good of the individual is contained in the good of all; (ii) that a lawyer's work has the same value as the barber's, inasmuch as all have the same right of earning their livelihood from that work; (iii) that a life or labour, i.e., the life of the tiller of the soil and the handicraftsman is the life worth living.[74] It is clear that Gandhi tried to put the teachings of Ruskin into practice in his life, because it tallied with his own convictions, which he already found present in Gita and other Indian scriptures.

According to Gandhi's own statement, his first acquaintance with Gita began in 1888-89 with the verse translation by Sir Edwin Arnold, but later on he read as many translations as he could lay hold of.[75] Out of various commentaries and interpretations of Gita that Gandhiji read, the 'Karma-Yoga' of Tilak, seems to have left great influence on Gandhi. He himself says that he read it reverentially.[76] His emphasis on non-attached action (anāsakti) as the prime teaching of Gita seems to be the development of idea of Karma-Yoga, which came to him from Tilak. Gandhi's firm faith in Gita is reflected in a categorical assertion that he made in reply to a letter from a revolutionary Sachindranath Sanyal. Therein Gandhi writes: "I owe much to Tolstoy and much to Buddha. I still somehow or other fancy that 'my philosophy' represents the true meaning of the teachings of the Gita."[77] Now in a very elaborate study, Dr. Betai has shown how almost all the teachings of Gandhiji have been deduced from the fundamental tenets of Gita.[78]

From this brief description, it becomes evident that the basic thought structure of Gandhi and his philosophy of life, came from Gita and he tried to blend various noble ideals into that. The *Anāsakti Yoga* is the net outcome of this great synthesis. It is the high philosophy of Gita, re-rendered according to the various cultural interactions. Gita itself asserts that the "essences, the essential principles never die ; but like the discarding of old garments, and wearing the new, only their manifestation changes."[79] In *Anāsakti Yoga*, the essential principles of Gita, which carry behind them the vast panorama of the Upanisadic and epic traditions of various philosophical ideals and cultural heritages of India, have been revivified and reproduced (punar-janma) to suit the modern conditions.

References

1. Desai, Mahadeva, *The Gita According to Gandhi* ; Also Radhakrishnan, S., *Bhagavadgītā*, p. 152. All great teachers like Gautam, the Buddha, and Mahāvīra, Saṁkara and Rāmānuja are content to affirm that they are only restating the teachings of their former masters.
2. Toynbee, Arnold., *A Study of History*, Vol. II, p. 178.
3. Peterson, William., *The Realities of World Communism*, p. 26.
4. Schumpeter, Josheph, *Capitalism, Socialism and Democracy*, (2nd Ed.), p. 1.
5. Bonar, James, op. cit., p. 349. (Mr. Brij Narain, a great economist has also brought out in his book '*Marxism is Dead*' the deep impact of Bazard on the Marxian Thought.
6. Beard, Charles A., *The Economic Basis of Politics*, Chap. 3.
7. Cohen, M.R., Faith of a Liberal in *Selected Essays* (New York, Holt etc. 1946).
8. Sorokin, P.A., *Modern Historical and Social Philosophies*, p. 148.
9. Marx, Engels, Lenin, *On Historical Materialism*, p. 454.
10. Marx, Engels, Lenin, *On Historical Materialism*, p. 453.
11. Ibid., pp. 453-4.
12. Marx, K., *Critique of Political Economy*, p. 13.
13. Marx, K., *Early Writings*, pp. 43-4.
14. Eric Roll, *A History of Economic Thought*, p. 254.
15. Marx, K., *Toward the Critique of Hegel's Philosophy of Right*, p. 263.
16. Tucker, Robert C., *Marxian Revolutionary Idea*, pp. 7-8.
17. Marx, K., *Capital*, p. 873.
18. Marx and Engels, *Selected Works*, Vol. I, p. 372.
19. Ibid., Vol. II, p. 333.
20. Bonar, James, op. cit., p. 328.
21. Marx, K., *Early Writings*, p. 202. (Tn. Bottomore).
22. Wetter, Gustava A., *Dialectical Materialism*, p. 11.
23. Tucker, Robert C., *Philosophy and Myth in Karl Marx*, p. 86.
24. Marx, K., *Mega*, p. 175.
25. Marx, K. and Engels, F., *Selected Works*, Vol. II. p. 333.
26. Ibid.
27. Tucker, Robert C., op. cit., p. 86.
28. Hook, Sidney, *From Hegel to Marx*, p. 272.

29. Feuerbach, Ludwig, *The Essence of Christianity*, p. 218.
30. Marx, K., *Early Writings*, p. 195 ff.
31. Marx, K., *MEGA*, p. 428.
32. Hegel, G.W.F., *Logic of Hegel*, p. 55.
33. Marx, K. and Engels, F., *Selected Correspondence*, p. 169.
34. Marx, K., *MEGA*, p. 157.
35. Ibid.
36. Gide, Charles, and Rist Charles, *A History of Economic Doctrines*, (VII Ed.), p. 434.
37. Ibid., p. 150 and Foot-note, p. 134.
38. Ibid., p. 145.
39. Ronald, Meek L., *Marx and Engels on Malthus*, pp. 60 and 115-53.
40. *Communist Manifesto.* The whole of the manifesto is charged with such pronouncements.
41. Engels, F., *Anti-Duhring*, pp. 309-10.
42. Titus, H.H., op. cit., p. 14.
43. Marx, K. and Engels, F., *Selected Correspondence*, pp. 125-6.
44. Engels, F., *Dialectic of Nature*, p. 208.
45. Marx, K. and Engels, F., *Selected Correspondence*, p. 411.
46. Lenin, V.I., *Materialism and Empirio-Criticism*, p. 284.
47. Radhakrishnan, S., *Bhagavadgītā*—Introduction, p. 1.
48. Tilak, B.G., *Gita Rahasya*—Introduction.
49. Ibid., p. 698.
50. Radhakrishnan, S., *Indian Philosophy*, Vol. 1, p. 532.
51. Ibid., p. 529.
52. Aurobindo, *Essays on the Gita*, p. 43.
53. *The Gita According to Gandhi*, p. 127.
54. Marx, K., *Selected Correspondence*, p. 15.
55. Rao, M.B., *The Mahatma : A Marxist Symposium*, p. 17.
56. Ibid., p. 5.
57. Ibid., p. 18.
58. Damodaran, K., *Indian Thought—A Critical Survey*, p. 338.
59. Theodore De Bary, *Sources of Indian Tradition*, pp. 596-7.
60. Toynbee, Arnold., op. cit., Vol. IV, pp. 1-2.
61. Radhakrishnan, S., *Eastern Religion and Western Thought*, p. 305.
62. Marx, K., 'The Future Results of British Rule in India', in *Selected Works*, Vol. I, p. 496.
63. Ibid.
64. Gandhi, M.K., *Harijan*, 6-3-1937.
65. Sarma, D.S., *Renaissance of Hinduism*, p. 639.
66. Sorokin, P.A., op. cit., pp. 306-307.
67. Gandhi, M.K., *Young India*, 5-4-1926.
68. Gandhi, M.K., *My Experiments With Truth*, pp. 12-13.
69. Ibid., pp. 90-3.
70. Ibid., pp. 197-8.
71. Ibid., pp. 322-4.
72. Ibid., pp. 364-5.

73. Ibid.
74. Ibid.
75. Gandhi, M.K., Preface to *Anāsakti Yoga*, p. 14.
76. Desai, Mahadeva, *The Gita According to Gandhi*, p. 126.
77. Gandhi, M.K., *Young India*, 12-2-1925.
78. Betai, Ramesh S., *Gita and Gandhiji*, pp. 204-56.
79. *Gita*, II. 22.

4

The Ideal Social Order

Both communism and Gita propose to release man from his alienated existence. What would be the ideal social order in which man would seek his *summum bonum* ? What is the form of future existence beyond the realm of necessity, contradictions and conflicts. Both Gita and Communism have their own answers.

Communist Social Order

The ideal order of man's social existence, as brought out by Marx can be understood into two phases : (i) the lower phase of society in which the alienated man will strive for the realization of his humanity. This is called 'Socialism'. This is also called the transitory period of the 'dictatorship of the proletariat' ; (ii) The higher phase in which man will exist after his full transformation. This is called 'Communism'. It is in the final stage of communism that the State will 'wither away', division of labour, leading to class struggle will finish, and the private property which is the source of dehumanization will be abolished.

The idea of the withering away of the 'state reflects Marx' moral concern for human freedom. Hegel in his system, has upheld that "for freedom it is necessary that we should feel no presence of something, which is not ourselves,"[1] because the 'limitations' or 'being limited by the other' are the signs of human bondage. Marx retained this idea in his theory of alienation. For Marx alienation of man from his 'species being' is a social separation from socially generated characteristics and propensities.[2] But Hegel went wrong when he conceived the 'world-self' as a 'self-comprehending totality',[3] the political implications of which lead to the worst type of 'totalitarianism'. The purpose of Marx was to remedy this position. "The point of Marx's analysis is to reidentify the true subject (the acting individual, living in the 'real' material world) and to trace the process of his 'objectification' in the political institution of the State."[4]

Accordingly, the State is conceived as an alienated form of political activity. This alienation takes place when, in the words of Marx himself, "the State power makes itself independent in relation to society whose mere instrument it was originally intended to be."[5] Once it has come into being, it is perpetuated to foster the vested interests, and accordingly, it is, as Marx himself called it, "simply the official form of the antagonism in civil society."[6] According to this view, the State becomes an instrument for continuing the class struggle from above. The possessing class, with the help of the existing social order of production, resists all the efforts of the producing class to transform the society. This is the repressive function that they assign to the State. But man wants to realize his productive freedom and for that it becomes necessary to break the repressive bonds. Marx did not like that man's creative freedom should be subjected to the iron laws of political expediency. He made his position very clear when he said, "In order to free their creative powers from the existing despotic regime of production (and) in order, therefore, to assert themselves as individuals, they must overthrow the State."[7] What he wanted to say in this assertion was, that when man becomes really 'human' by sheding off his inhuman tendencies, he will not stand in need of any control from any political authority. Thus, the withering away of the State is not a political but a moral necessity. It is due to the misunderstanding of this moral postulate that many superfluous theories about the 'withering away' of State have flooded the market. For example, a great economist like Mises, after analysing communism, comes to hold that it "is a programme of transforming the economic life and constitution of society according to a defined ideal."[8] Accordingly, he sees communism as some economic order in which all private property will come to an end. With the abolition of class interests and private property, the political institution, which has so far defended it, will not be needed. Such an analysis of the Marxian theory of State is put forth on the grounds that Marx considered the political institutions to be an element of the superstructure and thus generally dependent on the operative forces in a society's economic structure. This is, however, not the whole story. Marx had a complex view of the relations between economic and political forces. No doubt, Marx upheld the view that "the totality of the relations of production constitutes the economic structure of society, the real foundation. The modes of production determine the general characteristic of the social, political and spiritual process of life."[9]

But, it may be recalled that this type of determinism is operative in the realm of dialectical necessity only. Beyond that the economic factors will cease to determine human conduct and, therefore, it will not be the economic grounds on which State will wither away, but according to the logical law of Quantified Negation, the negation of the economic determinism will negate the political institutions as such. Marx has referred to this point at various places in various ways, suggesting thereby that from the communist point of view, it is something more than economics which is working behind the formation of a new social order. Marx writes : "Every 'economic' phenomenon is at the same time always a social phenomenon and the existence of a particular kind of 'economy' presupposes a definite kind of society."[10] It means that there are certain social exigencies, which require the State to wither away. All confusion about the theory of State arises, when we ignore the antecedent of Marxian conditional proposition, which may be formulated to read as : "If man is to be freed from his alienated existence in his practical life, then State must be made to wither away." Without affirming the antecedent, the consequent cannot be logically affirmed. Marx expresses the view that abolition of State is required to assert the existence of man as a social being. Marx writes, "when the proletariat announces the dissolution of the hitherto existing order of things, it merely announces the secret of its own existence."[11]

It shows that man does not exist as a social being so long as the State authority regulates his conduct from above. Once the rule of law is accepted as a matter of social habit, the force automatically dwindles away. It is a moral mode of existence like the 'Kingdom of the ends' of Kant. Marx is very clear on this point in Xth Theses on Feuerbach wherein he writes : "The standpoint of the old materialism is 'civil' society ; the standpoint of the new materialism is human society or socialized humanity."[12]

Marx does not talk of an 'economised humanity' but he talks of a society of such individuals, who have realized their essence as 'species being'. In the civil society, man exists as an atomized individual with his egoistic interest. It is intrinsically a sphere of unrestrained egoism, where each man is pitted against every other. Under these conditions of acute competition, State enforces an order and man, if he wants to live in harmony, has to subordinate himself to that political agency, the State. Hegelian concept of civil society also requires the State to regulate the life of man, as the embodiment of 'universal rights'. In Hegelian account, therefore, the State is presented as something severed from the lives of individuals in civil society. This severed existence of State appeared, as a sphere of man's alienation. According to Marx, 'man, as a citizen in the modern state, is but an idealization of the real man and hence an 'abstraction'. Hegel's mistake was, that he treated State, as the foundation of civil society, whereas the truth is just the contrary, i.e., that the civil society is the foundation of State, and State is nothing but the externalization of the powers of the species. But it exists as a special political organism, separating itself from the society and dominating over it.

Engels explains : "Once historically established, the political power is endowed with a movement of its own and strives for as much independence as possible."[13] This 'special organism' of political rule is considered by Marx to be a "parasitic growth on the body of society."[14] This type of the 'parasitic excrescence' was to be finished by destroying the underlying causes of that. The continued existence of the State has a great degenerative effect on man. Criticising such mode of dehumanized existence, Marx goes beyond politics and bases his argument on moral considerations. He writes :

"When the political State achieves fully developed form, man not only in thoughts, in consciousness but in *reality*, in life, leads a double life, heavenly and earthly, a life in the political community, in which he recognises himself as a communal being, and a life in civil society, in which he acts as a private person, treats others as a means, reduces himself to the role of a means and becomes the plaything of the alien forces."[15]

It is, therefore, to end this condition of immoral living, viz., living as 'mere means', which will have to be finished by making the State wither away. Here tacitly, Marx is reflecting Kantian categorical imperative that when man treats others as means or allows himself to be treated as mere means, then that is an immoral condition, which needs to be remedied. The cure for this political alienation is that the repressive organs of the old government power should be amputed and its legitimate functions may be restored to the responsible agents of society. This is the state of "the return of man to himself as a social, i.e., really human being. a complete and conscious return which assimilates all the wealth of previous development."[16] By this, man will repossess the social power that has hitherto forth been externalised in the political institutions. When the 'real' individual takes back into himself the abstract citizen of the State, and as individual man, in his individual labour and in his individual relations, becomes a 'species being', then no political authority will be needed. Marx further clarifies "when man recognizes and organizes his *forces propres* as social forces and so ceases to separate social power from himself in the form of political power—only then will human emancipation take place."[17] Tacitly, Marx is going back to Machiavelli's position that natural man, being grossly egoistic, competitive and atomized individuality, needs a strong political authority, which may put his selfish tendencies under control. The difference is that Machiavelli thinks that man, by nature is egoist and selfish and, therefore, he will always stand in need of strong political authority, the absolute State. But Marx is optimistic and hopes that man will realize his essence, the social nature one day. Then, he will be freed from the acute competition for the goods ; he will give up his acquisitive and egoistic needs. Visualizing that future mode of human existence, Marx writes : "When, in the course of development, class distinctions have disappeared and all production has been concentrated in the hands of a vast association of the whole nation, the public power will lose its political character,"[18] and as a consequent of that, having become superfluous, the State will by itself wither away.

Dictatorship of the Proletariat :

In order to reach the final stage of the communist society where State will be rendered superfluous, mankind will have to pass the ordeals of the lower phase of communism, viz., socialism. This transitory stage will be needed as a 'means' to prepare man for his final jump to communism. Writing in the *Critique of The Gotha Programme*, Marx points out that, "between capitalist and communist society lies the period of the revolutionary transformation of the one into the other. Corresponding to this is also a political transition period in which the State can be nothing but the revolutionary dictatorship of the proletariat."[19] This stage cannot be bypassed, because man will need adequate training in order to enable him to enter the 'realm of freedom'. According to Lenin, "from capitalism, mankind can pass directly only to socialism."[20] During this transitional period, all the prerequisites for final stage, viz., a highly developed material and technical basis and improved social relations between man and man, will be achieved. Freed from the capitalist exploitation, humanity will need a pause to sift out as to who are eligi ble to traverse the higher path and who are not.

Although so much emphasis has been laid on the inevitability and necessity of this socialist stage of development by Marx and Engels both, in the course of history's planned march to communism, yet they have made very vague statements about the political set up, the type of government and the constitution of this workers' State. What they have tried to show, is that it is a form of polity destined to endure through the entire historical epoch of 'transition' to communism and that this 'dictatorship of revolution', would have a short life at the close of man's pre-history. In *The Class Struggle in France*, Marx proclaimed : "This socialism is the declaration of the class dictatorship of the proletariat as the necessary transit point to the abo ition of class distinctions generally."[21] He further confirmed the transitory character of this stage, in one of his letters to his friend. Marx in that letter declared *inter alia* that this dictatorship itself constitutes only the transition to the *abolition* of all classes and to classless society.[22] The intermediary stage between the realm of necessity and realm of freedom is conceived, as the period of revolutionary transformation, during which 'the State can be nothing but the revolutionary dictatorship of the proletariat.'[23]

All this shows that although the transitory stage of dictatorship was so important in the march towards the ideal social order, yet the founders of communism were not interested to go into detail of this phase, because of its transitory character and left it for the politicians to play with this vague and uncertain idea. The whole controversy in Marxists' circles today is regarding the working out of concrete forms of this stage. The only clue about the blue print of dictatorship is found in one of the letters of Engels. Writing on *Gotha Programme,* Engels wrote to one of his contemporaries : "So long as the proletariat still uses the State, it does not use it in the interests of freedom, but in order to hold down its adversaries and as soon as it becomes possible to speak of freedom the State as such ceases to exist."[24] From this statement it is evident that like all previous historical forms of the State, the proletarian State was also looked upon by the founders of communism as an instrumentality of class struggle. Accordingly, the workers' State is a means of holding down a class in society and to crush the adversaries. However, being a repressive force, it must wither away when man becomes morally perfect and the repressive techniques are not needed. These pronouncements do not make the position of Marx clear about the necessity of the continuation of State.

There may be two implications and justification for positing this 'lower phase' of communism or the 'dictatorship'. Either State would exist as long as the evil exists. This is the negative function of State, according to which State exists because evil exists and when evil is eliminated, it will not be needed. As a second alternative, it exists for making man a social being. This is the positive function of State. This distinction did not occupy any attention of Marx although it has great political implications. His concern was less political and more ethical, because he had a faith that when an individual prepares himself for his final realisation, this dictatorship will disappear. Marx himself expressed this contention when he said that "in place of the old bourgeois society, with its classes and class antagonism, we shall have an association in which the free *development* of each is the pre-condition for the free development of all.[25]

What is State :

A question may be raised here that when the idea of this 'dictatorship' was so insignificant that Marx did not like to waste his efforts in working out its details, was it at all necessary for his theory to postulate this ? If at all this stage was essential, why Marx assigned it only a transitory role and thought that it should wither away after performing its function ? The answer to this problem can be traced in Marxian concept of alienation as applied to political field which appears in the form of State. According to Marxian concept, State is the expression of man's alienated existence. In "Gotha Programme", Marx clarifies, what he means by 'State' : "By the word 'State' is meant the Government machine or the State in so far as it forms a special organism separated from society through the division of labour."[26] In finishing the State, Marx wants to finish this artificial separation between the political power and the society from which it has arisen. The State machinery, viz., the bureaucracy, is the product of society, but when this machinery starts exploiting the society itself, the social forces must revolt against that. Society is much above the government machinery. Inverting the Hegel's idea of State by his method of transformational criticism, Marx arrived at the conclusion that the State is a manifestation, an outgrowth of civil society. Hegel proceeded from the State and turned man into a subjectified State. But democracy must proceed from man, and it would turn the State into an objectified man. How can man's own objectified form be allowed to swallow man's dignity. Marx retorted, on this ground, against the State. He wrote : "Just as religion does not create man, but man creates religion, so the political system does not create the people, but rather the people create the political system."[27]

This statement of Marx has a great significance, because he wants to cut the political power to size. When the executive power in the society becomes so corrupt and despotic that it starts thinking itself quite separate from the people, then it asserts itself as a specially privileged class : When it applies the laws not for human welfare but simply for the sake of the letter of the law and the humanity is crucified at the altar of blind and abstract laws, it becomes a tyranny. This type of the outgrowth makes State, in the opinion of Engels, "an organization of the possessing class for its protection against the non-possessing class."[28] Marx is, therefore, justified in asking for the end of such State machinery in so far as it feels itself separated from the demos. Mill, a contemporary of Marx also advocated that State can be and should be democratically converted into an instrument for the social improvement of the living condition of masses.

But Marx's zeal for freedom as a supreme human value was so intense that it led him to conclude that the continued existence of State is incompatible with the realization of freedom. This could be realized only if the State is replaced by communes. In commune, Marx found a revolutionary substitute and a revolutionary movement to destroy the State as 'parasitic excrescence' on the body of society. What are these communes ? In one of his letter to August Bebel, Engels clarified that "they would propose to replace 'State' everywhere by 'community' a good old German word (Gemeinwesen) which can very well represent the French word 'commune.'[29] The position becomes clear that in advocating that the 'State' will wither away, Marx and Engels wanted to finish the 'separateness' between the political authority and the community. It signifies the end of 'alienation' between the political and the social. It is in this sense that State will ultimately yield place to 'Communes'. In so characterizing 'State' and its withering away, Marx advocated that the communes would restore "to the social body all the forces hitherto absorbed by the State parasitic feeding upon and clogging the free movements of society."[30] The concept of community living is considered more consistent with the freedom and growth of man than the idea of 'State' machinery, which is considered to be "a separate and powerful section of the nation."[31]

When man becomes conscious of community living and he is prepared to break the fetters of political alienation which State has imposed on him, then he becomes fully capable of entering the higher phase of society. Only then, the communism is achieved. What are then the outlines of the communist society, the final phase of human history ?

Socialization of man :

According to the view of marx, final stage of human existence will be achieved in the communist social order when man will be liberated from the vagaries of his dehumanised conditions. If the capitalist system was the negation of humanity, the transition period may at best be called '*negation of negation*'. But this is not a positive state of affairs. It is merely 'blowing off' the bondage. We have already seen that it is considered a necessary pre-condition for the emancipation of man. The cancellation of the capitalism and its replacement by the proletarian state, is a pre-requisite for clearing the way for his free and genuine human development. What is then the positive side of it. Marx tells us that "at the stage of final communism, man is to be affirmed in the objective world, not only in the act of thinking but with all his senses."[32] In the tacit reference to the process of affirming men in the act of thinking only, Marx seems to have been indicating that previous theories like Christianity have been showing man the vision of distant 'Kingdom of God', but they were Utopian. This higher phase of communism is a stage of the jump of humanity 'from the realm of necessity' into the 'realm of freedom'.

As against the imaginary affirmation of man in an extra-terrestrial world of religion, Marx wanted to affirm man's existence as a species being. According to the image of this ideal social order projected in *Das Capital*, we can say that "it is a society of freedom with common ownership of the means of production, consciously using their individual powers of labour as a social function."[33] It is sometimes conceived as the perfectly socialised stage of humanity. In the 10th Thesis, on Feuerbach, Marx pointed out that "the standpoint of new materialism is human society, or socialized humanity."[34] When the humanity is socialized, what Marx seems to say, the difference between the 'egoism and altruism' will be obliterated. This has been a great problem for all the ethical thinkers of utilitarian school, may it be Mill's utilitarianism, or Sidgwick's rational utilitarianism. Mill tried to resolve this problem with the help of his principle of utility, i.e., 'the maximum happiness of maximum number,' and Sidgwick posited the two principles of 'rational self-love' and 'rational benevolence'. But these attempts led to paradox, which Sidgwick called the 'duality of practical reason'. Marx resolved this problem in his communist formula when he says : "Now the development of each is the pre-condition of free development of all."[35] Such a vivid picture of communist society implies that communism according to Marxian concept would be a social order of harmony and unison within humanity at large. It will be the emergence of a unified society consisting of a vast association of 'complete individuals'. The word 'socialised humanity' also suggests that at this stage the alienated society, divided in class antagonism, will return to itself out of the inherent contradictions, which is the bane of capitalist system. A society free from the contradictions, will be the 'communist society'.

End of Private Property :

As it has already been shown, the real cause of human misery in the capitalist society is the lust or greed, the acquisitive mania. This manifests in the form of the desire of self-aggrandisement, a lust to have more and more money, and a desire to appropriate what legitimately belongs to the worker. The refuge of this lust is 'private property'. When man breaks his bondage, this severest and the prime source of bondage will also be finished. Marx considered the monopoly of the capital as a fetter upon the mode of production and upon the productive power of the working man. He, therefore, pronounced its doom under communism. Marx says : "This integument is burst asunder. The knell of the capitalist property sounds, the expropriators are expropriated." [36] Why Marx wanted to do away with the institution of private property ? Marx has not given any economic grounds for this.

It has already been discussed that Marx has not given any 'Economics of the communist society', because his conception of communism was that of a meta-economical social order. His argument for ending the private property is based on his moral considerations. It is to be finished because it has degenerative effects and corruptive influence on humanity. Marx himself writes : "This primitive accumulation plays in political economy about the same part as original sin in theology. Adam bit the apple and thereupon sin fell on the human race......and from this original sin dates the poverty of the great majority."[37] The religious analogy used by Marx shows his deep conviction that so long as man has the lust for private property, he will be impelled by his greed to commit all sorts of sins against humanity. This type of contempt for wordly accumulations is found in almost all the religious discourses, which shows that private property can be as well ended in the name of religion as in the name of communism. The difference is that religion negates the private property only in imagination whereas communism finishes this stigma in practical life.

The final stage or communism may thus be described as 'positive transcendence of private property. Men, in communist society, will be liberated from the compulsive acquisitive mania that has dominated the lives of men throughout the whole process of their development upto capitalism and has turned them into sinners.

Inner Dynamics of Communist Society :

What will be the laws regulating this 'socialized humanity' ? The State having withered away, some sort of regulatory laws are needed to keep the social cohesion. Nothing has been said by Marx anywhere about the question of planning, the distribution of goods, the organisation of public services or about the communal living arrangements. Marx has laid down the guideline of communism in his formula 'from each according to his ability to each according to his need'. The contemporary communist thinkers call it the fundamental principle of communism.[38] Marx assumed while laying down this principle that after having realized his real nature, man will not need any external authority to regulate his conduct. Man, of Marxian concept, being essentially a producer, will produce material goods for the sheer expression of his productive nature. Marx believed that man produces even when he is free from physical need. From this, it can be inferred that man, under communism, will produce to realize his inner essence and to express his '*svabhava*'. It will be an inner moral obligation for him. After producing the material goods in abundance, he will arrange his affairs not according to economic or political laws, but according to law of aesthetics.[39] Communist thinkers rightly hold that the maxim " 'from each according to his ability', under communism becomes also a kind of morality for citizens gradually to acquire the habit of observing the rules of the communist way of life."[40] When man becomes so much moralized that it becomes his habit to act according to the requirements of moral law, there will be no need of any political sanctions or the codified rules of economics. Thus speaking, the communist society presupposes, as Afanasyev also tells us, "a man, who combines in himself spiritual richness, moral purity and physical perfection."[41]

Socio-Political Institutions :

Marx describes the final stage of communism, as consisting of 'socialized humanity' that is 'a classless, stateless, and generally a structureless collectivity of complete individuals, who live in harmony with themselves and with each other'. Beyond this, little light is thrown on the institutional set up in the communist society. In presenting such a negative description of the final phase of human existence, Marx seems to have tacitly assumed the nature of the 'ultimate', which cannot be precisely described. It is due to this indeterminate conception of the communist society that the beliefs expressed by Marx appear to be very beautiful, but aesthetic or romantic beliefs. In the background of his desire to do away with State, private property, division of labour and thereby to put an end to the dehumanized conditions of existence, there seems to be the hope of casting the devil once for all out of the world. It is his fond hope that by eliminating the source of greed, man will become a moral being. Ridiculing the utopian scheme of Marx, Popper points out, "the anarchist dreamt that once in the State, the political system was destroyed, everything must turn out well. And Marx dreamt a similar dream of banishing the devil by destroying the economic system."[42]

However, such pseudo-simple and hasty conclusions are bound to be drawn when precise predictions are tried about the future state of existence. As a matter of fact, whenever the indeterminate is explained in the categories of determinate, many fanciful conclusions follow. Kant warned that if the categories of phenomenon are applied to noumenon, it is bound to lead into antinomies. That seems to be reason why Marx wanted to avoid any precise description of the socio-political structure of the institutions in the communist society. Since the prime concern of Marx was the transcendence of alienated existence and the regaining of self, he did not consider it necessary to lay down a clear-cut blue-print of the communist institutions. On the contrary, at one place, he pointed out clearly : "The socialists need not concern themselves with devising programmes for future but have only to give an account of what passes before their eyes."[43]

Marx, being a practical man, did not like the working man to indulge into fanciful speculations about the liberated state of man's existence, for the fear of the worker losing his zeal to break the bondage and to strive for liberation in practical life. Marx warned the working class against wasting their energies in these speculations about the future. Marx writes : "they (workers) have no ideals to realize, but to set free the elements of the new society with which old collapsing bourgeoise society is pregnant."[44] Since it is neither practically predictable nor it is scientifically tenable to work out the precise shape of the future social events, it is better to take care of the present conditions, and the future will take care of it by itself. Therefore, Marx thought it proper to work out only the outlines and the framework into which the working details will be filled by the posterity itself. Conceptualizing the whole picture of the future social order and summarizing the whole position about the communist society, Marx writes :

> "Here for the first time his natural existence is his human existence and nature has become man for him. Thus *society* is the complete essential unity of man with nature, the true resurrection of nature, the achieved naturalism of man and the achieved humanism of nature."[45]

Ideal Social Order according to Gita

Anāsakti Yoga of Gita does not reveal any dichotomy of the social orders as communism has put forth in the form of higher and lower phases. For communist thinkers the society is far above the Government, the State and the political machinery. If the social forces are weak, the state will become a tyrant and will exploit the people. Gita also accepts this sociological truth, and aims more to build a strong society of liberated and enlightened persons. That is why Gita does not discuss political problems.

For a superficial onlooker, the Gita may not present any sound social theory. But a closer and deeper analysis of the meanings of various verses of Gita read with the key aphorisms, supplied by Mahābhārata, reveals it is pregnant with an organic theory of society. The mystery centres round the concept of Brahman which remained a supra-mundane, transcendental Being because of the orientation given by the spiritualistic thinkers. Such a supra-rational, trans-empirical and qualityless Absolute, the Brahman did not serve any practical purpose at all. The practical discipline of Gita requires that the ideal must be such as may serve the practical needs of mankind. Some practical formulae must, therefore, be searched within the philosophy of Gita's Anāsakti Yoga.

There is nothing to be sceptic about this, because the practical considerations have been the dominating mark of Indian thought. The philosophy in India has originated under the pressure of a practical need engendered by the presence of moral and physical evil in life. It was due to the mystified interpretation of the Upaniṣads that some pious hands erected the dead walls of a deep mystery and made whole philosophical system something devoid of practice.

In the West, a mystifying horror was created by the grandiose system of Hegel. It remained an unresolved puzzle till Feuerbach used his 'method of transformational criticism' and tore off the veil of mystery. Under his hand, the God of Hegel became 'Man'. In his *Essence of Christianity*, Feuerbach transformed Hegel and re-read his aphorisms in a demystified way. He said, "Therefore, in the Being of God, it is only thy own being, which is object to thee and what presents itself before thy consciousness is simply what lies behind it."[46]

What Feuerbach did for demystifying Hegel, Mahābhārata has done for unravelling the mystery of Brahman of the Upaniṣadic thought. Revealing the secret of Brahman, Mahābhārata proclaims that there is nothing higher (superior) than man (*na mānuṣāt śreṣṭhataram hi kiñcit*). This concept of Brahman is the purgatory of all the mystifications and obscurities. Gita forms an integral part of Mahābhārata, and we have no reasons to believe that the author of Mahābhārata broke the logical law of identity and committed the fallacy of equivocation by using the term 'Brahman' in any other connotation. The demystifying clarification given by Mahābhārata, enables us to substitute the word 'Man' for 'Brahman'.

The word 'Man' can be used in its generic or collective sense, as human subjectivity or the species being. Such use of the term is very common even in ordinary language. When we say 'Man is the crown of creation', we use the word to stand for the class 'humanity'. Understood in this sense, it is the man, who is realizing himself, his true humanity, in the process of self-realization. The consistency in the use of the term 'Brahman' and the continuity of thought in Gita demands that the aim of Brahma nirvāṇa of Gita is to make man perfectly one with humanity. As already discussed, Bṛhadāraṇyaka Upaniṣad and Chāndogya Upaniṣad contain various verses, which are sufficient to show that man himself is Brahman in his essence. The identity of Brahman and man has been verily shown. Brahman differs from Ātman only in the sense that Ātman is the essence of all internal reality, whereas Brahman stands for the transcendent unity of mankind. Damodaran, after a detailed survey of the Upaniṣads, also comes to conclude that "Brahman is nothing but the human being."[47]

Taking this key concept from Mahābhārata, we can very well discern that Gita presents the organic theory of society. In the eleventh chapter of the Gita, the Divine presents itself before Arjuna in a human form. Gita says : "Then did Pāṇḍava see the whole universe in its manifold divisions gathered as one in the body of that God of gods."[48] Commenting on this verse, Radhakrishnan opines that "Gita stands for an organic as against an atomistic conception of society."[49] *Mahābhārata* substantiates this contention that the world of mortals is an interdependent organism (*saṅghātavān martyalokaḥ parasparam apāśritaḥ*).[50] The Māndūkya Upaniṣad also while describing the four states of self, corroborates that "world-manifested in waking state is Virāt or the Cosmic person."[51] Hundred of such verses fill the Upaniṣadic texts, which suggest that society is an 'organism' (puruṣa). Since Gita represents the essence of upaniṣads, we can have no objection in upholding that the doctrine of the Anāsakti Yoga of Gita is based on the principle that the reality is a social system. "A social system", according to Sorokin, "is an organised group that possesses a set of enforced, obligatory law norms defining in details the rights, duties, social position, and functions of each of its members towards one another and the world at large."[52] It is this organised character of the group that the concept of 'organism' denotes in Gita.

Organic Theory :

From an ordinary point of view, every man sees the factual plurality, the gross individuality but the social and psychic bonds are not empirically observed. This was the infantile disease of Hume's empiricism that he tried to search for the relations in his empirical modes The social unity is a matter of rational apprehension. How the existence of others is to be proved ? This is still a problem for the positivists who are again and again led to solipsism due to their over-emphasis on empirical observation. Arjuna is, therefore, clearly told that "you cannot see me with these your own eyes. I give you the eyes divine (divyam)."[53] The rational insight is considered divine, because it is the inability of the mechanistic and empirical modes to conceptualize the felt unity and that is the reason that in order to apprehend the underlying unity, man has to transcend his mechanistic modes.

Hartshorn also advocates the view that social unity is not empirically realizable. He says : "Nothing can be social that is without experience. The minimum of experience is 'feeling'. Therefore, the creatures are social if they feel."[54] This type of vision, which was given to Arjuna to see the organic unity, may be called, in Whitehead's language a 'prehensive unity'. The prehensive unity as Whitehead explains 'is a process of prehensive unification as working behind the atomic individuation.'[55] This type of prehension, is *ipso facto*, the process of realization. It is the realization of one underlying activity behind the interlocked plurality of modes. This Whiteheadian concept is suggestive of the fact that an individual can realize himself by realization of the organic unity of mankind. Gita's giving the 'divine' vision to the moral agents conveys the idea that the prehensive unity of society is a matter of realization.

The view that human society may be compared to a living organism is not exclusive to Gita. This idea occurred very early to the reflective minds right from the Republic of Plato. In west, there are many thinkers, who regarded the human society as an organic unity and rejected the idea of atomistic individuality. Pointing out the significance of this view, Mackenzie is very clear on the point "just as we recognise a common life animating all the members of which a living body is composed, so we must acknowledge a similar unity among the members of a human society."[56] Milne also lends support to this view. "Society", he says, "is organic in its nature and finite individual is a member of social whole."[57]

In the light of these various conceptions of organic unity available here, we may infer that according to the indications provided by Gita, society must be regarded as a unity, in fact, as an organic unity. The parts of it are necessary to each other, as the parts of an organism are. The human organism through which the divine revealed itself was indicative of this interdependence of the members of society.

Surprisingly enough, the Marxist view of society is also more or less the same in which the society has been seen as a 'self'. Prof. Tucker has rightly concluded that in the Marxist theory of society, "the possessing class and the proletariat class represent one and the same human self-alienation."[58] In communism, society has been treated as a self-system and the two antagonistic classes are conceived as collective expression of the conflicting forces within the same self-system. Communist theory thus subscribes to the organic conception of society.

Some of the scholars specially those of the Spencerian school of thought, have carried this analogy beyond its legitimate limits. This has been the source of many confusions about the organic theory of society. The theory is meant to convey only the interdependence of the members. Many sociologists like Comte etc. have shown that the unity of society and the participation of individual within it are to be thought in terms of organism.[59] The organic concept of society would not give rise to any objection if we use it only to personify a society, e g., 'Russia is marching ahead', 'Mentality of Pakistan is not understandable', or as the jurists use the term in 'jurisprudence' when they call a corporation or society as 'legal person'. In jurisprudence, any real or imaginary beings can be called a 'legal person', who for the purpose of legal reasoning. are treated in greater or lesser degree in the same way as human beings. It is in this sense that associations are also considered as 'persons'. Beyond this limit, this hypothesis should not be legitimately extended. McIver is right in saying that "so long as in fact we merely compare a group or community to an organism in order to bring out such aspects of society as interdependence of individuals within the unity of social system, we are using a simple and sometimes helpful analogy."[60]

Gita has used this analogical expression in this very sense to convey the idea that moral life is possible only as a member of society (*amśa*). The whole idea of *svadharma* is also an expression of this truism that man can realize himself by sublimating his narrow individualism, his isolated and atomized existence, before the social system. Milne also lends support to this contention and says that "by virtue of his being a member of the organic social whole, the social nature of the individual is derived."[61] Thus speaking, Gita uses the analogy of the divine manifesting itself in human form to convey the organic conception of the society and thereby it emphasizes that there is functional interdependence of all the members and that the social nature of man is to be derived by his partaking in the organic unity.

Divine Nature of Society :

Another problem may crop up here about the divinity of the society. Is social system divine ? To this pertinent question as to why the social system assumed the divine form, we find a very good solution in Durkheim's book *The Elementary Forms of Religious Life*. There, the society has been conceived of as possessing all the authority to command of a god and this authority is moral authority. Durkheim writes of society : "The empire which it holds on consciences is due much less to the physical supremacy of which it has the privilege than to the moral authority with which it is invested."[62] It is in this moral authority that the 'divinity lies'.

Accordingly, we can say that in 'divine' form it was the 'social system' that presented itself before the moral agent. Kṛṣṇa was addressing Arjuna, as a symbolised or personified form of social system. In order to understand the significance of the dialogue between Arjuna and Kṛṣṇa, we once again seek help from Durkheim's book. Durkheim rightly tells us that "it is society who speaks through the mouths of those who affirm them in our *presence* ; it is society whom we hear in hearing them."[63] Thus the divine manifestation is no other than the social system personified.

Democracy of the Enlightened

The ethical implication of the theory of Gita is that individual should seek his perfection by an active participation in the system. In the last discourse of Gita Arjuna is persuaded to sublate his personality to the social whole. The verse says : "On Me fix thy mind, to me bring thy devotion (*manmanā bhava madbhakto madyājī mām namaskuru*)."[64] The idea behind this verse seems to be that real dignity comes to man when he leaves the ego-centric consideration and acts with a sense of devotion that he is doing something for society. Muirhead also echoes the same idea when he says that "individuality must be sought for not in separation from the whole but in the whole-hearted acceptance of a definite station within it."[65] What would then be the best arrangement of the institutions through which the individuals can merge their egoism in the social system by finding their proper place in that? For this purpose, Gita has suggested the four-fold stratification of society. So says Gita, "The order of the four-fold varṇas was created by Me according to the different guṇas and karma of each."[66] This is the democratic principle of free choice which allows every individual to contribute his mite 'according to his congenital abilities' (*svabhāvajena*). Radhakrishnan has very correctly pointed out that "democracy is not the standardization of every one so as to obliterate all peculiarity. This would be dictatorship."[67] Democracy, on the other hand, requires the equal right of all to the development of their respective innate capacity and the talent with which nature has endowed them. Thus, the four-fold scheme of Gita affords the opportunity to every individual to manifest whatever is unique in him, and thereby recognises his dignity as a 'social being'. Recognition of man's dignity, that is, the recognition of the fact that every individual is equally capable of making contribution to society in his own way is one of the essential conditions of democracy. Democracy is not merely a form of government but it is a way of life that rests essentially on moral foundations which require us, in the words of Titus, "to respect and develop the free spirit of man, which is responsible for all progress in human history."[68] The organic theory serves both the purposes in Gita ; it provides a source of moral obligation by providing a social context in the form of the organic system and it also keeps the conduct of the individual duly regulated in so far as he finds himself as an interdependent part of society. This is a positive check on licentiousness. Hindu ethics, in general, recognises that the individual has the power to act on his own account as well as to control within limits, his own future, so as to aid others also in expressing their own power. Titus substantiates this view and says : "The Hindu philosophers seem to agree that overcoming selfishness is necessary in order to realize one's true self."[69] This assessment is true in case of the organic conception of Gita, because it is through the organimistic conception that the idea of interdependence and social interaction of the individual entities can be more approximately conveyed.

Moral Basis of Democracy :

For the successful functioning of democracy, it is essential that the demos should be morally strong and intellectually enlightened. People should realize their social responsibilities. Any weakness of democracy is an expression of the imperfection of human nature. An ideal form of democracy can be achieved if the people are freed from their frailties, the temptations of money and power. If the demos and their representatives forget the principles of participation in social life, they will take recourse to propaganda that replaces principles. In propaganda, without principles, there is nothing but mere mud-slinging. Men of integrity then withdraw from this mud-slinging game and eventually social life itself. Democracy then degenerates into the 'rule of the ignobles'.

To safeguard against this petrification, the *Gita* presents the concept of those ideal persons, who are free from the baneful influence of the temptations. Gita verily calls them '*Sthitaprajña*', '*Yogī*' and '*guṇātīta*'. An enlightened person, according to Gita, is that who has controlled his inclinations,[70] a yogī has been described as that who has freed himself from the possessions and tendency to possess[71] (*nirāśīraparigrahaḥ*), and a 'guṇātīta' is a man who, the embodied one, transcends the three bonds of materiality, which are born of his contact with the body, viz., his sensualities.[72] A deeper understanding of all these traits, prescribed by Gita, leads us to believe that these are the prerequisite characteristics of an 'enlightened demos' and the people should be imbibed with them if the democratic institutions are to function successfully and on some sound principles. The principle of conduct for them is to discharge their duties with a sense of non-attachment.

Summarizing these characteristics, as laid down by Gita, we may say that a morally trained person will be a man of secure understanding (*sthitaprajña*), ready to perform his duties with honesty and integrity (*yogī*), and will transcend all the materialistic temptations (*guṇātīta*), which instigate him to adopt corruptive means of living. He will be an *anāsakta.* Gita suggests that such persons, liberated from the narrow sensualities and instinctualities, will put away all the cravings that arise in their mind (*prajahāti yadā kāmānsarvānpārtha manogatān*) (II. 55). Although these persons will give up the tendency of exploiting people and thereby making money under the garb of social service, yet they will not withdraw from the world. Gita asserts this and tells, "the disciplined soul will move among sense objects (*viṣayānindriyaiścaran*) with the senses weaned from likes and dislikes (*rāgadveṣaviyuktaiḥ*) (II. 64)." It means that all sorts of temptations will be offered to them in the form of money and power but the people in their democratic functioning and in the discharge of their duties should not be allowed to become the victim of these petty ambitions of life. Similarly, when a man is contributing his share to the society, he should care more for principles than for the personalities, personal prejudices and preferences. Laying down the postulates of democracy, Gita further tells us that "the enlightened may not confuse the mind of the unenlightened, who are attached to action" (*na buddhi bhedaṁ janayedajñānaṁ karma saṅginām*) (III. 26).

According to Gita, the fight in democracy should be for principles only and the masses should not be confused by falsified propaganda or by mere vote-catching slogans. Those who confuse the uneducated masses by false propaganda are not only the enemies of democracy but of society as well. The trained intelligentsia and enlightened statesmen should not withdraw into indolence or inaction, but they should be the active guides and thereby the conscientious participants in the social life. As a moral agent, these statesmen will act in a very responsible manner, because their conduct and their examples are to be followed by the progeny. Gita says : "whatever the best man does, is also done by other man ; what example he sets, the world follows."[73] This is a very high maxim of democratic society. If the people's representatives, the legislators, the statesmen and the social educators are corrupt, the whole generation will become corrupt. Their precepts will have no effect on the new generation, but on the contrary the younger generation will resort to all sorts of corruption and quote these aldermen of society as their example.

If democracy is not to collapse under the burden of its own weaknesses, those at the helm should be men of exemplary character in their social affairs. Gita does not free even men of knowledge from the social obligations.[74] Many a failure of the democracy can be traced to the fact that intellectuals withdraw into ivory towers and the intellectual and spiritual darkness then befalls the society. It is, therefore, incumbent on men of knowledge not to withdraw but to guide effectively when the politicians go astray and the masses are being misguided. Freed from this narrow egoism, such enlightened persons and statesmen will act for the welfare of the society. Gita ordains : "Just as, with attachment, the unenlightened perform all actions, O Bhārata, even so, but unattached should the enlightened act with a desire for the welfare of humanity."[75] Such instances and descriptions can be multiplied where Gita expresses its faith in man and his fallibility, the two foundations on which a sound democracy can be based. To train such persons in democratic traditions, all the social institutions will work in an ideal society. Anāsakti Yoga of Gita advocates *democracy of the enlightened demos* as an ideal social order.

Nature of State Authority :

As we have already seen in the beginning, political problems did never bother the author of Gita. The presupposition seems to be that if the people are morally strong and well trained in democratic traditions, the state machinery cannot go wrong. Similarly, Gita presupposes that for a man who is law unto himself, neither any extraneous law is needed, nor he has any fear of the state coercion. This seems to be the consideration on account of which Gita left the political problem untouched.

Alexander Pope has also expressed the idea in another way. He says : "For forms of Government, let fools contest ; whatever is administered best is best." The morally enlightened people will themselves manage the organisational structure of their socio-political institutions. However, we find a reference in the *Mahābhārata* of which the *Gita* forms part, that "there was once a time when there was no state nor a sovereign."[76] The state was created when anarchy prevailed and is in fact a negative institution, which came into existence, because there was evil. It will continue so long as there is evil.

What was the regulative force when the state was not there? That force can still serve as regulative of human conduct if state withers away. We are told in *Mahābhārata* that it was dharma that protected the life of people in the absence of the state power (rājya).[77] In this way, *Mahābhārata* advocates the supremacy of socio-ethical laws over the political institutions. Gita, like other Indian scriptures, also recognises the superiority of dharma, which is more effective to protect the civil society and create law-abidingness even when the political authority is not functioning. The emphasis is on safeguarding the social fabric.

No one will doubt that obedience to some law is necessary condition of corporate and civilised life for the promotion of the common social interest. For the morally depraved, it will be legal law, the police force, whereas for the moral man, it will be ethical conviction. Thus, the existence of state will be a requirement for those, who are socio-paths and delinquents. However, the strong social forces can challenge the state power when it goes corrupt. This is the morale behind the fall of Duryodhana. The author of Gita has projected Duryodhana as corrupt and greedy (*lobhopahatacetasaḥ*) (II. 38), and a tyrant (*ātatāyinaḥ*) (II. 36). His fall is indicative of a moral dynamics that a "social force in the forms of some Avatātra[78] awakens and destroys the corrupt and tyrant state machinery, specially when it starts pursuing the ends which are against common good and when it fails to maintain a system of rights which are necessary for the free development of the individual. There is also an implicit assumption in *Gita* that the corrupt authority may be replaced by the alternative authority supported by dharma. Thus speaking, the state machinery can be regulated by rigid moral regulations and the social forces. The derelictions can be effectively cured by public censure. Morris Ginsberg comes closer to this position when he says that "a sound theory of justice will involve a definition of the limit within which the State power may be rightly exercised."[79] Accordingly, if the society is to be based on justice, then the state should derive its power from the people acting through law, and law itself should be subject to limitations. This is possible in a democratic set-up only where the well-trained people can exercise check on the tyranny of state authority and put limitations on it. Marx also visualised that when state is replaced by communes, the people will be able to exercise their power more effectively through universal franchise. Discussing the dimensions of real democracy, Marx himself writes : "Universal suffrage gives all the members of civil society a political existence and, therefore, *ipso facto* eliminates the 'political' as a separate category."[80] In the light of the above, the concept of the peoples' force as a regulative force is far superior to the idea of 'withering away of state'. In this way, Gita does not side with those who say that sun should banish from the sky because it sometimes becomes covered in clouds. If state machinery is being abused, the morally strong people should choose another government to regulate the affairs and thereby exercise their effective control over the executive power.

Private Property :

Freedom cannot exist in the societies where a few persons appropriate all the social product. Thus, in order to give equal share in national wealth and with a view to see that every one may be able to satisfy his primary economic needs, it is essential to watch that the economic resources and the means of production should not be owned privately. Marx denounced the political economy, because it incorporates the private property into the very essence of man.[81] The author of Gita condemns not only the '*corpus*' of possession but the '*animus possidendi*' also. In the opening verse of Gita, the use of the word 'māmakāḥ' has been made by Kauravas, who have been symbolised in Gita as the forces of greed (*lobhopahatacetasaḥ*). This shows that the very sense of 'mineness' is the source of evil. It is evident from the expostulatory attitude of Gita that the very idea of personal ownership is distasteful and derogatory to the author of Gita. The enlightened persons of Gita and the morally disciplined persons will never desire to bring the economic goods under their personal ownership. Radhakrishnan more specifically suggests that such persons "covet nothing and are jealous of none".[82] Comparing the demonic and the divine persons, Gita also upholds that those who have the pride of personal wealth (*dhanamānamadānvitaḥ*), are demonical persons, whereas the freedom from covetness (*alolupatvam*) is the sign of divine character.[83] All these show that Gita detests the concept of private ownership and the sense of possession. The things should be enjoyed and utilised with this sense that an individual is not their owner. The communist solution of abolition of private property may finish the '*corpus possessions*' only but Gita wants to finish the *animus domini*, the very intention to hold as owner. For this purpose, Gita has put forth the idea of 'aparigraha' or putting away every possession.[84] There are certain specific references in other scriptures which reflect over the problem of the private ownership of property. So far as the private property is concerned, the Hindu view is given in Bhāgavata wherein it has been said that we have a legitimate right only on so much as would satisfy our existential needs. If any one desires more, he is a thief deserving punishment (*yāvad mṛyeta jaṭharaṁ tāvat svattavaṁ hi dehinām adhikaṁ yo'bhimanyeta sa steno daṇḍam arhate*).[85] Thus, no one has a right over the surplus, but one's right is limited to only as much as his social requirements are. This is a human quality that he can adjust his requirements and desires to the social context. Marx also advocates the similar view and says that "our desires and pleasures spring from society : we measure them, therefore, by society and not by the objects which serve for their satisfaction."[86] In view of this, to enjoy wealth at the expense of society is considered by Gita a social crime. Therefore, Gita says : "A man who appropriates from society without contributing his share to social good and takes from society disproportionately, is a thief."[87] On the basis of such pronouncements, Gandhiji has traced his socialism in Indian traditions. He writes : "Socialism was not born with the discovery of the misuse of the capital by capitalist. As I have contended socialism, even communism is explicit in the first verse of Īśopaniṣad[88] (*īśāvāsyamidaṁ sarvam yatkiñca jagatyāṁ jagat ; tenatyaktena bhuñjīthaḥ mā gṛdhaḥ kasyasviddhanam*). According to Gandhi's interpretation, this verse means that we see this great universe as pervaded by God. Renounce it and enjoy it. Do not covett anybody's wealth or possession.[89] These verses indicate that misappropriation of wealth is highly disparaging according to Indian thinkers, and, therefore, it must be finished.

In a highly denunciatory tone, Gita devotes as many as eleven verses to express its indignation against those who make indulgence or lust as their sole goal (*Kāmopabhogaparamā*), who seek unlawfully to amass wealth (*anyāyenarthasañcayān*), who have unsatisfiable acquisitive mania (*duṣpūram kāmam*), and who are full of intoxication of their personal wealth (*dhanamānamadānvitāḥ*).[90] These are more or less the same characteristic which Marx attributed to the 'capitalist'.

Kṛṣṇa's call to the effect that these depraved souls (*naṣṭātmanāḥ*), and lowest of mankind (*narādhamāḥa*) are to be eliminated from the society (*vināsāye ca duṣkrtām*), is an assertion of the fact that social forces must manifest themselves in every age for the purpose of condemning the desire for private ownership and the creed of money worship. Numerous verses of Gita suggest that nobody should be allowed to monopolise the economic resources for personal and private use. All should equally utilise them for the public good (*lokasaṁgraha*). The Gita's concept of non-attachment is a guarantee that man will not fall victim to the acquisitive mania and will not appropriate the property. The idea of finishing the '*corpus*' private ownership still leaves a great lacuna that the '*animus*', the intention to possess and desire to misappropriate still remains. If the tendency of lust and greed is still there, and if man has not learnt to control his sensuous desires, then the abolishing of private property will not be sufficient, because he will commit sin against the public property and will misuse or misappropriate it for his own personal benefit at the cost of society. Gita, therefore, rightly suggests that the very desire to possess should be finished.

The significance of the concept can be grasped in the light of Salmond's theory of Legal Sanctions. In the Jurisprudence, 'Sanction' operates upon desire.[91] If 'A' is about to break a rule of imperative law, 'A' shall have the choice between two pains—either 'A' should keep within the law and thus suffer the pain of not getting the illegal advantage or 'A' should break the law and suffer the pain of punishment. Thus desire itself can be a source of pain. Accordingly, it is not only the '*Actus Reus*', the actual act of expropriation, but the '*mens rea*' the guilty mindedness and the desire to misappropriate the surplus value is to be negated if the crimes against society are to be checked. This is the standpoint of Gita's Anāsakti doctrine. "Rid of desires and possession", suggests Gita, "a man can discharge his duties sincerely".[92] Such freedom from longing for possession is an ethical state and not a material condition. However, the idea behind all this is that a man must control the appetite for possession and free himself from the tyranny of belongings. In that case, the very desire to have private property and the motive of private ownership of means of production will end. Thus speaking, the ideal of the 'anāsakti' and the ideal of 'aparigraha' is not restricted upto the mere abolition of the *corpus* of private property but to the cessation and eradication of the very '*animus*' thereof, which compels one to exploit. This will be wrong to assume that the tendencies cannot be cured. Since the tendencies are not uncaused, these can be finished *in toto*, because anything which has a cause, can be destroyed, As a matter of fact, they all arise due to a kind of āsakti, i.e., attachment arising out of the false knowledge of the self, its relation with other man and with objects. If the degenerative and dehumanizing consequences (*viṣayadoṣadarśana*) of the private ownership of wealth are exposed, it will lead to anāsakti.

From all this discussion, a conclusion may be rightly drawn that Gita suggests a type of social order in which the economic goods will be used for common good ; everything will be so used by the agents as it is not their private property but it has social ownership, and each individual will discharge his social task (*svadharma*) freely according to his talents and functional capacity. By whatever 'ism' it may be called.

References

1. Hegel, G.W.F., *Logic of Hegel*, p. 49.
2. Meyer, Alfred G., *Marxism, The Unity of Theory and Practice*, p. 57.
3. Hegel, G.W.F., *Philosophy of History*, p. 104.
4. Giddens, Anthony, *Capitalism and Modern Social Theory*, p. 5.
5. Marx and Engels, *Selected Works*, Vol. I, pp. 483-484.
6. Marx, K., *The Poverty of Philosophy*, p. 190.
7. Marx, K., *German Ideology*, p. 78.

8. Mises, Ludwig von, *Socialism*, p. 32.
9. Marx, K., *Critique of Political Economy* (New York International Library, 1904), p. 11.
10. Marx, K., *MEGA*, pp. 120-121.
11. Marx, K., *Early Writings*, pp. 58-59.
12. Marx, K., and Engels, F., *German Ideology*, p. 199.
13. Marx, K. and Engels, F., *Selected Correspondence* (Letter to C. Schmidt of October 27, 1890), p. 480.
14. Marx, Engels, Lenin, *On Historical Materialism*, p. 128.
15. Marx, K., *Early Writings*, p. 13 (Trans. Bottomore).
16. Marx, K., *MEGA*, p. 155.
17. Ibid., p. 599.
18. Marx, K., and Engels, F., *Manifesto of the Communist Party* (Soviet Ed.), p. 76.
19. Marx, K. and Engels, F., *Selected Works*, Vol. III, p. 26.
20. Lenin, V.I., *Collected Works*, Vol. 24, pp. 84-85.
21. Marx, Engels, Lenin, *On Historical Materialism*, p. 111.
22. Marx, K. and Engels, F., *Selected Correspondence*, p. 57.
23. Marx and Engels, *Selected Works*, Vol. II, p. 30.
24. Marx and Engels, *Selected Correspondence*, p. 337.
25. Marx and Engels, *Selected Works*, Vol. I, p. 54.
26. Marx, K. and Engels, F., *Selected Works*, Vol. II, p. 31.
27. Marx, K., *Writings of the Young Marx on Philosophy and Society*, pp. 173-174.
28. Engels, F., The Origin of Family, Private Property and the State in Marx and Engels, *Selected Works*, Vol. II, p. 291.
29. Marx, K. and Engels, F., *Selected Correspondence*, p. 337.
30. Marx, K. and Engels, F., *Selected Works*, Vol. I, pp. 520-521.
31. Marx, K., Civil War in France, in Marx and Engels, *Selected Works*, Vol. I, p. 484.
32. Marx, K., *MEGA*, p. 119.
33. Marx, K., and Engels, F., *Selected Works*, Vol. II, pp. 144-145.
34. Marx, Engels and Lenin, *On Historical Materialism*, p. 13.
35. Marx, K., *Selected Works*, Vol. I, p. 54.
36. Marx, K. and Engels, F., *Selected Works*, Vol. II, p. 144.
37. Marx, Engels, Lenin, *On Historical Materialism*, p. 150.
38. Afanasyev, S., *Socialism and Communism*, p. 126.
39. Marx, K., *MEGA*, p. 88.
40. Afanasyev, S., *Socialism and Communism*, p. 127.
41. Ibid., p. 133.
42. Popper, K.R., op. cit., pp. 333-334.
43. Marx, K., *Poverty of Philosophy*, p. 136.
44. Marx, K., *Selected Works*, Vol. I, p. 523.
45. Marx, K., *MEGA*, p. 126.
46. Feuerbach, Ludwig, *The Essence of Christianity*, p. 230.
47. Damodaran, K., *Indian Thought : A Critical Survey*, p. 53.
48. *Gita*, XI. 13 (Anāsakti Yoga bhāṣya).

49. Radhakrishnan, S., *Bhagavadgītā*, p. 161.
50. *Mahābhārata*, XII. 298. 17 (Hindi version).
51. Radhakrishnan, S., *Eastern Religion and Western Thought*, p. 124 ff.
52. Sorokin, P.A., op. cit., p. 202.
53. *Gita*, XI. 8.
54. Hartshorn, *Reality as a Social Process*, p. 34.
55. Whitehead, A.N., *Science and the Modern World*, p. 81.
56. Mackenzie, J.S., *A Manual of Ethics*, p. 279.
57. Milne, A.J.M., *A Social Philosophy of English Idealism*, p. 63.
58. Tucker, Robert C., *Philosophy and Myth of Karl Marx*, p. 175.
59. McIver & Page, *Society*, p. 43.
60. Ibid., p. 44.
61. Milne, A.J.M., op. cit., p. 63.
62. Durkheim, Emile, *The Elementary Forms of Religious Life* (1915), p. 207.
63. Ibid., p. 208.
64. *Gita*, XVIII. 65 (*Anāsakti Yoga* bhāṣya).
65. Muirhead, J.H., *Elements of Ethics*, p. 178.
66. *Gita*, IV. 13 (Cāturvarṇyaṁ mayā Sṛṣṭaṁ guṇa karmavibhāgaśaḥ).
67. Radhakrishnan, S., *The Hindu View of Life*, p. 83.
68. Titus, H.H., op. cit., p. 418.
69. Titus, H.H., op. cit., p. 511 ff.
70. *Gita*, II. 58 (*Anāsakti Yoga*) (indriyāṇi indriyārthebhyaḥ saṁharate).
71. *Gita*, VI. 10 (*Anāsakti Yoga*).
72. *Srimadbhagavadgita* (Hindi), XIV. 19-20.
73. *Gita*, III. 21 : (yadyadācarati śreṣṭhastattaddeve'taro janaḥ sa yatpramāṇaṁ kurute lokastadanuvartate).
74. *The Gita According to Gandhi*, p. 187.
75. *Gita*, III. 25 (*Anāsakti Yoga* bhāṣya).
76. *Mahābhārata* (śānti parva), 58. 14 (na vai rājyaṁ na rājāsīnna ca daṇdo na daṇdikaḥ).
77. Ibid., 58. 14 (dharmeṇaiva prajāḥ sarvarakṣantesma parasparam).
78. Avatāraś, for Gandhi, are the embodiment of some extraordinary service to mankind—Gandhi, M.K., *Young India*, 6-8-1931.
79. Morris. Ginsberg, *Justice in Society*, p. 70.
80. Marx, K., *Writings of Young Marx on Philosophy and Society*, p. 202.
81. Marx, K., *Early Writings*, pp. 137 ff. (Trans. Bottomore).
82. Radhakrishnan, S., *Bhagavadgita*, p. 126.
83. *Srimadbhagavadgita* (Hindi), XVI. 17 ; 2.
84. *Gita*, IV. 21 and VI. 10.
85. *Bhāgavata*, VII. 14.8.
86. Marx, K. and Engels, F., *Selected Works*, Vol. I, p. 94.
87. *Gita*, III. 12 (*Anāsakti Yoga* bhāṣya).
88. Gandhi, M.K., *Harijan*, 20-2-1937.
89. Gandhi, M.K., *In Search of the Supreme*, Vol. III, pp. 105-106.
90. *Gita*, XVI. 9-19. (*Anāsakti Yoga*).
91. Salmond, *Jurisprudence*, 9th Ed., pp. 26-27.
92. *The Gita According to Gandhi*, VI, 10.

5

Concept of Social Justice

Social justice is one of the most crucial concerns of our times. The gross inequalities are being vehemently condemned everywhere. Russell is representative of these voices when, he says : "An uneven distribution causes envy and hatred in the less fortunate and fear and hatred in the more fortunate."[1] The fear in the more fortunates, who are also called the class of 'haves', might have been generated by their own unconscious, the repository of their sins against humanity. The masses, however, are groaning under drudgery and baneful living conditions. The wealthy are also suffering from mental torture, always aware of the impending danger of being deprived of their possessions. The rise of giant multi-nation aggregates, equipped with tremendous resources, has disturbed the global equilibrium. The growth of a peculiar nexus of rights and duties, which is the outcome of the complex forms of corporative state, and private property as well as hitherto unknown types of labour, have projected new versions of inequalities. We are living in a world where few men receive their just desserts, mighty nations wage unjust wars against their smaller neighbours and the bounty of nature is unfairly distributed among the people of the earth. The social problems in our midst today, result in and are in large part the result of injustice, unfairness and inequality.

Part of the difficulty in ameliorating these conditions lies in our inability or unwillingness to obtain accurate factual description and causal explanation of men's conduct and partly in our lack of reflections as to how our institutions really work. But an equally perplexing part of the difficulty in overcoming injustice is the seeming abstractness, instability and variegated description of the ideals of justice. Nevertheless, the social thinkers are bringing to light enormous instances of individual and institutional injustice. In doing so, they assume certain social ideals, which help them in making their evaluations. It, therefore, brings before us the problem 'what facts about men and society must a theory of justice and equality take into account ?'

Communism and Gita both have given their own social ideals, and on the basis of that, we are now in a position to consider what do these ideals say about the problem of social justice ? How far the juridical system under the ideal social order suggested by communism and also by the Anāsakti Yoga of Gita will approximate to justice and how the legal institutions will implement the jural laws, is a question for comparative jurisprudence to decide. Hence, it is not relevant to the discussion of social justice from sociological and ethical point of view ; justice cannot be equated with legal and juristic laws. Because, sometimes the law itself may be unjust or unjustly administered. What are then the dimensions of social justice ?

Justice and Dharma :

After discussing in detail various problems, which can fall under the scope of justice, a great jurisprudent, Ginsberg puts all these into three forms. Briefly stated, these are (i) control of power or rather arbitrary exercise of it ; (ii) distribution of the means of well-being ; and (iii) provision for the compensation of injuries.[2] Taken all these three forms together, justice will approximate to the concept of Dharma in Indian thought. Dharma, in the sense of moral justice, stresses on the worth of human personality and on the right of man to the conditions, necessary for his personal fulfilment. The first form of justice is concerned with the political order. In the preceding chapter, it has been discussed that under communism, there will be no state, but during the transition period, humanity will have to pass through the ordeal of 'dictatorship of the proletariat'. Gita also conceives of the society where the democracy of the enlightened people prevails. What type of the constitutional set up—the executive, the judiciary, the legislative—will meet the requirements of justice in the two alternative ideal social orders, has neither been worked out by Marx nor by the author of Gita. It appears that their sole concern was to stress on the 'freedom of man' as a producer of goods. Accordingly, any political system, which hampers the productive freedom of man, will be considered undesirable and unjust. How the control is to be exercised on the arbitrary use of power ? Whether it should be done by decentralization of power or by replacing the state authority by social units, i.e. communes etc.? These are the questions, which have been left solely for the posterity to decide.

The first form of justice, viz., the just exercise of the political power and keeping the state within its legitimate jurisdiction, has been left indeterminate after laying down the broader guidelines and moral considerations. The third form of justice is concerned with the remedies, which a society will provide to an individual when his civil rights have been eroded. This is a question for the Law of Torts to discuss and decide. It is the second one, which is concerned with the problem of assuring an equitable distribution of the conditions without which none of the major ideals can be attained. Ginsberg has, therefore, rightly pointed out about the problem of social justice that "it is the problem of assuring an equitable distribution of means."[3] Accordingly, social justice seeks to distribute the products of society so that all men may have an opportunity for self-development. Using Aristotelian terminology, we can say that social justice approximates 'distributive justice'. In the light of these observations, it will be relevant to evaluate the communism and the Anāsakti Yoga of Gita as to how they deal with the problem of social justice, i.e., the problem of the distribution of goods.

Distributive Justice and Communism :

Many have assumed that the distributive justice is the chief value underlying the value judgement, pronounced by Marx against the existing society. His indictment of capitalism and call for its replacement with communism is generally attributed to his concern for justice in the sense of a fair distribution of material goods. It is natural that when such questions are asked as to why there ought to be a world revolution ? and on what standard it is pronounced that the present social system is evil ?, one is led to believe the 'distributive justice' to be the theme of communist theory. Laski, for example, writes that "the main passion by which he (Marx) was moved was the passion for justice."[4] Some other eminent thinkers like E.H. Carr, Lindsay and Sidney Hook also bring forth the passion for justice in the pronouncements of Marx.[5] According to these writers, the ethics of Marx did not merely express a demand for social justice but a specific *kind* of justice dependent upon the objective possibilities created by capitalism. The central theme of communism to many a great minds then is the fight for social justice and for the equal distribution of goods.

However, a close examination of the doctrine of communism would reveal that 'distributive justice' never occupied such an important place in this theory. The misconception that Marx was a fighter for justice arises from his use of the word 'exploitation' conventionally associated with injustice. He defines capitalism as a way of production founded on the 'exploitation' of wage-labour for the accumulation of capital. His theory of exploitation is more concretely a theory of 'surplus value'. If the principle of 'surplus value' under capitalist economy is proved untenable, his whole theory of exploitation will also fall as under. Engels clearly states their key problem is that of 'surplus value'. He writes :"The exploitative relation of capital and labour is expressed in surplus value."[6] This exploitation is considered by them as the basic evil, which the social revolution will end by abolishing the capitalistic modes of production. It is evident that in this pronouncement the emphasis is not on the fair or unfair, equal or unequal distribution of goods, but on the elimination of a mode of production in which profit is the sole motive. For Marx, as we have already seen, capitalism is a system of the 'accumulation of capital and dehumanisation of man', and in asking for the elimination of capitalism, he is actually emphasizing the need of a system, which will remove profit motive and acquisitiveness, as the motivating factors in production. After a thorough study of *Das Capital,* it becomes all the more evident that Marx dismissed the slogan of 'fair distribution' as 'obsolete verbal rubbish'. He violently rejected all the suggestions that the struggle being raged by the working class has to do with distributive justice. The only possible solution of such a conflict was the ending of it by abolition of the force that made the two hostile entities out of one, i.e., labour and capital out of mankind. Prof. Tucker seems to be right in his assessment that "the issue for Marx was not justice but man's loss of himself under enslavement and dehumanizing force and his recovery of himself by the total vanquishment of this force."[7] It is obvious from his description of communism that Marx wanted man to transcend his limitations, without which the exploitation cannot end.

Further it also can be seen that Marx was averse to the idea of distributive justice. If we emphasize the 'just distribution', 'fair distribution', i.e., the 'distributive justice', then the very c ncept of justice implies mutual adjustment of claims between contending individuals and groups within the existing system and, therefore, this adjustment will mean a compromise with the forces of evil. That was the reason on account of which Marx ridiculed the idea of justice as 'utopian'. He writes : "It was in general a mistake (of vulgar socialism) to make a fuss about so-called distribution and put the principal stress on it."[8] Engels also made a denunciatory note against those, who believed that "the capitalist's mode of production is quite good and can remain in existence, but the capitalist's mode of distribution is evil."[9] In their indictment against the seekers of 'distributive justice', the founders of communism were obviously referring to the socialism of Saint-Simon and Fourier in France and Robert Owen in England, which was 'distribution oriented' and was concerned with the problem of 'uneven distribution in society'. Marx was very much convinced that under the sway of greed, profit motive and acquisitiveness the possessing class can go to any extreme in doing the things that satisfy its megalomania. *Das Capital* paints the disparaging picture as to what extent a man can become inhuman, when the sole motive of his activity becomes the acquisition of private capital. That is why Marx was allergic to the very talk of 'justice' under such system of production. He also denounced all his contemporary socialists for using the pseudo-concepts. He ridiculed the slogans of 'fair distribution', 'equal right', and 'undiminished proceeds of labour', as meaningless phraseology. Rejecting all these slogans as 'obsolete verbal rubbish', Marx said, "the German party's hard won realistic outlook should not be perverted by ideological non-sense about 'right' and other trash so common among the democrats and French socialists."[10] Such denunciatory attacks were made by Marx on Proudhanism also, which upheld the position that wage workers were being robbed under capitalism, of something that 'rightfully' belonged to them. Engels came forward to corroborate the stand of his partner in exposing the futility of the idea of justice. He says : "To go on talking about the idea of justice in relation to economic matters (as Proudhan does) is to create the same hopeless confusion, as would be created, for instance, in modern Chemistry, if the terminology of the phlogiston theory were to be retained."[11] It would be tantamount to saying that the distribution oriented socialism was an unscientific approach according to him. The ridiculing attitude towards the 'application of ideal of justice to economic relations' has been verily expressed by Marx in his various other writings,[12] which shows that he was not in favour of making this distributive justice as the *raison d'etre* of communism.

Moral Positivism :

From what has been stated above, it also becomes clear why Marx did not like the idea of justice to be discussed. He believed that in every age the standards of morality and justice have their connotation according to the relations of production of that age. This may be called 'moral positivism', according to which the moral institutions of an age are nothing but the reflection of the economic forces around them. The standards of 'ought' are nothing more than the ideological rationalization of 'isness'. Marx affirms this positivism in saying that "Law, morality, religion are so many bourgeois prejudices behind which lurk in ambush just as many bourgeois interests."[13] In Marxian vocabulary, these terms are considered ideological, which means that they are part of the conceptual system through which a particular social and economic order expresses itself in man's consciousness. In the light of this type of economic determinism, each mode of produc tion will have its own mode of distribution and as a consequence of that, its own form and criterion of equality. The evidences of this type of moral positivism are found at various places in Marx's own writings. He says that "right can never be higher than the economic structure of society and its cultural development thereby determined."[14]

Accordingly, it would be meaningless to pass any true judgement of right or wrong, just or unjust on it from some other point of view. According to the definition of capitalism given by Marx, the capitalist modes of production are such that under them, man is moved solely by his acquisitive desire. Consequently, the capitalist, under the force of this acquisitive mania, is bound to exploit. Labour also becomes compelled to sell its humanity under the force of money. This state of affairs will continue and must continue till capitalist system and its main ingredients, the very forces of lust and greed are negated. It means that there is no injustice if the capitalist misappropriates the surplus value, because his mode of production is such as he cannot help it. Marx accepts this position. His surplus value theory says that "the value, which its use creates during a working day is twice the value of a day's labour power." Marx upholds that there is nothing unjust in it. He says : "So much the better for the purchaser but it is nowise an injustice to seller."[15] The same thing is confirmed by Engels in his *Anti-Duhring*.[16] Marx did not approve of the approach of the other schools of socialism nor of the reformists, who vainly thought that distributive reforms can be introduced in the existing system by making the distribution of goods more equitable. The capitalist mode of distribution is inhuman and evil and on this moral consideration, Marx and Engels advocated the complete abolition of bourgeois property and capitalist system. Hence Marx denounced other socialist thinkers as 'utopians'. It was a wild-goose chase to think that without changing the capitalist system of production, the exploitation will come to an end.

Justice under Communism :

On this basis, it may be said that talking of 'distributive justice' in an economic system, where *per se*, it was impossible to be found, is a useless effort. But a relevant question may be raised here. Will not the higher phase of communist society be a realm of distributive justice ? And Marx tells us to our great dismay that 'it will not'. In describing communist ideal, Marx has not raised the problem of the distribution of goods. At one place, in his *Critique of Gotha Programme*, Marx conceives of a new social order, the higher phase of communist society, which shall dawn after the enslaving subordination of the individual to the division of labour has vanished and antithesis between mental and physical labour has ended. Under the communist society, the productive forces will also be increased due to the all round development of the individual and all the springs of co-operative wealth will flow more abundantly. In a very romantic tone, Marx writes : "Only then the narrow horizons of bourgeois right be crossed in its entirety and society inscribes on its banners *from each according to his ability to each according to his needs*."[17] The last portion of this aphorism was the slogan of French Socialism also. Since the French Socialism was 'distribution-oriented', and this maxim has been adopted in its original form, some thinkers, on this basis, have been led to believe that it is a princip'e of 'distributive justice'. They forget that such distribution-oriented interpretation of this maxim raises many problems. For example, one may ask, are all the needs of a man limited to his biological satisfaction ? But the communist thinkers do not restrict them to these narrow horizons.

Man, according to them, will need many things to "widen, to enrich and to promote his individual existence."[18] Then what types of the needs man will be able to satisfy in order to promote his existence ? Some of his baneful needs may be injurious to the welfare of others. Will it be decided in economic terms ? The reoly is again in negative. A Soviet scholar tells us that "the formation of healthy and reasonable needs presupposes a struggle against pernicious needs whose satisfaction frequently leads to misdemeanours that clash with the standards of communist morality."[19] Thus, the distribution of economic goods will not be the criteria of the satisfaction of need and the question of economic justice will not arise. Moreover, when the communist society will be a realm of 'abundance', the distribution will not be made according to the laws of economics, viz., the law of substitution and laws of equimarginal utility, which operate in the society where the problem of distribution may really puzzle. The criterion of "each according to his need", therefore, cannot be understood as a criterion of 'distributive justice'.

The communist society with its super-abundance will provide generously not only for all the needs of the citizen in the matter of food, shelter, clothing, but will, as we are told, also "provide him no less generously with everything needed for his cultural advancement, and for his leading a rich and satisfying life."[20] It is natural that in a society where there is super-abundance of goods and where man adjusts his needs according to communist morality, there will not be needed any principle of distribution. What this society will need? It will require proper training to man to adjust his needs in consonance with social good, and harmonize them with the communist social order.

Fundamental passion of the founders of communism then was not a passion for 'economic or distributive justice'. Distributive justice occupies a secondary place in communism. Prof. Tucker rightly tells us that "the ending of worker's material imprisonment was incidental to the real goal, the ending of his dehumanization."[21]

Myth of Economic Equality :

Communism has often been misinterpreted as an attempt towards the creation of equalities. So far as the question of formal equality is concerned, nobody has ever disputed, on ethical grounds, the right of every one to be equal. Similarly, nobody will question the equal right of every man to the minimum conditions of life. But when the question of 'substantive' or the 'proportionate' equality, i.e., the question of equal distribution of goods arises, then the problem comes what is the measuring rod to this. Thus the question of distributive justice overlaps into the realm of the question of the equality of man. Some communist thinkers try to search for an emphasis on economic equality in Marxism in the extensive treatment of the law of increasing misery given by Marx in *Das Capital*. Therein Marx stated : "Absolute general law of capitalist accumulation is the accumulation of wealth at one pole of society and a simultaneous accumulation of poverty, labour, torment, slavery, ignorance, brutalisation and moral degradation at the opposite pole."[22]

Inequalities no doubt are clearly visible in the economic sphere specially in the sphere of 'private possession'. But will equality come by the mere abolition of property ? To be more realistic, "on practical considerations, the inequality will have to be tolerated as a necessary evil."[23] Rigid equalization may discourage creative endeavour, and initiative and decrease efficiency. If absolute equality of per capita distribution is introduced, then those who contribute less, because they are weak, infirm etc., will get more in reward because of their more needs, viz., the need for medicines etc. and thus will draw additional benefit without corresponding additional work. This will cause inequality in distribution, and inequality in treatment.

Distribution of Happiness :

To resolve the problem of the 'economic equality', two alternatives may be possible : (i) that goods are distributed by counting the heads, or (ii) the economic goods are nationalised and every individual is given equal opportunity to utilise them for his development. The first alternative was suggested by Bentham also in the form of his calculus which crudely asserted the principle of 'every one of count for one and nobody for more than one'. But soon it was realised by his successor Mill that the pl.asure of Socrates cannot be equated with the pleasure of a pig. Realizing the difficulty of crude utilitarianism, Rashdall had to modify the principle of utilitarianism to read as "every body's good to be treated as of equal value with the like good of every one else."[24] But this reformulated principle of Rashdall does not lead to 'economic equality' because the good of a man cannot be measured in economic terms. If physico-biological capacities differ and economic equality is enforced on them, they may become equally unhappy. Similarly, a man, who is working in a research laboratory may need more economic goods to conduct his higher research, than a man tilling a farm, or a man who is imbecile. The society will doubly suffer by treating them economically equal.

But when we come to the second principle, the principle of giving equal opportunity, the same difficulty is faced. Given equal opportunity to utilise the public good, some people may consume and appropriate more so as to create dearth for others. If 'equal opportunity' is made the criterion of equality, then the question will again be raised, how can we change the conditions of a man, living in the remote regions of Sahara desert to match with the facilities available to a man living in the fertile regions of the Indo-Gangetic plane. Thus, every man will have to avail the opportunity according to the available conditions and the talk of perfect equality in opportunity will be a utopian scheme.

After a great deliberation on this issue, Rashdall came to the conclusion that "the concept of 'equality of opportunity' cannot be pushed to its logical consequences without absurdity."[25] Thus speaking, the unequal opportunities and unequal distribution of economic 'goods' may lead to more equal distribution of *good.* Rashdall, therefore, suggested that "some inequality is a condition of well-being."[26] Even Kant, the great equalitarian in the realm of moral decisions, has emphasized the blessings involved in the fact of human inequality. "He saw," as Popper brings out, "in the variety and individuality of human characters and opinions one of the main conditions of moral as well as material progress."[27] Such advocates of communism, who vainly claim that communism will create 'economic equality', will be greatly dismayed to learn that even the communist thinkers do not find the economic equality practicable. In one of his speeches dated 26-1-1934 when Stalin was convincing the workers to surrender some of their wages to meet the cost of administration and the salaries of the managerial staff, he said, "in actual practice, it is time it was understood that Marxism is an enemy of equalization."[28] The context of the speech, where equality is being denied, is the context of economic equality between the wages of the 'Managers' and those of workers. It does not mean that Stalin also denied the equality of man *qua* man. From this, it is evident that communism does not believe in the equalization of wages, viz., 'the economic equalization'.

Dispelling all the misconceptions about the notion of equality Engels differentiated the bourgeois demand for equality from the proletarian demand for equality, and then specifically pointed out that, "the real content of the proletarian demand for equality is the demand for the 'abolition of classes'. Any demand, which goes beyond that, of necessity passes into absurdity."[29] Thus, according to Engels, equality does not mean 'economic equality' in the realm of micro-economics, which, as they see it, is a vulgarity, but it means the 'equality to overthrow the conditions of dehumanising existence'. Marx has nowhere asserted that all men have 'equal ability' nor has he emphasized the 'equality of needs'. Therefore, it would be unjustified to carry the communist maxim to prove 'economic equality' on the basis of that. In fact inequality is inherent in the very principle from each according to his ability and to each according to his needs. Afanasyev, a modern communist thinker accepts this factual reality and asserts, "People differ from each other by the occupation, level of education, way of thinking, character and many other indications."[30] Afanasyev further redefines the Marxian concept of wealth, "What is wealth, if not the absolute bringing to light of man's creative talents without any prerequisites except preceding historical development, i.e., the development of all human powers as such."[31] If this is the definition of 'wealth', then any talk of 'economic equality' as the aim of communism only distorts its essence.

Equality is Spiritual :

The concept of economic equality is clearly a myth. When men differ physically and intellectually, then what does their 'equality' signify ? The only equality, which can be conceived in communism, is the equality of breaking the bonds of the dehumanizing conditions. It means that it is in possessing the human dignity that all men are equal. Hearnshaw elaborates the notion of 'equality' thus : "In conflict with the same corporeal and spiritual foes, in contemplation of the same enigmas of life and destiny, all men are equal, and differences, which distinguish man from man dwindle into imperceptibility.[32] The position of Marx and Engels still goes beyond this. They assert that the only equality, which communism recognises is that all men are *equal* in realising that they are human beings. In Kantian language, we may render this to mean that they are equal in realising that they all are equally capable to become the members of the 'Kingdom of Ends'. In the opinion of the present author, this is not economic but spiritual equality.

Social Justice and Equality in Gita

The Anāsakti Yoga of Gita does not lay down a 'need-oriented' formula as the basis of 'distributive justice'. The author of Gita has avoided the pitfall into which the vague concept of 'each according to his need' may take. The need of an individual may be in inverse proportion to his abilities and to his contribution to society. Therefore, Gita decrees that no one will be allowed to enjoy the benefit of his share from the net product of the society unless he has contributed his due share to the productive process of society. Those, who live on 'unearned incomes', are condemned as thieves. Gita says : "He who enjoys their gifts without rendering aught unto them is verily a thief."[33] Thus speaking, those, who do not work for society, have no right to take anything from it. This principle will presuppose that individuals will claim from the society only as much as is commensurate to their work. If the need oriented formula is adopted, problem of measurement of needs crops up. Who will judge as to what are the needs of an individual or a class ? This measurement may differ from individual to individual.

In order, therefore, to check the vagaries of the 'needs', Gita has offered the formula of *aparigraha*.[34] The underlying assumption in Gita is that only an unenlightened egoist will appropriate the share of others. But the men of superior social integrity will make use of the wealth in the public interest. 'Aparigraha' stands for this type of the attitude of indifference towards accumulation. According to Indian ethics, *aparigraha* arises from the consciousness that all material possession is tainted by the fault of deceit and cruelty etc.[35] This was the standpoint of Proudhan also. who enunciated that 'property is theft'.[36] When the desire to misappropriate that which legitimately belongs to others is sublated, the man will take from the society only as much as is needed for the discharge of his allotted social duty. Gita holds : "The righteous men, who eat the residue of the sacrifice, are freed from all sin."[37] Accordingly, a man is supposed to take from the gross products of society as much as is left after investing it into the productive process of the society. This seems to be the ideal projected by the modern protagonists of communism, who uphold that in communist society, "the needs of every person will be truly human" and behaviour in the spirit of the lofty principles of communists morality will itself be an inner need."[38] When the needs are so regulated in the service of the society and the desires are socialised, the problem of distributive justice will not arise. The problem of distributive justice arises only when man is in bondage of the competitive goods. But for a man, who performs all his obligatory actions without preconceiving his personal profit, there is no such problem. The author of *Gita* suggests that a socialized man 'has ill-will towards none ; he will be friendly and compassionate, (*adveṣṭā sarvabhūtānāṁ maitraḥ karuṇa eva ca*).[39]

The use of word 'maitraḥ' is very significant here, because among friends everything is held in common – their pleasures as well as their pains, and therefore, the problem of fair or unfair distribution does not crop up. This word reminds of Aristotle's famous dictum that if friendship prevails, justice will not be needed, but if justice prevails, friendship will still be a boon. *Gita's* emphasis is on this aspect. Accordingly, if the social sentiment is aroused and men are made to feel friendly to each other, the problem of distributive justice will not be raised. This is the message of *Anāsakti yoga*.

Justice and Svadharma :

But the whole question of justice has been seen in Gita from totally different perspective. Here the question of rights has not been raised but instead, it has been presupposed that if every one discharges the duties of his social station (*svadharma*) sincerely, the rights will automatically flow from them. Apart from society, a man by himself has no right to anything whatever. He derives his rights when he is a part of social whole. Mackenzie, therefore, rightly points out, "he has a right only to that which it is for the good of the whole that he should have."[40] Therefore, the formula adopted in Indian traditions is that 'let every one take care of his duties and the rights will automatically take care of themselves'. According to Gita, it is 'by performing action without attachment that man attains the supreme' (*asakto hyācaran karma paramāpnoti pūruṣaḥ*).[41] This statement implies that if man is to seek the highest state of his existence, and if he wants to realize an optimum of the socialized conditions, then he should take precaution that he is not violating his duties towards the society. If the social equilibrium is to be maintained, every one must discharge his duty sincerely. It naturally follows that if someone in society is not getting his rights, his due share, then somewhere some body has broken the chain of discharging his social obligation. The social order will function undisrupted if every one is doing his allotted work. The emphasis is laid on it in third chapter when Gita says' : "Do thou thy allotted task" (*niyataṃ kuru karma tvam*).[42] This allotted task is not to be performed for profit motive or for the sake of satisfying the selfish ends.

In such discharge of work, he should not look to others as to whether or not they are discharging their job sincerely. 'The others are negligent of their duty', is no excuse for a man for not doing his own job. *Gita*, therefore, tells us "Better one's own duty, bereft of merit than another's well-performed ; better is death in the discharge of one's duty ; another's duty is fraught with danger."[43]

Interaction of rights and duties also follows from the Gita's organic conception of society. Unless the individual realizes the organic interdependence, his ego-centric actions may continue to disturb the social equilibrium, which is the *raison d'etre* of social justice. Gita tells us clearly that if every individual discharges his social responsibility sincerely and honestly, then a perfect state of social existence can be achieved.[44]

The norms of social justice are broken by the criminals who want to appropriate everything for their own selfish ends. Gita reserves the severest words for them; doomed to devilish wombs (*āsurīṁ yoni-māpannā*) (XVI.20) are those who say 'this have I gained today; this aspiration shall I now attain; this wealth is mine; this likewise be mine hereinafter.'[45]

The whole society is a web of relations sustained by the *svadharma*, in which rights will occupy the secondary place. In Gita the social justice, i.e., the distributive justice is dependent on the discharge of *svadharma*. This is a far superior conception to that suggested by communism, viz., 'from each according to his ability to each according to his need'. The communist dictum will approximate *Gita*, if it is re-rendered to read that 'because each according to his ability', 'therefore, each according to his need'.

Through the law of Karma, Gita offers to the individuals full freedom to enjoy the goods in such a way as may be helpful in the discharge of their dharma. This means that man should be given equal opportunity, in principle, to realize his hidden capacities. Beyond this, the principle of equality cannot be stretched. In the words of Radhakrishnan "equality refers to opportunity and not to capacity."[46]

It is the equality of essence, which has been proposed in *Gita*. Humanity speaks through the mouth of Kṛṣṇa that "he who sees Me, everywhere and everything in Me, never vanishes from Me nor I from him."[47] This would come to mean that all men have the same essential principle of humanity underlying their apparent individualities. *Gita* wants to convey that the same human dignity can be found in every individual. The enlightened men will take this fact into cognisance in all their social dealings.

It is only when man becomes spiritually blind that he denies humanity of others in practical considerations. Such an assertion of the equality of men is the assertion of the fundamental principle of democracy also. When this principle is applied to the practical life-situation, it is tantamount to say that all human beings *qua* human beings should have equal opportunity to exercise their free choice to determine as to what sort of administration they consider most suitable for them. They should also have equal freedom to select their profession according to their capacities and aptitudes. If the administration plans as to which man is to be fixed in which job-performance, then it would mean that men are being treated like cogs and nuts to be fixed in a vast machine by some skilled mechanics. Such attitude grows from fascism, which despises the masses and denies them the equality of right to decide their socio-political fate. This is, as a matter of fact, the denial of equality. Democracy does not permit this type of regimentation, but rather expresses a faith that every man has equal right to assert himself as a human being, the only equality, which man ought to strive for, is ethical and spiritual equality, i.e., the equality to realise that '*I am a human being*'. All other equalities are subordinate to and derivatory from it.

References

1. Russell, B., *Human Society in Ethics and Politics*, p. 133.
2. Ginsberg, Morris, *Justice in Society*, p. 73.
3. Ibid., p. 37.
4. Laski, Harold J., *Karl Marx*, p. 46.
5. Carr, E.H., *Karl Marx : A Study in Fanaticism*, p. 83.
   Lindsay, A.G., *Karl Marx's Capital*, p. 144.
   Sidney Hook, *From Hegel to Marx*, p. 53.
6. Marx, K., and Engels, F., *Selected Works*, Vol. I, p. 558.
7. Tucker, Robert C., *Philosophy and Myth in Karl Marx*, p. 222.

8. Marx, K. and Engels, F., *Selected Works*, Vol. II, pp. 23-24.
9. Engels, F., *Anti-Duhring*, pp. 443, 445.
10. Marx, K., and Engels, F., *Selected Works*, Vol. II, p. 23.
11. Ibid., Vol. I, pp. 624-625.
12. Marx, K., *Capital*, pp. 59-60 ; *Selected Correspondence*, p. 128 ; and *Selected Works*, Vol. II, pp. 20, 23, 24.
13. Marx, K., *Economic and Philosophic Manuscripts of 1844*, p. 129.
14. Marx, K., *Selected Works*, Vol. II, p. 23.
15. Marx, K., *Capital*, p. 188.
16. Engels, F., *Anti-Duhring*, p. 305.
17. Marx, K., *Selected Works*, Vol. II, p. 23.
18. Marx, K., *Communist Manifesto*, p. 119.
19. Afanasyev, V., *Scientific Communism*, p. 325.
20. Afanasyev, V., *Socialism and Communism*, p. 128.
21. Tucker, Robert C., op. cit., p. 22.
22. Marx, K., *Capital*, p. 714.
23. Ginsberg, Morris, op. cit., p. 99.
24. Rashdall, H., *Theory of Good and Evil*, Vol. I, p. 222.
25. Rashdall, op cit., p. 231.
26. Ibid., p. 233.
27. Popper, Karl, *The Open Society and its Enemies*, Vol. II, p. 357.
28. Stalin, Joseph, *Problems of Leninism*, p. 635.
29. Marx, Engels, Lenin, *On Historical Materialism*, p. 207.
30. Afanasyev, V., *Scientific Communism*, p. 297.
31. Ibid., p. 292.
32. Hearnshaw, F., *Democracy at the Crossways*, p. 33.
33. *Gita*, III. 12 (*Anāsakti Yoga* Bhāṣya) (tairdattānapradāyai bhyo yo bhuñkte stena eva saḥ).
34. *Gita*, IV. 21 (tyakta sarvaparigrahaḥ) ; VI. 10 (Nirāśīraparigrahaḥ)
35. Maitra, S.K., *The Ethics of the Hindus*, p. 198.
36. Proudhan, P.J., *What is Property ? An Enquiry into the Principles of Right and Government*, pp. 256-257.
37. *Gita*, III. 13 (*Anāsakti Yoga* Bhāṣya) (Yajñaśiṣṭāśinaḥ santo mucyante sarva kilbiṣaiḥ).
38. Afanasyev, V., *Scientific Communism*, p. 326.
39. *Gita*, XII. 13 (*Anāsakti Yoga* bhāṣya).
40. Mackenzie, J.S., *A Manual of Ethics*, p. 290.
41. *Gita*, III. 19 (*Anāsakti Yoga*).
42. *Gita*, III. 8 (Hindi version).
43. *Gita* (*Anāsakti Yoga* bhaṣya), III. 35.
44. *Śrimadbhagavadgita* (Hindi), XVIII. 45 (sve sve karmaṇyabhirataḥ sansiddhiṁ labhate naraḥ).
44. *Gita* (*Anāsakti Yoga*), XVI. 13 (idam adya mayā labdham imaṁ prāpsye manoratham ; idam astī'dam api me bhaviṣyati punar dhanam).
46. Radhakrishan, S., *Eastern Religion and Western Thought*, p. 368.
47. *Gita*, VI. 30 (*Anāsakti Yoga* bhāṣya).

6

Varna Vyavastha vs. Classless Society

Varna Vyavastha

The concept of the four-fold division of society (catur varṇa) is a much maligned one and considered not consistent with the norms of social justice. The Anāsakti-Yoga of Gita on the other hand, emphasizes its need on the basis of variety of *guṇa* and *karma.* The whole social system, according to this scheme, is divided into four strata (*cātur varṇyaṁ mayā sṛṣṭam guṇakarmavibhāgaśaḥ).*[1] The historians, anthropologists, sociologists, and Indian thinkers in general have all subjected this controvertial subject to their critical gaze. In this present study we are not concerned with its real origin. Let us analyse it, as it has come down to be accepted in Gita, and then compare it with the communist ideal of a classless society. Gita takes it for granted that the four-fold division (*varṇas*) was created according to the different *guṇas* and *karmas* of the individual members of society. The principle has been re-asserted in the closing chapter where the duties of Brāhmaṇas, Kṣatriyas, Vaiśyas and Sudras are distributed according to their innate qualification.[2] This sort of criterion serves as a guide for social stratification, role assignment, and thereby for sustaining the ideal order of society in Indian social thought. Since Gita incorporates the essence of Upaniṣads, epic and other philosophical traditions, we have no reason to doubt that the author of Gita, before adopting this criterion, had not taken all the theories current at that time, viz., the theory of metaphysical origin, the skin theory, the theory of hereditary determination of status etc. into consideration before arriving at the theory of *guṇa-karma* as the basis of varṇa. Accordingly, there should be no objection in holding that out of all the theories of varṇa-vyavasthā, Gita subscribes to the theory that guṇa-karma are the basis of varṇa system and rejects all others. What this criterion suggests and what is its significance, is a problem to be examined in detail.

Uniformity not tenable :

Gita subscribes to the principle of the unity of mankind. A yogī, according to Gita, is one, who has become one with the *Ātman* in all the creation (sarva bhūtātma bhūtāmā).[3] The same principle of unity has been further asserted : "He who sees Me everywhere and everything in Me, never vanishes from Me nor I from him (*yo mām paśyati sarvatra sarvaṁ ca mayi paśyati tasyā' haṁ na praṇaśyāmi sa ca me na praṇaśyati*)."[4]

But a unity does not mean absolute uniformity so as to reduce all the varieties to negation. Whitehead warned not to confuse between 'unity' and 'uniformity'. He said, "The Gospel of Uniformity is dangerous for social progress. A diversification among human communities is essential for the provision of incentive to human spirit."[5] If all men shed their inherent 'differentia', the society will be a dull, and monotonous lump and not a real living unity with richness of personalities.

Aldous Huxley has presented a caricature of such a society in his book, *The Brave New World.* He conceives of a society, with standardised inhabitants, who think, feel and act alike ; their interests are same and so are their opinions. Obviously, in such societies, the civilization would never advance and culture would always remain rudimentary. Will it be possible to tolerate such state of affairs and its boredom of monotony ? It is, therefore, an undersirable state for men, who have 'variant individualities, and the individual differences of guṇa and karma.

It was in the primitive societies that 'likeness' was considered to be the dominant condition of social cohesion. But, as Durkheim rightly points out, "in more advanced societies where members possess some individuality, with more elaborate division of labour, the structure is built on difference as well as likeness."[6] Tribal societies where the occupations are not specialised and division of labour is rudimentary prove the point. Any one there can eke out his existence by doing any job. But as civilization advances, social roles get demarcated. A general survey of cultural anthropology shows that as the division of labour proceeds, the individuals tend more and more to develop their distinctive functions and genuine personalities. But the social cohesion is still maintained. Durkheim explains this phenomenon thus : through this division of labour, "society acquires an organic rather a mechanical unity".[7]

The theory of *varṇa vyavasthā* is the expression of the same synthesis of the functional differences of man and the organic unity of the society. Radhakrishnan says "human society is an organic whole, the parts of which are naturally dependent in such a way that each part fulfilling its distinctive function conditions the fulfilment of the function by the rest and *vice versa*."[8] Gita convinces us of the efficacy of this sort of special stratification. Accordingly, when the parts of the social organism discharge their allotted function, they provide a good scheme for the individual to select his task according to his own nature (*svabhāvaprabhavair guṇaiḥ*).[9] Thus choosing their place in the vocational institutions of their choice, men can discharge their respective social obligations more skilfully. The problem of misfits will not arise By wilful selection of their roles, the individuals it is assumed, can feel a sense of unity with the society. The individual can merge his atomized individuality into the larger context of humanity through some intermediary groups. Integrated and harmonized, these institutionalized groups contribute to the healthy growth of both the society as well as the individuals. In support of Gita's organic theory of the society Radhakrishnan sums up : "spiritual wisdom, combined with executive power plus skilled production and devoted service are indispensable elements of any social order."[10] Accordingly, it would be an undesirable effort to enforce an unwarranted uniformity on mankind. The day when man is reduced to 'robot' to act in a perfectly uniform manner, will be an unfortunate day and then, it would be a society of robots not of human beings. For a human society, the variegated tastes and temperaments, the individual differences in talent and aptitude must be honoured.

Varṇa and Caste :

The criterion of determining one's status according to his guṇa-karma, saves this theory of social stratification from falling into crude casteism. Differentiating between caste and class, McIver points out that "when status is wholly predetermined so that men are born to their lot in their life without any hope of changing it, then class takes the extreme form of caste."[11] Prabhu, in his elaborate discussion, has also recognised the distinction between caste (jāti) and varṇa. According to his view, "a caste is comparatively a more rigid social class, to which transition from another class becomes well-nigh an impossibility."[12] We have seen that the principle of birth is not the criterion of the social division in Gita. The emphasis here is on guṇa and karma. Gita repeatedly stresses in about 14 verses that men rise and fall in this world according to the preponderance of three guṇas in their nature.[13] These guṇas have been presented as the three tendencies of prakṛti. The criterion of birth determining one's social role is ruled out. It becomes evident that Gita never confuses *varṇa* with *jāti*. Accordingly, the varṇa vyavasthā, to which Gita subscribes, cannot be confused with the petrified and degenerated caste structure of the present day Indian society.

In ideal society, according to Gita, the principle of guṇa and karma determines the role of stratification. Dignity does not come to a man by his birth in a particular lineage, but by discharging one's obligation to the social system. Gandhiji puts it aptly, "the real dignity of man comes from his capacity for superior service, not superior status. The moment the superior status is arrogated, it becomes worth to be trampled under feet."[14] The class of Anāsakti Yoga determined by temperament and vocation should not be equated with a caste determined by birth.

Psycho-Social Efficacy of Vārṇa :

The efficacy of this system will depend on the psychological make-up of man and the vocational or economic structure of the society. Commenting on the efficacy of varṇa system Radhakrishnan suggests that "it cannot be regarded as anything more than insistence on a variety of ways in which the social purpose can be carried out. Functional groupings will never be out of date."[15] In order to make every one find his social position according to his nature (*svabhāvaniyatam*) (XVIII. 47), a correct understanding of human psychology becomes essential.

The Western psychologists, like Adler, Jung, Freud, Allport, Vernon etc. have been maintaining that individuals differ in their personality traits, in aptitude, and in the level of intelligence. The latest methods of testing the intelligence and aptitude have also proved that every person is not fit for every job because individuals differ in their innate endowment and capabilities. Accordingly, the best adjustment would be to adopt in life those lines of activities for which a person is best suited by virtue of his intelligence and aptitude, taste and temperament.

The idea of such 'intelligence testing' may appear disparaging to those scholars who interpret Marxism as a denial of all the innate differences. But these persons may be shocked to learn that the modern communist thinkers have also confirmed on pschological grounds the theory of individual differences. For example, the fact that men differ according to their temperaments, has been well recognised by Soviet psychiatrists. They uphold that the "individual features of personality are associated with temperaments. Fedotov tells us that "the temperaments influence thinking, volition and other psychic processes."[16] Accordingly, the men of different temperaments will manifest different traits in their personality, which, in turn, may influence their social activity. Fedotov presents the theory of Pavlov in a new light, recognising the four types of temperaments and four personality types resembling to that : (i) choleric, (ii) sanguine, (iii) phlegmatic (iv) melancholic.[17]

Through the institution of varṇas, the individuals, with their temperamental differences, will be able to express their individuality in its sociological context. Such an expression will depend on the varying qualities of independence of judgement, degree of initiative and the strength of their character. Gita recognizes this psychological fact that "all creatures follow their nature (*prakṛtiṁyānti bhūtani*)."[18] This is to say the individuals will act according to their natural tendencies, their talents and their aptitude. Accordingly, if they are not allowed to select their life-vocation according to their temperamental and characterological traits and if constraints are put on this these, will only help to create maladjusted personalities. As a consequence of that, the society will also suffer, because the unwilling performance of duty by the vocational misfits will leave their social duties half-done. Therefore, a good social system will have to take these temperamental differences into consideration. McIver substantiates this position and says that "more highly organised societies supply a far greater variety and range of contacts ; of occupation, of interests and of opportunities.[19] Obviously, this variety of contacts comprises the general and specific channels, in which the differences involved in the individuality, can appropriately find their fulfilment.

Coming from psychology to ethics, it is Rashdall, who says "the perfection of human society demands the interaction of many different types of human excellences, moral as well as intellectual."[20] This means that not only in vocational field, but in moral considerations also there should be certain departments of conduct in which a certain type of conduct only becomes right. In moral judgements, the society should take this fact into consideration that certain conduct is practically possible only for the persons of a certain temperament.

In view of widely recognised formula of psychological differences, Anäsakti Yoga of Gita has given due consideration to the human factors in laying down the code of duties according to the *guṇas* of a man, which is a code of *varṇa* duties. In an ideal social order, these temperamental differences will not be crushed under an iron law of totalitarian planning. The man will contribute to the social good only if he is working willingly and thereby feeling that he is not a fragmented personality. According to Gita, when "each man feels complete absorption in the performance of his duty, then he shall win perfection" (*sve sve karmaṇyabhiratah samsiddhim labhate naraḥ*).[21]

Svadharma and Varṇas :

It is on the basis of this psychological principle of individual differences that Gita has laid stress on *svadharma*. It prescribes that better is death in the discharge of one's duty (*svadharme* nidhanaṁ śreyaḥ).[22] If a man having aptitude for intellectual work is asked to do farmer's job and a man having an aptitude for farming is posted to do intellectual work, then the society will suffer from the unhealthy consequences, and the social equilibrium also will be disturbed. During these days of advanced technology, this type of the classification becomes all the more obvious. Accordingly, when Gita classifies the personality types according to guṇa and karma and then prescribes certain avenues for selecting their social roles, then it is, as a matter of fact, conveying that in an ideal social order, there should neither be conscriptions, nor regimentation, but freedom to develop according to one's capacities.

Varṇas as the Levels of Realization :

Varṇa Vyavasthā can also have its efficacy in the process of self-realization, which is the process of realization of individual's lost unity with mankind. A question may be raised here. When a man starts in search of the actualization of his social nature and when he strives for seeking his perfection by doing the duty according to his nature, does he find appropriate institutions for that ? Does social order permit the various levels of realisation ? Gita has an affirmative answer to this. This perfection can be achieved, according to Gita, "by offering the worship of his duty to Him who is the moving spirit of all beings and by whom all this is pervaded,"[23] i.e., to the humanity and to society. Man can realize himself by offering his services to the social system. Milne supports this contention and holds that 'a man realizes himself through the contributions that he makes to the system, in his work, in his leisure pursuits and in his interests, in his personal relations.'[24] This type of assertion presupposes that the social order must, in turn, have various levels of realization conforming to various types of obligations. These have been duly provided by *Gita* in the form of the types of social functions to which the individuals should conform in accordance with their natural endowments.

A long list of the social functions, which the different varṇas will perform, has been laid down in verses 42-44 of the eighteenth chapter of Gita. These duties coincide with minor modifications, with the ancient Indian classification of the varṇa dharma. Among the several duties, prescribed therein, the most commendable are :

propagation of knowledge (jñānaṁ vijñānam) for Brahmaṇa; capacity to protect (Iśvarabhāva) for a Kṣatriya; and agriculture, animal husbandry and trade (Kṛṣigaurakṣyavāṇijya) for a vaiśaya. The unskilled, who has not received initiation in any of the above, is supposed to serve by his manual labour (paricaryātmaka).

Moral Basis of Varṇas :

The four-fold scheme of social obligations stands for the motto that vocation is the service of humanity. As Radhakrishnan points out, "this idea of vocation, as service, never encouraged the notion of work, as a degrading servitude, to be done purely from the economic motive."[25] When work becomes a business and not a source of joy and inner satisfaction, then the worker wants to escape from it to seek satisfaction elsewhere. This is the state of demoralisation. The principle of varṇa dharma conveys the same idea that morality means the contribution to the true good of society, and as Rashdall rightly suggests: "it lies in the principle of specialisation of character."[26] The four-fold division is based on the recognition of the fact that, in general, the highest amount of good cannot be realised by each individual and for that a comprehensive synthesis of the persons of various skills is needed. It is the requirement of democracy also that each should be allowed to develop the best in him by finding proper opportunity in the social system for that. If we are to respect the 'personality', which is the requirement of highest morality, then the principle of uniqueness should also be recognised, so that each may be free to tread towards the ideal according to his own characteristics. It is through this varṇa vyavasthā that the individuals can realize a functional unity. When a man realises that he is a member of a system, which is not inimical to his nature but rather is providing adequate avenues for the expression of his talents and for fulfilment of his capacities, he feels elevated in identifying himself with that. Thus, the concept of varṇa dharma is helpful in giving value to one's life. Fedo, the Soviet psychologist has voiced similar feelings in saying that "the social status of a person and his concrete role in society depends on his awareness and evaluation of his position."[27] This is in agreement with Gita's stance. In the light of this, the varṇa vyavasthā of Gita is the assertion of the fact that society is the source of moral obligation and man draws his obligation by becoming aware of his position in society.

Varṇa and Division of Powers :

The principle of varṇa can be applied *mutatis mutandis* can be applied to answer a nagging problem of our era, namely that of concentration of power. When an individual or a group of individuals grab power and become corrupt they drag the masses into degradation. Principle of varṇa vyavasthā made operative facilitates decentralization of power. Varṇa vyavasthā demands that functions should be divided according to inherent capacity of the individuals. Accordingly, the spiritual and intellectual power (equivalent to Church in West), political power (State) and the economic power should not be concentrated at one place in the hands of one group. Different groups should wield these different powers so that they may exercise effective check on the tyranny of each other. In the absence of this principle, the mighty dictators may reduce the masses to the level of dumb-driven cattle.

Varṇa system would be a sign of healthy social order. The principle of varṇa vyavasthā conceives of a society in which the highly complex and developed institutions may work in harmony without losing their internal autonomy. This type of the division of power between the '*sacredotium*' and '*imperium*' was the hallmark of the Conciliar Movement of the medieval European history. The jurisdictions were mutually settled on the basis of the principle 'render unto Caesar the things that are Caesar's and unto God the things that are God's'. The varṇa vyavasthā can also put the constitutional limitation on the exercise of the power by those who are considered competent for it.

Varṇa Vyavasthā—A Sociological Necessity :

The description of varṇa vyavasthā, as provided in Gita, in its sociological implications, points to the richness of social life. It presents a contrast which lends charm to harmony. It rejects any scheme of life which attempts to reduce everything to a uniformity of any kind and thereby threatens the essential vitality of social life. Hartshorn tells us that "any proposal to universalise strict equality is perhaps a proposal 'to render life insipid' in this respect."[28] Thus speaking, for a successful functioning of the democracy, the institution of *varṇas* will be most helpful.

Radhakrishnan has provided various grounds to show the democratic character of this scheme.[29] This scheme of varṇa is democratic in its essence, because it presupposes the spiritual equality of all men, and also suggests that every human being has the right to grow in his own way. Thus, varṇa vyavasthā honours the individuality in its positive sense. However, chief merit of this stratification is that it recognises that all work is socially useful.

To my mind, the four-fold division has another deeper significance. The dharma is considered to be a principle of sustaining the society. If it is so, then there must be some potentiality in this principle to save society from destruction. The societies may go to decay and to ultimate ruin due to four factors : (*i*) Ajñāna (lack of intellectual excellence and fallen standards of knowledge) ; (*ii*) abhāva (shortage of material goods and scarcity of the necessities of life; (*iii*) adharma (general lawlessness and the condition of anomy) ; and (*iv*) ālasya (non-utilisation of resources and talents). To counteract these four hazards which may jeopardise the survival of a social order, every society will need four types of concentrated and well-organized efforts.

(*i*) To keep the intellectual standards high, a band of scholars, devoted to the cause of higher researches, will be needed. They may be called brāhmaṇas. They will create new intellectual and cultural values. Even today when global utilization of knowledge is possible, the problem of brain-drain is viewed with grave concern, because it exhausts all the creative talents. (*ii*) The strong administrative machinery to save society from lawlessness is a protective force without which the productive process cannot function well. (*iii*) Similarly the sincere and devoted producers and distributors will always be needed if the economic crisis and the man-made shortage of economic goods is to be overcome, and (*iv*) Labour power in any society will counteract the non-utilisation of the available resources. If varṇa vyavasthá is resorted to, then the society can be saved from any impending intellectual, political and economic crises as well as the general decline due to slothness and indolence. Accordingly, some scheme like *varṇa vyavasthā* will always be applicable and operative

tive in all the societies. For the efficient operation of this *scheme*, certain specialisation of the various functions will be equally imperative. Here lies the justification for its continued existence in all the times and in all the societies.

Classless Society under Communism

The concept of the classless society is one of the most controversial themes of communism. Marx and Engels categorically asserted : "The history of all hitherto existing societies is the history of class struggles."[30] Accordingly, if humanity is to get rid of the existing miseries, then this class-division will have to go. Marx asserted in very explicit terms that he wanted to prove *inter alia* that "dictatorship itself constitutes the transition to the abolition of all classes and to a classless society."[31] To understand the significance of these pronouncements, it becomes essential to ask what does the notion of 'class' signify. McIver tells us that "social classes are more or less spontaneous formations expressive of social attitude."[32] According to this description, the class system will influence the whole mode of life and thinking within the community. But this is not the sense in which the concept of 'class' and class-struggle has been used in communism.

In formulating his theory of communism, Marx started from the position that the forces of lust, greed and acquisitiveness have bifurcated the humanity into two camps, one of those is of the exploiters, who expropriate the goods for their personal ends and the other is that of the exploited who have been denied all the means of subsistence, nay even their humanity. Thus, the whole society, as Marx tells us, stands "divided into a 'non-working' minority class of owners and non-owning majority class of workers."[33] This is an inexorable law of social dynamics that an incessant conflict is going on between them. In this conflict, the capitalist class by virtue of its ownership and control of the means of production becomes able to appropriate the producers' surplus product as private property. Chesnokov, a communist philosopher tells us that "the division of society into classes, which is the most fundamental and profound division of people in a society is based on the rule of private property."[34] The emergence of a polarised class structure is the historical process of the expropriation of the producers from control of their means of production. It was on this consideration that Marx said that all history hencetoforth is the history of class struggle and that the future communist society will end this antagonism.

What is a Class :

Although the struggle of classes is the key to the understanding of all the social processes at pre-communist level, yet the precise definition of 'class' occupies a secondary importance in the writings of Marx. Verily Marx uses the term 'Klasse' in an equivocal sense. It was at the end of his intellectual career that he confronted the problem of defining his term precisely. It, however, appears that he took its meaning for granted. In one of his letters to Weydemeyer, in 1852, he wrote, "No credit is due to me for discovering the existence of classes in modern society, nor yet the struggie between them."[35] This means that Marx adopted the concept in its prevalent connotation. Some references suggest hat he was trying upon a systematic analysis of the concept of class, in the last volume of *Das Capital* which he left incomplete at the time of his death. But even there, it appears that section on 'The Classes' is a mere fragment.[36] What, then constitute a class ? Is it a division of people according to their occupation, education, political views etc. ? The communist theoreticians tell us that these are 'groups', not 'classes'.[37] Whatever Marx has said about 'class' is mainly negative, but one thing is clear from his negative definition that his classes are not income groups. Anthony Giddens substantiates this position and also holds that "class must not be identified with either source of income or the functional position in the division of labour."[38] If this criterion is adopted, then it would mean that the class distinction can be finished by eliminating the discrepancy of incomes. It is obvious that Marx rejected all such approaches, as merely 'obsolete' and 'utopian'. In order to become a 'class' in Marxian sense, the groups must have antagonistic relations in the matters of the production. Marx points out, "In so far as millions of families live under economic conditions of existence that divide their mode of life, their interests and their culture from those of the other classes and put them in hostile contrast to the latter, they form a class."[39] It means that hostility of their attitude towards each other is one of the conditions and the other is that their interests in the mode of production should also be divergent. Lenin also defines 'class' in terms of the conflicting relations in the productive process. According to him, "the classes are groups of people, one of which can appropriate the labour of another owing to the different places they occupy in a definite system of social economics."[40] It is in this context that we can say that the capitalists form a class. Marx affirms that "capitalists are in economic competition with each other in the pursuit of profit in the market,"[41] but they form a 'single class', because they are compelled to carry on a struggle against another 'class'. Similarly, Marx also recognises the existence of various and variable subordinate gradations in all classes,[42] but these groups do not disturb the homogeneity of a particular class. The classes of Marxian concept are constituted by the grouping of individuals according to their relation to the private ownership of property in the means of production.

Classes and Division of Labour :

Since the Marxian concept of a class is based on the property relations, it becomes necessary to reflect in brief on the process of emergence of the private property and its dehumanizing effects. Marx has projected in *Das Capital*, the creation of a large mass of propertyless wage labourer as a necessary precondition for the rise of the capitalism. He writes : "The absolute general law of capitalist accumulation is the accumulation of wealth at one pole of society and a simultaneous accumulation of poverty at the opposite pole, where dwells the class that produces its own product in the form of capital."[43] Marx wants to say that when the capitalist modes of production prevail in the society, the whole of humanity is sharply divided into two mutually exclusive classes. Thus speaking, capitalism is founded upon a class division between the proletariat or the working class on the one hand and bourgeois or the capitalist class on the other. These classes are in endemic conflict as regards the distribution of the fruits of industrial production. As Marx himself points out, "wages on the one side and profits on the other are determined by the bitter struggle between capitalist and worker."[44] In the whole process of production, the class that owns the capital becomes dominant. The result is that more the capitalism grows, the more impoverished the workers become. The worker is separated from the product of his own labour and the owning class expropriates the enormous wealth produced by capitalist modes of production. The worker is treated as a marketable commodity, and as Marx shows, "the worker becomes ever cheaper commodity the more goods he creates."[45] This is the state of man's dehumanized condition which must end.

From this brief description of the process of the creation of classes, it becomes evident that the classes are the product of the division of labour between two groups of the individuals. The worker, through his labour, acts to modify the world of nature, and the capitalist because of his acquisitiveness, acts to alienate the worker from his products, so much so that, as Marx points out, "what is embodied in the product of his labour is no longer his own."[46] In the precommunist societies, this type of the division works in the sphere of material production. Elaborating the emergence of the classes on the basis of such a division, Marx points out that "the division of labour implies the division between capital and labour and the different forms of property itself."[47] Thus the class division of the society is the prime expression of the division of labour. Engels corroborates this fact when he says that "it is the law of division of labour, which lies at the root of the division into classes."[48] Accordingly, it is the social division of labour in the productive process which determines the class-structure of society. This, in turn, gives rise to the experience of otherness, which is the experience of bondage. Till the capitalist modes of production continue, this type of alienation of the worker from his product will continue. In Marx's concept, 'alienation' is inseparable from the division of labour. In explicit terms he states "the division of labour is nothing but the alienated form of human activity."[49] Thus, in the ultimate analysis, the formation of the classes is the expression of the alienated existence of mankind.

Finishing the Division of Labour :

The alienated existence of man, which is perpetuated under capitalism, can be overcome by the revolutionary reorganisation of the society and by socialisation of the production. Thus the formation of a classless society is necessary for the abolition of the division of labour and thereby ending the alienated form of human existence. Anthony Giddens also substantiates this view that "the expansion of the division of labour is synonymous with the growth of alienation and private property."[50]

Although all class societies are built around a primary line of division between two antagonistic classes, yet in the capitalist society. as Marx puts it, their relation becomes that of "naked, shameless, direct brutal exploitation."[51] Consequently while the capitalist class accumulates more and more wealth, the wages of the working class can never rise far above subsistence level. Therefore, the abolition of the division of labour is the prerequisite to as well as the expression of the alienation.

This state of affairs cannot be transcended till a class, which represents the universal essence of man, emerges with class consciousness and with a determination to finish the very ground of the class division, that is the private property and the acquisitiveness. When the new order is achieved, it will end the expropriation and therewith the antagonism of the classes. Efforts are to be made to achieve this. This will need a group of workers, who are ready to overthrow the system, which perpetuates the division between man and man. For this, the idea of communism, as a classless society, was projected. Emphasizing the need of such a class of workers, Marx writes : "while the idea of communism has been expressed a hundred times in history, the real possibility of a communist revolution presupposes the existence of a revolutionary class."[52] With the overthrow of capitalism, the division of labour will be finally abolished and man will be released from the bond of class-categorisation. Marx spares no words to condemn this class structure ; "All the houses of Europe are now marked with the mysterious red cross. History is the judge—its executioner, the proletarian."[53] In saying so, Marx wants to present the future revolution as an act of retributive justice against a civilization which is so criminal in character that it deserved nothing less than 'execution' and capital punishment.

Role of Specialization :

Why was Marx so disgusted with class division that he thought it impossible that these classes can exist side by side ? Giddens has an answer : "Under this system of production, the worker exchanges with capital his labour itself ; he alienates it. The pr ce he receives is the value of this alienation."[54] Marx himself gives a more specific reason. It is due to this division that "the capitalist wage labour becomes transformed into a simple, monotonous productive force that does not have to use intense bodily or intellectual faculties."[55] It means that the division of labour makes the personality of a man fragmented by making him an appendage of some specialized job in the total process of social production. Justifying as to why he considered the 'division of labour' as evil, Marx writes that it serves "to mutilate the worker into a fragment, degrade him to the level of an appendage of a machine, destroy the content of work by his agony, and alienate him from the spiritual potentialities o th labour-process."[56] What Marx wants to convey is that under capitalist society, the division of labour becomes highly specialized and the workers are forced to develop some sort of specialized dexterity at the cost of the all round and general development of his personality. Whatever he wants to produce, he can produce only in the large-scale factories. It becomes impossible for him to develop the productive activity independently. It, however, increases the relative mass of industrial production. The capitalist goes on perpetuating it and thereby keeping the working men under the bonds of machines. Condemning the dehumanizing effects of the division of labour, Marx pointed out :

> "Just as it was written upon the brow of the chosen people that they were Jehovah's property, so does the division of labour brand the manufacturing worker as the property of the capital."[57]

What Marx wants to emphasize here is that due to division of labour, man becomes a slave to machines under capitalist mode of production and he becomes a 'means' to the satisfaction of capitalist's desire for acquisitiveness. Therefore, in order to realize the real productive essence of man, the specialisation must end. Engels also attacks the evil effects of occupational specialisation. According to his view, "the manufacturer splits up each trade into its separate fractional operations, allot each of these to an individual labourer as his life calling, and thus chains him for life to a particular tool."[58] Not only this specialisation and the division of labour is a bondage for the worker, but through the division of labour, other class also becomes subjected to the tools of its production. The bourgeois becomes bound to his own capital and his own thirst for profits. It was in this context that Marx called the communist revolution as an act of 'universal emancipation'.

Disgust with machines :

Explaining the dynamics as to how the division of labour is evil and how it causes degeneration, Marx starts with his major premises that "the motive force of capitalist production is a passionate hunt for value or urge towards absolute enrichment."[59] The labour process under the capitalist system is a productive activity performed as a wage labour in the service of a drive to infinite accumulation of capital. This labour-power of an individual is the aggregate of bodily and mental capacities of the human beings. With this labour power, the worker produces 'surplus value'. But the greedy capitalist purchases machinery out of the surplus profit and thereby turns the 'living labour' into dead. Marx describes this process vividly : "By transforming money into commodities which form the material elements of a new product or serve as factors in the labour process, and by incorporating living labour power with their dead substance, the capitalist transforms value into capital."[60] The more the mechanized industries produce, the more grows the greed of the capitalist as the capitalist is "a greed incarnate". Thus, under the pressure of his acquisitive drive, he goes on repeating the same process of converting surplus labour into dead machines and the vicious circle goes on. The prolongation of this process beyond a limit makes it a perpetuating process of creating surplus value. Marx comes to uphold that "the end and aim, the driving force of capitalist production is an endeavour to promote to the uttermost the self-expansion of capital."[61]

By this method of the mechanized production, it becomes possible to create large amount of surplus value, and therefore, it leads to the maximum possible exploitation of the labour power by the capitalist. Once the lust for profit becomes the motivating force, the capitalist becomes so inhuman that he tries to suck as much from labourers energy as possible. In Marx's own words, "capital, in its unbriddled passion for self-expansion, develops a greed for 'surplus labour', an impulse to suck labour dry' or a vampire thirst for the living blood of labour."[62] The moralists and the religious preachers have also been warning man against the undesirable and dehumanizing effects of the forces of greed. But the capitalist cannot help it. He, being the embodiment of greed, introduces increasing mechanisation of the labour process to satisfy his 'unbriddled passion' for surplus value, and the labourer, in this process, loses his humanity, *vis-a-vis*, the machines. Marx points out that in the large scale industry based upon machine production, "the instrument of labour comes to confront the worker during the labour process as capital, as dead labour which controls the living labour power and suck it dry."[63] There can be no vehement criticism of the evil effects of the machine-oriented civilisation and large scale industry as this. This shows that Marx was ready to finish the machine-oriented industrial civilization if it comes in conflict with the human values.

He repeatedly condemns the tendency of the capitalist to give preference to machines over human beings as the 'despotism of the capital'. The more the lust for wealth increases, the more the worker sinks into poverty. The machines, which are nothing but 'objectified labour', or 'the surplus produced by the labours turned into dead capital', start weighing down upon their own creators like an incubous. The capitalist attaches more importance to his tools and the machines dominate the living embodiments of labour power. Analogically speaking. Marx says that "in the sphere of capitalist production, man is dominated by the creature of his own hand."[64] What may be the more degrading than this that the producer surrenders whatever he produces spending his 'life energy' to the acquisitive mania of the capitalist and then faces his own creature, the machines. But still the unsatisfied lust goes on increasing and exploiting them. "The victim", says Marx, "having sold his productive powers to the inhuman force, is reduced to 'living raw material' or 'personified labour time'."[65] Slowly and gradually under the despotism of capitalist system, the worker is agonisingly destroyed in the monster's deadly embrace and he is driven deeper and deeper into an abyss of servitude, degradation and misery, from where there is no escape. When the position goes beyond the level of tolerance, the worker becomes compelled for a world-wide rebellion to overthrow this despotism. The lustful deeds of capitalist become the cause of his own destruction. As Marx puts it, "What the bourgeois, therefore, produces above all is its own grave diggers. Its fall and victory of the proletariat are equally inevitable."[66]

Proletariat Class :

The existence of this dehumanized group is a prerequisite of revolution. Marx himself writes : "An oppressed class is the vital condition for every society founded on the antagonism of classes."[67] This does not, however, mean that every poor and oppressed man forms the proletariat class. The *Manifesto* defines this class as "a class without property". This proletariat alone is considered the revolutionary class, because it can stand face to face with the bourgeois.[68] In defining the main characteristics of this class, Marx sought inspiration from Hegel. Hegel's heory also laid down that the modern civil society had a dangerous tendency to the concentration of disproportionate wealth in a few hands, at one pole and the creation of a rabble of paupers at the other. But Hegel clearly pointed out that "poverty itself does not make a rabble, for, a rabble is created only when there is joined to poverty a disposition of mind, an inner indignation against the rich, against society, against the government etc."[69] Accordingly, this class is not only the victim of exploitation, but also unreconciled to its lot. While writing his introduction to *Hegel's Philosophy of Right*, Marx adopted the idea from him and gave his own version about the proletariat. Marx writes : "It is proud, resentful and defiant, possessing that revolutionary valour which hurls in the face of the adversary the insolent challenge, 'I am nothing, but I have to be everything'."[70] Thus, it is class which is *aware* of his 'dehumanisation', and is ready to transform it. When it takes over the means of production and the private property is finished, the capitalist will be emancipated from his unbridled lust and the worker will be liberated from the alienated existence, his dehumanized life-situation.

The search for such class was the main task of Marx to make his philosophy true and practical and his ideal of classless society realizable, as against the utopians, who harped upon the theme of seeking justice within the corrupt system. In the light of this, the proletariat class represented the real aspirations of humanity. In the absence of this proletariat, the utopians used to run in vain to philosophy, religion and politics for the solution of their problem of alienation. Communism the proletarian-oriented "true philosophy" unmasks these illusions. "It makes man think and act and shape his reality like a man, who has been disillusioned and has come to reason so that he will revolve round himself, and therefore, round his true sun."[71] In the light of this, the persons, who have the consciousness that they are men and they ought to realize themselves as men, are the class-conscious workers. Accordingly, it is the proletariat only that knows the truth ; it only knows that dignity of man lies in overthrowing his bondage. Elaborating the role that this class will play in the process of self-realisation, Marx says :

> "*Philosophy cannot be made a reality without the abolition of the proletariat, the poletariat cannot be abolished without philosophy being made a reality.*"[72]

Marx underlines the role of his philosophy in giving the proletariat the courage to fight the dehumanizing life-situation and expropriates the expropriators, and thereby achieve the establishment of a classless communist society.

This is a matter of strange coincidence that communism is echoing the same aphorism at which Gita concludes. Gita says :

> "*yatra yogeśvaraḥ kṛṣṇo yatra pārtho dhanurdhoraḥ ; tatra śrirvijayo bhūtir dhruvānītir matiramama.*"[73]

This means that success on the path of realisation lies only when Kṛṣṇa, the spiritual weapon, finds its material weapon in Arjuna. A despondent Arjuna, unwilling to fight against his degrading conditions, and trying to reconcile himself in recluse, does not fall under the category of 'proletariat'. The role that Kṛṣṇa was playing was to turn him into a 'proletariat' by making him conscious that he should be ready to rebel against his demoralised conditions. Since Arjuna in Gita is only a medium (*nimitta*), it means that through his medium, Gita wants to inspire all those who are living under the dehumanizing conditions to break the bonds of their degenerative conditions and assert themselves as 'man'.

Varṇa Vyavasthā and Classless Society :

What would be the position of catur varṇa if the classless society of Marx is established ? A closer analysis of both the theories shows that these schemes do not come into conflict with each other. In the philosophy of Marx, a concept like that of dharma as a regulative force over the powers of acquisitiveness, is absent. The class conflict on the basis of the property relations will arise only in a perverted and diseased society. If the forces of the community are so strengthened, the exploiters will not be able to play their dirty role. If each individual discharges his function with this idea that he is dedicating it to the social whole, the conflict of interests will not arise. Marxian theory, therefore, can be best applied to the perverse societies where people have forgotten their dharma. In an ideal social order, the varṇa vyavasthā can operate without coming into contradiction with the classless society.

The classes of Marx are exclusively based on property relations and not on guṇa and karma. But this approach leaves much to be desired. The identification of the social stratification with the economic division is not sociologically adequate.[74] Even if the two antagonistic classes are abolished, the principle of *svadharma* will still be a requirement of communist society for social coherence. The unity and solidarity of a class in Marxian consideration is largely a product of class-struggle. No reason has been given by Marx why the individuals, who form the proletariat class today, should retain their unity when the common class enemy has ceased. Any latent interest may divide the previously united proletariat. Popper attacks Marxian concept of classless society and says : "Marx has assumed (falsely) that class consciousness is a thing that can be accumulated and afterwards stored ; that it can survive the forces that produced it."[75] Popper's criticism ignores, however that in the communist society there will be no proletariat class in the sense in which Marx conceived it, viz., a 'dehumanised but ready to revolt' class. Popper has drawn attention to the inherent need to which the communist society will stand i.e., the principle of its very subsistence and cohesion. This principle has been well laid down in varṇa vyavasthā. Therefore, even in communist society varṇa vyavasthā can function effectively.

Here a criticism may be raised that Marx and Engels were against professional specialisation. Marx has been repeatedly saying that division of labour is a hostile social relation of man to man, and class war is the multiplication of this hostility on the social scale. How it can be adjusted with the varṅa vyavasthā which requires the men of different innate temperaments to handle different vocations. But the whole position will be clear if we make subtle distinction between 'division' and 'distribution'. The distribution of work according to guṅa and karma is not a 'division of humanity'. Each man discharging his function allotted to him is fully human.

To divide that, which is indivisible, is called 'māyā' (bewilderment) in Indian thought. Therefore, to say that the class 'division', of which Marx has spoken, is the same as the 'distribution of work' according to one's nature, will be mistaken. The humanity is an indivisible wholeness and due to his selfish interests, the capitalist wants to divide it by denying human conditions of existence to labour. This is called negation in Marxian system. But such an effort will be *māyā* or *adhyāropaṇa* in Indian thought because he is trying to impose false divisions where they do not exist. In cancelling the class division, therefore, the negation created by the capitalist will be negated but the principle of the rational distribution of work will not be destroyed. So far as the question of professional specialisation is concerned, it is admitted that sometimes the communist thinkers spoke in such a way as it appeared to come in conflict with varṇa vyavasthā. Engels, for example, writes : "...man is divided. All other physical and mental faculties are sacrificed to the development of one single activity."[76] Marx also denounced the professional specialisation as "*enslaving subordination of man to the division of labour*."[77]

This idea was based on his assumption that every social division of labour enforces occupational specialisation as a way of life. He writes in *German Ideology*, "for, as soon as labour is divided, each man has a particular exclusive sphere of activity, which is forced upon him from which he cannot escape...he must remain so, if he does not want to lose his means of livelihood."[78] But what will be the practice prevalent in communist society ? Explaining this, Marx says, "the communist stage will liberate the natural human tendency to become a universal man to do one thing today and other tomorrow, to hunt in the morning, fish in the afternoon, rear cattle in the evening, criticise after dinner."[79] Similar scheme has been voiced by Engels. He says : "In time to come, there will be no longer any professional porters or architects...the man who for half an hour gives instructions as an architect, will also push a barrow for a period until his activity as architect is once more required."[80] Because when man is liberated from the drive for accumulation, he will produce in order to realise his nature as a being with manifold creative capacities.

But impracticability of this approach is so obvious that it needs hardly any argument to refute it. As Prof. Tucker has pointed out that "seeing the difficulty that a sound society cannot work without specialisation, there is trend in Soviet Marxists of denying that Marx was opposed to occupational specialization as a way of life."[81] The confusion seems to have been caused by Hegel's idea of 'world-self' perfecting its power in every direction. Hegel wrote : "What powers it inherently possesses, we learn from the variety of products and formations which it originates."[82] Marx, under his influence simply replaced the word 'man' for 'world-self'. But he forgot that in such propositions as "man is a free conscious producer developing its power in every direction", he should have used the term 'man' in the Feuerbachian sense i.e., in the generic sense, to mean human race, the species. Correctly understood, it would mean that 'humanity' in its connotation as the 'totality of society' and not the 'individual man' is manifesting, developing its power in every direction. Gita has also emphasized this aspect that the individual can seek his perfection by sublating his productive activity to the demands of the system. Understood in this sense, the architect will be realizing in his own way the same human values, which the porter be realizing in his own. If this confusion between 'Man' and 'man' is removed from Marx's pronouncements, it will accommodate the *varṇa vyavasthā* and the *svadharma*, without destroying its own characteristic.

References

1. *Gita*, IV. 13.
2. Gita, XVIII. 41 (*Anāsakti Yoga*).
3. *Gita*, V. 7.
4. *Gita*, VI. 30 (*Anāsakti Yoga*).
5. Whitehead, A.N., *Science and Modern World*, p. 259.
6. Durkheim, Emile, *The Division of Labour in Society*, pp. 41-43.
7. Ibid., p. 399.
8. Radhakrishnan, S., *Hindu View of Life*, p. 76.
9. *Gita*, XVIII. 41.

10. Radhakrishnan, S., *Eastern Religion and Western Thought*, p. 356.
11. McIver and Page, *Society*, p. 356.
12. Prabhu, P.H., *The Hindu Social Organisation*, p. 324.
13. *Gita*, XIV. 4-18.
14. Gandhi, M.K., *Young India*, 24-11-1927 .
15. Radhakrishnan, S., *Bhagavadgita*, p. 161.
16. Portonov, A.A. and Fedotov, D.D., *Psychiatry*, p. 334.
17. Ibid., pp. 334-335.
18. *Gita*, III. 33 (*Anāsakti Yoga*).
19. McIver and Page, op. cit., p. 52.
20. Rashdall, H., op. cit., Vol. I, p. 141 ff.
21. *Gita*, XVIII. 45 (*Anāsakti Yoga*).
22. *Gita*, III.35.
23. *The Gita According to Gandhi*, p. 377 (XVIII. 46).
24. Milne, A.J.M., *The Social Philosophy of English Idealism*, p. 39.
25. Radhakrishnan, S., *Hindu View of Life*, p. 80.
26. Rashdall, H., op. cit., Vol. II, p. 148
27. Protonov, A.A. and Fedotov, D.D., op. cit., p. 330.
28. Hartshorn, Charles, op. cit., p. 47.
29. Radhakrishnan, S., *Eastern Religion and Western Thought*, p. 367 ff.
30. Marx and Engels, *Manifesto of the Communist Party*, p. 40.
31. Marx, Engels, Lenin, *On Historical Materialism*, p. 284.
32. McIver and Page, *Society*, p. 348.
33. Marx, K. and Engels, F., *German Ideology*, p. 69.
34. Chesnokov, D., *Historical Materialism*, p. 202.
35. Marx, K. and Engels, F., *Selected Correspondence*, p. 57.
36. Marx, K., *Das Capital*, Vol. III, pp. 862-63.
37. Chesnokov, D., op. cit., p. 202.
38. Giddens, Anthony, *Capitalism and Modern Social Theory*, p. 37.
39. Marx, K. and Engels, F., *Selected Works*, Vol. I, p. 334.
40. Lenin, V.I., *Collected Works*, Vol. 29, p. 421.
41. Marx, K. and Engels, F., *German Ideology*, p. 69.
42. Marx, K. and Engels, F., *Communist Manifesto*, p. 132.
43. Marx, K., *Capital*, p. 714.
44. Marx, K., *Early Writings*, p. 69.
45. Ibid., p. 40.
46. Ibid., p. 122.
47. Marx, K. and Engels, F., *German Ideology*, pp. 22, 65.
48. Engles, F., *Anti-Duhring*, p. 418.
49. Marx, K., *MEGA*, p. 181.
50. Giddens, Anthony. op. cit., p. 23.
51. Marx, K., *Communist Manifesto*, p. 135.
52. Marx, K. and Engels, F., *German Ideology*, pp. 51, 62.
53. Marx, K. and Engels, F., *Selected Works*, Vol. I, p. 360.
54. Giddens. Anthony, op. cit., p. 49.
55. Marx, K. and Engels, F., *Selected Works*, Vol. I, p. 102.
56. Marx, K., *Capital*, Vol. I, p. 645.

57. Marx, K., *Capital*, pp. 381-82.
58. Engels, F., *Anti Duhring*, p. 436.
59. Marx, K., *Capital*, pp. 137-38.
60. Ibid., p. 189.
61. Ibid., pp. 346-47.
62. Ibid., pp. 235, 237, 239, 259, 270.
63. Ibid., pp. 451-52.
64. Ibid., p. 685.
65. Ibid., pp. 347, 244.
66. Marx, Engels, Lenin, *On Historical Materialism*, p. 94.
67. Ibid., p. 82.
68. Ibid., p. 93.
69. Hegel, G.W.F., *Philosophy of Right*, pp. 150, 277.
70. Marx, K., *Towards the Critique of Hegel's Philosophy of Right*, p. 263.
71. Ibid., p. 263.
72. Ibid., p. 266.
73. *Gita*, XVIII. 78.
74. McIver and Page, *Society*, p. 349.
75. Popper, K.R., op. cit., p. 138.
76. Engels, F., *Anti-Duhring*, pp. 435-36.
77. Marx, K. and Engels, F., *Selected Works*, Vol. II, p. 23.
78. Marx, K., *German Ideology*, p. 22.
79. Ibid., p. 22.
80. Engels, F., *Anti-Duhring*, p. 87.
81. Tucker, Robert C., *The Marxian Revolutionary Idea*, p. 20.
82. Hegel, G.W.F., *Philosophy of History*, p. 73.

7

Ideals of Human Life

In judging a system, the analysts and the analytical sociologists take recourse to analysing the existing institutions. They make predictions in social context on the basis of the factual data and then pronounce their judgement about that. Both Marx and Gita feel dissatisfied with such a descriptive analysis. For them, the worth of a system lies in its providing opportunities to man for self-actualization. What values an individual will realize in a system for his self-development ? On this depends the moral worth of that social system. Thus, for both these philosophies, it is the ideal that is more real for the normative evaluation than the actually existing institutions. It is from this point of view that we may study what ends and what values of life are put before man by each of these systems.

Ideal More Significant than Actual

Man is not a chance product. He lives with certain ends to realize, which keep him inspired. A man who has no ideal before him, finds his existence meaningless. He feels himself to be a burden on the earth. Man is not born with a purpose, but it is by pursuing some ideal, that he adds meaning to his existence. The worth of a man's life does not depend on how much he eats or how much he consumes, but on what are the ideals for which he is living. When man chooses some ideal for him, he exercises the choice from the point of 'better' and 'worse'.

Marx and Gita have both placed certain ideals in their philosophies to inspire a man to regulate his conduct according to them. Both, however, come to agree on one point that in marching ahead towards the highest goal, the lower is to be sublimated by the higher. It does not, however, mean that the lower self is to be negated. Radhakrishnan suggests that the "lower self is not to be destroyed. It can be used as helper if it is held in check."[1] Similar opinion has been expressed by Marx when he says that the "laws of animal society cannot be applied to human society."[2] Man's conduct is regulated by much more dignified norms than the normal animality. In this way, Marx and Gita both recognise the dignity of man.

The Teleological Approach :

The materialistic aspect of Marxism has been over-emphasized in such a distorted manner that sometimes it has led to a misunderstanding that his system was not value-oriented. Even Lenin and Kautsky believed that the scientific socialism of Marx was different from the 'ethical socialism' of others.

Prof. Tucker has shown that "Marx was a teleologist and ethical idealist ; he has moral contents like the idea that the historically inevitable is morally desirable."[3] Werner Stark also supports the contention that "Marx was an idealist,"[4] i.e., one who lays more emphasis on the ethical ideal. These thinkers do not consider him a metaphysical idealist. Nor do they think that ideas are prior in ordering the objective world. Marx is an idealist in ethical sense that the ideal is higher than the facts and that the facts ought to be oriented towards and judged through that ideal. His ideal of communism was the sole measuring rod to judge how far a historical stage is approximating it. The actual serves only as a stepping stone for the ideal. To Marx, the most fundamental thing is to liberate the individual from the bonds of his alienated existence so that he may realize his essential nature as 'producer'. Everything else is to be approximated to this. Marx has always applauded that conduct as 'progressive', which conforms to the progressive realization of the ideal lying ahead. Marxism thus has a teleological interpretation.

Similarly, in Anāsakti Yoga of Gita, when emphasis is laid on Brahmanirvāna, perfection (Saṁsiddhi), it does not deny the pursuit for other things, which a man verily needs for his successful living on this earth. Gita has nowhere indicated that the pursuit of prosperity is not a legitimate human aspiration. Radhakrishnan tells us that "the Hindu code of practice links up the realm of desires with the perspective of the eternal. It binds together the kingdoms of earth and heaven."[5] In a balanced life, there should be a synthesis of the mundane prosperity and the realization of the human dignity. Both Anāsakti Yoga and communism have provided grounds for the individual to realize the various values of life. The point for consideration, therefore, is as to what are the ideals, which are placed before the individual by communism and by Gita.

Communism, a Society of Abundance :

It is generally believed that the ideal to be realized by communism is the emancipation of man from economic worries. But this ideal requires to be more elaborately understood. Marx has conceived man essentially as 'producer'. He writes that men begin to "distinguish themselves from animals, as soon as they begin to produce their means of subsistence, a step which is considered by their physical organisation."[6]

This essential nature of man remains unrealized when he is not free. When men are freed from the bonds of the forces of acquisitiveness, they will naturally produce in order to realize their essence. They will create the conditions of abundance of the goods. This is the conception of the end of economic emancipation that men will realize under communism. The communist thinkers tell us that "communism is a cup of abundance, which must always be full to the brim."[7]

Unity with Mankind :

However, to limit the horizons of the communist ideal to mere economic freedom will not be justified. No doubt that the freedom from economic worries is one of the foremost conditions for the realization of any higher goal of life. No one would also deny that men should first create the conditions necessary for their very survival before realizing the lofty intellectual and moral values. But to stop short at the level of economic satisfaction is not the communist ideal.

Communist ideal as Economic Emancipation

The *Summum Bonum* of human life, communism places before man, is his release from the bondage of his dehumanized existence. From the realm of necessity, he is supposed to jump into the realm of freedom. This realm of freedom, according to communist thinkers, denotes "the individual's freedom to participate creatively in social production, the creation of material and spiritual values and the formation of new social relations, to develop and improve culturally and morally."[8] Thus speaking, the communist ideal is not confined to the economic freedom only. Progressing ahead towards the higher type of society, when man reaches communism, he "acquires genuine spiritual freedom"[9] also. It is for the realization of this freedom that a man ought to strive for. The final condition of man will be to go beyond all ownership, and beyond the property principle. Thus speaking, the highest ideal for man is to go beyond all limitations and finitude. Describing the nature of the human bondage, Marx points out that "alienated labour is the antithesis of the free, spontaneous creativity, in which man realizes his nature as man. This labour process, where the production of object is taken as loss of object to an alien power, is an activity of suffering. It is servitude."[10] Accordingly, in order to break the bondage, the man, who has lost the created world to the forces of greed, must perform an act of reappropriation in order to change his life-situation. This is the real meaning of *Engels' dictum* that *communism will give "freedom from the snare of the realm of necessity"*. When the bonds of his servitude are broken, the individual 'man' can merge himself with the species-being—'Man'. Thus, *the ideal to be realized in communism, is the ideal of becoming fully 'Man'*. In brief, it has been described by the communist thinkers that "the new society develops a full-blooded active man—a man, who is entitled to say "*Humani nil a me alienum puto*" (Nothing human is alien to me).[11] This leads us to conclude that the highest ideal of human life, laid down by communism, is to become one with the mankind by shedding one's alienated existence. Man ought to strive for the re-establishment of his lost identity with humanity.

Ideals of Human Life in Gita

The ideals of life, which inspire men for their achievement, are called puruṣārthas in Indian culture. Gita has laid down Dharma, Kāma Artha as the values to be pursued by a common man, who is holding his position in between two extremes, i.e., a man of Rajo-guṇa.[12] But the *Summum Bonum* is Mokṣa. Indian philosophy, in general, also subscribes to these four ideals, which, according to Prabhu, form the psycho-moral basis of āśrama dharma"[13] also. For the working out of method of realization of these ideals, the scriptures have also been divided into four-fold scheme viz., (i) Dharmaśāstra, (ii) Arthaśāstra, (iii) Kāmaśāstra, and (iv) Mokṣa śāstra. Laying emphasis on their importance in Indian life, Gokhale points out that "Hinduism has not established any organised church. Hindu life is full of the conception of dharma, artha, kāma and mokṣa."[14] Gita starts with the first ideal dharma. It opens with the very word dharma (*dharma kṣetre kurukṣetre*). Therefore, it would be in the fitness of the things to start with the first puruṣārtha 'dharma'.

Dharma :

This term has very rich and wide connotations. On the one hand, it is commonly believed, to consist of a series of sacrificial and ritualistic function, as laid down in the Brāhmaṇas, and other scriptures. On the other side, Vaiśeṣika Sūtra defines dharma as that which leads to the secular prosperity and moral uplift (*yato 'bhyudayāniḥśreyasa siddhiḥ sa dharmaḥ*).[15] Since Dharma is the source of mundane happiness also (*dhanāddharma tataḥ sukham*),[16] it follows that those, who destroy dharma, are destroyed, and those, who preserve it, are preserved (*dharma eva hato hanti dharmo rakṣati rakṣitaḥ*).[17] Dharma, therefore, is a principle of great significance in Indian life. Various philosophical systems, pūraṇas, etc., have used this concept in diverse ways. In Gita, its significance has been emphasized in saying "whenever the decline of dharma and adharma prevails, then the divine forces manifest themselves into concrete form (*yadā yadā hi dharmasya glānir-bhavati bhārata, abhyutthānam adharmasya tadātmānaṁ sṛjāmy-aham*).[18] This manifestation takes place for the destruction of the wicked and to establish dharma (*vināśāya ca duṣkṛtām, dharma-saṁsthāpanārthāya*).[19]

The question would naturally arise what is that 'dharma', which declines from age to age. The Gita being silent over the nature of dharma, this may mean various things. Some suggest that Gita is saying something against moral absolutism and may call it 'historical relativism'. When Gita says that in every age the dharma is re-established, it may be, in the words of Westermark, a bid "to persuade people not only that their moral ideas require improvement, but that their laws as far as possible, ought to come upto the improved standard."[20] It may also mean that in the changing society, the obsolete moral codes should be brought up-to-date to meet the requirements of the changed times. The Absolutists, who advocate that morality has some 'absolute standard', forget that we cannot act in disregard to the social consequences of our acts.

Communism has been subscribing to the similar contention that ethical codes in every age reflect the relations of production of that age. In whatever way this assurance of Gita is understood, it is certain that the source of dharma is not God. It is not the commandment of any authority, but it flows from the social exigencies.

Searching for the sense in which 'Dharma' has been used by Gita, we will have to go back to another piece of dialogue of Kṛṣṇa and Arjuna, where the meanings of Dharma have been explained by Kṛṣṇa. Three verses in *Mahābhārata* elaborate, what is dharma, for the establishment of which Kṛṣṇa promises in Gita. There Kṛṣṇa says : "Dharma has been created for the well-being of all."[21] It has been further pointed out that "all that saves from any harm all the beings, is dharma."[22] Thereafter, it has been told in a more elaborative way, "Dharma is that, which sustains people (prajāḥ) ; definitely that principle, which sustains the creation, must be taken as dharma."[23] If Kṛṣṇa continued to maintain the same position without falling into the fallacy of equivocation, then in Gita, dharma would come to mean a "principle that sustains society and safeguards it from being destroyed." This has been interpreted as 'righteousness' by Radhakrishnan.[24] In view of these definitions put forth by Mahābhārata, it can be said that *Gita* wants to emphasize that whenever the social equilibrium is disturbed and society is threatened, the social forces concretise themselves in the form of some historic personality to destroy the evil doers (duṣkṛtām) and to restore a value-system duly revivified according to social needs. An implication of this assertion is that moral chaos and social imbalances have been recognised as evil in Gita. Wherever there occur serious tensions in life, when a sort of value-negativism invades the human hearts, then the moral norms are reinterpreted to inspire the people in general. Radhakrishnan points out that "to preserve the equilibrium, an answering manifestation of wisdom and righteousness is essential."[25] Some historic entities representing the aspirations of masses emerge on the scene. By virtue of this fight for justice and right cause, these moral men are exalted to the status of divinity in the eyes of the people.

Commenting on this verse of Gita, Gandhiji says: "Here is comfort for the faithful and affirmation of the truth that right ever prevails."[26] Such assertion of faith is essential to keep the society reverberated with moral enthusiasm and thereby save it from falling into the state of 'anomie'. In a practical discipline, if the ideals placed in it do not inspire faith, people will hardly follow the course suggested by that. In *Communist Manifesto* also, Marx has provided similar assurance. He says: "Its (bourgeois) fall and the victory of the proletariat are equally inevitable."[27]

Dharma is Social:

Another end to be realized along with Dharma is *svadharma*, which occupies very important place in Gita. It has been categorically asserted by the author of Gita that, "Better one's own duty (*svadharma*) bereft of merit than another's well performed ; better is death in the discharge of one's duty ; another's duty is fraught with danger.

(*śreyāṁ svadharmo viguṇaḥ paradharmāt svanuṣṭhitāt* ;
svadharme nidhanaṁ śreyaḥ paradharmo bhayāvahaḥ).[28]

The same assertion has been reiterated in the concluding chapter wherein it has been said that "better one's duty, however bereft of merit (*śreyān svadharmo viguṇaḥ*).[29] Emphasis has been laid by Gita that if a man fails in his duty, he loses his honour and incurs sin.[30] By laying emphasis on the concept of *svadharma*, Gita suggests that one should search for his role in the social whole according to his own nature and find as to how he can contribute to the principle of the sustenance of society (dharma). In this way, the Gita conveys the idea that when a man comes to understand as to how he can be conducive in maintaining the social equilibrium, he can make it a law of his conduct (*svakarma*) (XVIII. 46), and (*sve sve karmaṇi*) (XVIII. 45). This resolves the crisis of choice of one's conduct. But wherefrom should man draw his moral obligation ? What is its source ? A deeper study of Gita would show that roots of morality lie in the social context. An individual then needs to take an honest judgement himself as to where his duty as a social being lies. Such a choice will bring a sense of social responsibility in him. Milne substantiates this view and says that the "morally responsible agent, properly so-called the morally autonomous agent, is he, who takes full responsibility of what he does."[31] Kantian principle of categorical imperative makes it very difficult to decide as to who is to be treated as means, and who as the end, because in social context, one's action will definitely affect the others. Similarly, the principle of "maximum happiness of maximum number," leaves one unable to decide as to who would be happier and whose happiness would be decreased in society by his action unless a man conducts a public opinion in advance. Sartre's formula of 'involvement in organised situation' is certainly a better guide. Sartre holds, that "Man finds himself in an organised situation in which he is *himself* involved. His choice involves mankind in its entirety...it is impossible for him not to take complete responsibility for his choice."[32] This formula may approximate the principle of *svadharma* with the exception that here in Gita the involvement is according to Guṇa and Karma. Unlike Sartre Gita does not preach 'abandonment'. The law of *svadharma* instead is a principle of the recognition of one's public responsibility.

In a larger society, the conduct of one man will definitely affect other people even those whom he does not and cannot *ipso facto* know. His contact with them may be impersonal but it is nonetheless real. For example, the conduct of a farmer tilling his farm will affect even those whom he does not know. Accordingly, if he neglects this responsibility, many whom he does not want to injure deliberately, will be adversely affected. Thus for regulating one's conduct *in absentia*, he would require a guide to carry out his obligation sincerely and as a service to the society. The best possible course for him would be to discharge his obligation according to the social position in his varṇa. Rashdall sounds a similar contention : "a man's duty consists in performing some special function marked out for him by his position in the social organism."[33]

The efficacy of the concept of *svadharma* can be realized all the more in modern times, when battering attacks on ethics are being made by the positivists. Joining their camp, Russell also suggests that "moral meanings must be isolated from philosophy,"[34] as the discursive intelligence will not be able to decide the issues involving 'ought'. But by so saying, he does not deny morality *per se*. The only idea behind his verdict is that the source of moral obligation should be searched somewhere else than in the field of scientific investigations, methodological discussion and analytic intellectualism. He, therefore, says : "While it is true that science cannot decide the question of value, that is because they cannot be decided intellectually at all and lie outside the realm of truth and falsehood."[35] In the light of this, any endeavour to find an intellectual basis for ethics will be a 'terrible business'. That seems to be the reason that Indian thinkers in general have not indulged in the dispute of meanings of moral judgement but they have concerned themselves with the source of moral obligation. Such pitfalls can be avoided if the source of moral obligation is localized in the social context. In the light of this discussion, it may be inferred that, in Gita, the obligation flows from the prehension of organic unity and in searching for one's place in society according to Guṇa and Karma. This is an end to be realized by man in his life as the basis of all other *puruṣārthas*.

Artha :

The social obligations cannot be discharged without some material resources. So, the concept of dharma presupposes *artha*. Quoting vedic testimony, Gokhale has defined *artha* as the "material goods for the discharge of one's obligation."[36] Prabhu understands *artha* "as referring to all the means necessary for acquiring worldly prosperity."[37] Artha is important because deprived of artha, the material resources, a man will be deprived of his dharma also. Gita has made a sweeping reference to *artha*, presumably because it has taken it for granted that artha is presupposed by *dharma.* That dharma and artha go together has been upheld by other Indian schools also. For example, Mahāparinirvāna tantra holds that dharma, artha and kāma go together (*dharmārtha kāmadaṁ vighnaharaṁ nirvāṇakāraṇam*).[38] Thus, in laying emphasis on the discharge of *svadharma*, the instrumentality of artha is presupposed.

Apart from this, importance of artha and kāma has been emphasized by Gita in another way. Gita expresses grave concern to save the institution of family from being ruined (in consecutive seven verses in Ist Chapter) wherein Arjuna argues that "their wits wrapped by greed, see not the guilt that lies in destroying family" (*lobhopahata cetasaḥ kulakṣayakṛtam*).[39] It has been shown that as a natural consequence of the destruction of the institution of family, the whole society would degenerate. This shows the great significance of the family as a social institution and of the duties that family is to perform. Accordingly, in laying emphasis on family, the value of artha and kāma is also automatically recognised, because the main purpose of family formation in Hindu ethics has been to realize artha and kāma along with dharma (*dharme ca arthe ca kāme ca nāticaritavyā tvayeyam*).[40] Thus, the concept of artha as a social value is very important in Indian thought. The Indian thinkers have not repudiated economic prosperity, nor they have eulogised poverty. On the contrary, wretchedness (dāridrya) and poverty have been recognised by Indians as curse.[41] Kauṭilya has also denounced the irrational tendency of vairāgya in his Arthaśāstra because it is considered harmful for the material progress of society. He goes to the extent to prescribe that "one who takes recourse to asceticism and mendacity without fulfilling his social and family responsibilities must be punished by the State."[42] The material well-being of society has not been out of tune with Indian life, and poverty has never been a national ideal in India. No body would doubt this fact that the lives, which are starved and strained, cannot be the lives of dharma. Therefore, artha is a presupposition for the fulfilment of *dharma.* In the light of this, what Gita repudiates, is not artha as such, but the greed for money (*lobha*), attachment (*āsakti*) craving (*rāga*), false pride of their wealth (*dhanamānamadānvitaḥ*) etc. It wants to convey that when money becomes the sole motto of life, degeneration follows.

Rashdall expresses the similar views and says: "It is often forgotten that the influence of excessive wealth upon the moral well-being of its possessors may be as injurious as its influence in decreasing the moral and physical well-being of the poor."[43]

In modern times, probably there is no thinker other than Marx, who has so vehemently condemned the tendency of acquiring money for money's sake. Condemning this tendency, he writes: "Enslaved by the acquisitive mania, the human species pours the whole wealth of its species-power into the *worldly god,* and impoverishes itself in the process. The inner world of the working man is progressively devalued."[44] This condemnation comes from Marx, because he thinks like Gita that once the greed takes over man, it goes on perpetuating and there is no end to it. According to Marx, a greedy man, the capitalist "worships money as the externalised potentiality of mankind, and 'almighty being' that confers unlimited power upon its possessor."[45] Accordingly, money becomes the divine power for them that overturns all things. When people take money as the criteria of evaluating the worth of man, then it is with the rod of money that they measure or even purchase fidality, love and intelligence. Therefore, it is this tendency of money for money's sake, that Gita has considered undesirable and that seems to be the reason that it has not affirmed 'artha' as an exclusive ideal detached from synthetic scheme of puruṣārtha. Thus speaking, Artha may be acquired only as part of higher social good, as part of dharma, and it should not form the intrinsic incentive for the conduct.

Kāma :

The concept of kāma also follows from the concept of dharma and as a psycho-moral base of āśrama theory. Detached from its context and seen in isolation, it becomes the cause of man's fall. Within the scheme of normal human life, its efficacy has been well recognised in Indian systems. Kāmadeva is not a demon, but a god of Hindu pantheon. Kāma is a principle of procreation. Denouncing kāma as sinful, is to say that whole humanity is the product of sin. This attitude is totally un-Indian. On the contrary, the Hindus recognise the 'sexual communion of male and female power' (*śivaśaktimithunapiṇḍa*)[46] as the sacred communion. The tantras go to the extent of saying that underlying human personality, main factor is Śakti, which is of the nature of erotic waves (*saundaryalaharī*).[47] This may be called the libidinal energy of Freudian concept. This Saundarya Laharī is said to be of the nature of uncreated bliss (*ātmānanda*).[48] Referring to the nature of this ānanda, Radhakrishnan tells us that it is a 'procreative effort'.[49] In tantra, the Devī has also been referred to as kāma-*kalā*. This kalā has been conceived as the psycho-motor-energy that moves the body (*prasāraṇāṁ preraṇam sā kurvatī tamsaḥ* kalā).[50] Putting all these passages together, it comes to mean that the libidinal energy (*Saundarya Laharī*) is the primary motor force (*kāmakalā*), a creative power, from which all the human faculties are activated. Thus, in recognising that Śakti is the first and the supreme principle of the universe, and identifying Devī as Kāmakalā, the Indian thinkers have recognised that sex energy is the primary principle of human personality.

Freud also recognised the primacy of sex as the foundational factors in personality formation. He went to the extent that the erotic desire in man is the expression of the highest ideal that he wants to achieve. Freud held that "the pleasure principle is nothing but the expression of Nirvāṇa principle."[51] Freudians still use the word 'Nirvāṇa' in the field of psychiatry to denote the desire of man to realize his real basis of personality.

If such is the importance of *kāmakalā* in Indian philosophy, why it has been denounced as something immoral ? Gita has included kāma in the scheme of puruṣārtha (XVIII. 34). But at various places, Gita has denounced it as the enemy of man,

(*kāma eṣa krodha eṣa rajoguṇasamudbhavaḥ* ;
mahāśano mahāpāpmā viddhyenamiha vairiṇam).[52]

It has been denounced as enemy (*kāmarupam durāsadam*) (III. 43), and gate of hell (*narkasye'daṁ dvāraṁ*) (XVI. 21). The reason for this denunciatory attitude towards kāma is evident. For when it is detached from the regulatory sphere of dharma, it can play a corruptive role in society. Kāma, as a separate end isolated from social need and not as an integral part of *trivarga*, is not acceptable to Gita. Gandhi points out that "when artha and kāma are divorced from Dharma, they lead not to Mokṣa but to predition."[53]

Accordingly, any society that wants to consolidate its energies, will need some control and regulation over the sex norms. This need has been recognized by communist planners also. Clarifying the attitude of communist party towards the problem of sex norms, Lenin wrote in one of his letters in 1920 that "he did not like an extension of the bourgeois brothel to communist societies." Lenin, therefore, suggested in that letter in a highly moralising tone, "sexual licentiousness belongs to the bourgeois world. It is an evidence of decay. Self-control, self-discipline, is not slavery."[54] Such a denunciatory attitude towards free sexuality by a communist thinker of the status of Lenin shows the evil consequences to which it could lead.

Therefore, the correct attitude would be that kāma should remain rooted in dharma and should not be allowed to be separated from it. Thus speaking, it is not the procreative principle, that Gita has denounced in repudiating kāma, but it is out of context satisfaction. Gita does not preach asceticism or celibacy to Arjuna. For the continuation of normal procreative life in society, the efficacy of kāma has to be recognised. To understand Gita's view correctly, we seek help from *Praśastapāda*, the law giver. According to his classification, 'although kāma signifies the sexual craving in ordinary usage, yet when it is particularised, it may designate 'longing', e.g., longing for happiness in heaven (*svarga kāmanā*), for wealth (*artha kāmanā*) etc.''[55] It is in this sense of the kāma that it is the cause of bondage and, therefore, denunciatory. The creation of the fine arts for aesthetic enjoyment (*rasa śāstra*) and to satisfy the procreative desire within the prescribed limits of dharma would be necessary to enrich life. Thus speaking, the three ideals, dharma, artha and kāma will have to be practised as a harmonious synthesis to make the life rich.

Life Affirming Scheme :

A general reflection on these three ideals shows that these puruṣārthas have been built up by a process of constructive imagination out of success and failures of social life. When we go through in seeking to satisfy our basic needs, then if we stop short at the level of satisfaction of the physiological drives, we are reduced to the animal level or to the level of morones. But if some higher ends are there, then a hierarchy will have to be laid down in order to allot priority to them. This needs a socio-ethical insight. Ginsberg has put forth the same suggestion when he says that "the ethical principle is involved in constructing a systematic hierarchy."[56] Quoting the testimony from Manusmṛti, Prabhu has rightly summarized the view of the Indian thinkers that "the real good of man consists in a proper aggregate of these three puruṣārthas."[57] Accordingly, this scheme of *trivarga* is the most positive and life-affirming approach, as it provides rich avenues to satisfy the emotional, biological and social aspects of individual. The *summum bonum* does not require us to cancel our mundane desires. It only requires that we should learn to place them in proper perspective. The recognition of these ends is the expression of the fact that psycho-biological and economic satisfactions may be there, but the life must be regulated according to the higher principle of social cohesion, and human dignity. By emphasizing dharma as the basis of all puruṣārthas, Gita wants to convey that a regulated life is a means to the real freedom and prosperity.

Mokṣa :

The ideal of *mokṣa* occupies central place in Indian philosophy. It is a well accepted tradition in Indian thought that Mokṣa is placed as the highest end of human life—*Summum Bonum.* As Dr. Maitra puts it, "It is customary indeed to distinguish four kinds of puruṣārthas or ends—dharma, artha, kāma and mokṣa ; out of this, mokṣa is considered to be parama puruṣārtha—*Summum Bonum.*"[58] Various schools of Indian thought present this ideal in various ways, but the underlying idea seems to be that man wants to get freedom from the vagaries of environmentalism, from his narrow limitations, and from his alienated existence. This type of dissatisfaction with the present is a moral craving. Man's relative unhappiness with the finite categories and limited modes of his existence is the expression of his greatness, which he wants to realise. Accordingly, those, who regard mokṣa as something pragmatic fiction, show their distrust in man's capacities to rise beyond the present conditions. If a man knows what is the cause of his misery, and why he has fallen victim to these limitations, it may be possible for him to remedy those conditions. Man is not condemned to remain as he is. Maitra therefore rightly points out that "those, who say that there is no release from the chain of miseries, are wrong. This is possible through *pratipakṣa bhāvanādi.*"[59] In this way, Mokṣa serves as the heuristic ideal (*apavarga*) and every system tries to explain it in its own way. Gita in line with Indian thought has put forth the idea about *mokṣa* in various ways. Accordingly, it requires a bit elaborate description to assess Gita's standpoint about mokṣa.

(a) *Transcending the dialectical modes*: According to Gita, man is suffering because of the dialectical existence (*icchā dveṣa samutthena dvandva mohena bhārata)* and the ideal before him is to transcend the dialectical process (*te dvandvamoha nirmuktā bhajante māṁ dṛḍhavratāḥ*).[60] The same idea is reflected in verse 5 of chapter fifteenth, which says that those go to the imperishable heaven who have transcended the dialectical modes of existence (*dvandvair vimuktāḥ*). From these passages, it appears that Gita does not place some supra-mundane or some metaphysical ideal before man. The man is tired of the conflicts and antagonism of his practical life and wants to find a way out of that antagonism. To go beyond the contradictions (*dvandvair vimuktāḥ*) does not mean to go beyond this world, but it only means to resolve the contradictions. Marx faced the same problem and his views are very clear. He said, "He (Proudhan) has failed to comprehend the real meaning of the dialectical idea, which looks to the overcoming of all dualism, all contradictions."[61] It shows that Marx was also searching for a world 'beyond' all the conflicts, but 'beyond' does not mean that it must be a transcendental world. At psychological level also, the same idea has been expressed in another way. Modern psychotherapy emphasizes that the environmental factors put stress and pressure on human personality and cause great conflicts in him. The neurogenic tensions and psychogenic frustrations create many abnormalities, and the aim of the therapeutics is to take man once again to his tension-free existence, which is 'beyond' the conflicts. This seems to be the meaning of mokṣa also

(b) *Bid to Perfection*: The ideal of mokṣa has been conceived from another angle. The awareness of tensions is the symptom of man's imperfection. If the bonds of his limitations are broken and the horizons of man are widened, it brings a blissful feeling to him. The limitations of human life can be broken by developing our capacities in a way that we may reach perfection. This can be possible when an individual brings his atomized existence in harmony with the social existence. The discrete individuality is the product of man's own ignorance. The 19th century *laissez faire* type of individualism, was the product of the dehumanising and petrified socio-economic conditions. If this limitation is cancelled and man realizes that he is one with the *humanity*, he feels released from the narrow egoism. This theme has been presented in the twelfth chapter of Gita. It says : "performing actions for my sake, you shall attain perfection" (siddhi).[62] The ideal placed in this way is highly practical ideal. It wants to say that a cultured man would be that who has conquered the petty personal ambitions and the shallow temptations of life. At another place, Gita suggests that perfection (saṁsiddhi), can be achieved by discharging by every one his allotted task.[63] Thus, for realizing the highest aim of life, perfection, man is not to go to another world, but he is supposed to discharge his social task. Such a sense of perfection (siddhi) comes when man discharges his duties honestly and sincerely; not with profit motive, but with a sense of service to humanity. This idea that man attains to the highest by doing work without attachment (*asakto hyācaran karma paramāpnoti puruṣaḥ*) forms its manifestation in various forms at various places in Gita. They all refer to a high ideal before the man. When the false egoism determined by one's limitations disappears ; when he realizes the prehensive unity of mankind, and when the finite man realizes that his interests are identical with the interest of society, he then acts as a social being, not confined to any particular group but working for the society as a whole. The realization of this prehensive unity is the release (mukti) from the vagaries of one's own limitations. The underlying assumption is that the narrower is our point of view, the more likely we are to fall into inconsistencies, contradictions and conflicts. Mackenzie has rightly pointed out that "the wider universe may be regarded as higher or better than the narrower one, since it enables us to maintain a more consistent point of view in our actions."[64] Explaining the efficacy of this high ideal as a practical guide for human conduct, Radhakrishnan tells us that "on the attainment of perfection, the historical existence terminates ; when one individual completes his purpose, he develops the universality of outlook, the characteristic of perfection, but retains his individuality, as centre of action."[65] When a man regains his lost humanity, he feels united with mankind and the resultant dignity of existence as a 'real human being'. This is the real meaning of self-realization. This type of underlying unity of mankind cannot be apprehended by empirical methods. The sciences in all their inductive generalizations have assumed the underlying uniformity behind the particular facts, as a formal ground of induction. But they are unable to prove this underlying uniformity empirically. For this purpose, man is to apprehend rationally. The social bonds are the psychic nexus, and the social unity is a 'felt unity'. The organic unity of society is not a matter of empirical observation. The empirical method concerns itself with 'facts' but the unity of mankind is 'ideal' and 'essential'. For the realization of that prehension is needed which takes us beyond the particularised modes of our empirical existence. It is in this sense only that mokṣa can be called trans-empirical (*pāralaukika*). This is the 'methodological transcendence' of the empirical.

(c) *Mokṣa as Happiness* : Describing the nature of this ideal, Gita further tells that "he who finds happiness only within, rest only within, light only within—that yogī having become one with nature, attains Brahma-nirvāṇa (V. 24). This is the process of 'attaining oneness with Brahman'.[66] This blissful state of existence can be attained while living in this world by resisting the flood tide of lust and wrath (*Kāmakrodhodbhavaṁ vegam*) as laid down by Gita.[67] This ideal of searching for happiness within by resisting the allo-erotic tendencies cancels all sorts of frustrations of life. It is a psychological fact well recognised by all the therapeutic disciplines that unless the man resolves his inner conflicts, he cannot enjoy the material comforts of life. To a neurotic or a pathological person, the whole world appears to be putting stress on his personality. When the underlying conflicts, repressions and vagaries of the unconscious which trouble a man from within, are purged, man feels an inner enjoyment of amelioration. Without that, the external objects cannot give happiness to man. The materialism has so much dominated us that we have forgotten that man is far greater than any material object. If today he is feeling satisfaction with a radio, tomorrow he will feel disgusted from it and run after televisions, only to be dissatisfied from it after some time. This sort of dissatisfaction with one thing after the other shows that his happiness, the happiness that he is searching for, is far higher. In his hectic search, he tumbles sometimes on this object and sometimes on that but soon he realizes that these are far inferior to the happiness that he requires. If pleasures are conditioned by external objects, the people will always remain frustrated and more they are frustrated, the more the society will remain torn by strife and jealousy. Gita, therefore, is right in saying that the source of happiness should be one's own feeling of dignity and realization that he is a 'man', the producer of the material modes and not the slave of them. This is the enjoyment of his own creativeness.

Marx also expresses similar opinion. It may be relevant to recall the standpoint of Marx, according to which man produces a world of alien wealth, and in so producing, enslaves himself under the task master of greed to the objects of his own creation. The crux of Marxian thinking is that the 'world of objects' deprives man of his humanity. He cares more for the objects than his own real worth as if the objects are not existing for him, but he is existing for the objects. He reduces himself to 'means'. Once his human dignity is lost, he starts searching for it in the objects. Sometimes he thinks that dignity would be restored to him if he has an abundance of furniture and sometimes he thinks that ornaments will bring him the lost dignity. But soon he feels dismayed and starts searching afresh new objects. Tucker rightly summarizes the Marxian position and says that "slaving under the task master of greed, he produces a world of alien wealth wherein ultimately he is to find himself."[68] But when the alienated worker starts searching himself in the objective world, he instead of becoming happy, becomes more conscious of his bondage, his oppression and exploitation. He wants to overthrow his bondage which is the cause of his suffering. Marx himself says : "Thus, alienated man is enslaved man, enduring torment in his productive activity. He develops no free physical and spiritual energy, but mortifies his body and ruins his spirit."[69]

Gita, in emphasizing that happiness is to be sought from within, wants to break the fetters on the ever-developing productive power of man. It conveys that in order to prevent undue frustrations, man should enjoy the world of objects from the point of view of a 'creator' and producer (janaka) and not as an 'enslaved consumer'. This is the attitude of 'anāsakti'. That will be the blissful state of his perfection. Johnson also emphasizes "that the achievement of an unselfish 'self' frees much vital energy which is ordinarily wasted in the pursuits of narrow goals."[70] Thus speaking, the real happiness should be searched in the expression of one's inner capacities with a sense of non-attachment and for the sake of realizing one's essence as the 'species being'. Gita, therefore, suggests that "real happiness (*sukhamuttamam*) comes to that who has become one with Brahman (*brahmabhūtam*)."[71]

(*d*) *A heuristic Ideal* : The efficacy of *mokṣa* as an ethical ideal can be well understood in the light of assessment made by eminent social philosophers, who say that "if culture ceases to be the supreme self-value and becomes mere means for the 'practical improvement of life', for prosperity and happiness, it is a degradation of culture to the level of third class *means-value*."[72] What they want to convey is that when some sort of social entropy develops, the culture turns into an uncreative civilization. With a view to avoiding this petrification of culture and in order to resist the petrified civilization from swallowing 'man', the *trivarga* of dharma, *artha*, *kama* is to be transcended. If man is to enjoy 'the full real existence', he will have to go beyond the utilitarian point to the realm of values. Mokṣa has been called 'parama' from this angle that it will always remain a heuristic ideal preventing the culture from falling into degeneration. To this heuristic ideal, Gita has given various names, viz., unity of 'man' with 'Man' (*Brahma-nirvaṇa*) (II. 72), highest bliss (*parama nirvāṇa*) (VI. 15) ; highest mode of humanity (*parama gati*) (VI. 45), (VIII. 15) ; state of perfection (*saṁsiddhi*) (VI. 43) (XVIII. 45), and highest mode of human existence (*brahma-sthita*) (V. 19), (*parama sthāna*) (VIII. 2‵) etc.. etc.

In the light of this, the urge for mokṣa is the urge for merging one's separate, isolated individuality into humanity. It is not the realization of something 'other', something other-worldly, but it is the realization of the foundations of one's own being. In the light of the above discussion, it may be concluded that behind the bid of Mokṣa, Anāsakti Yoga wants to break through all the limitations which separate man from man. It is a guiding idea which keeps the mankind filled with a moral zeal to strive towards a fullness of life in a more comprehensive happier world. *Mokṣa* is the urge of man towards wholeness, to become something more than 'I'. By merging his transient individuality in the essence of collective humanity, an individual can derive moral strength to shed off the false discriminations. Then only they become delivered from all gropings, and all bewilderments.

Dharma as Regulative Principle

From all this discussion, it can be observed that for the regulation of individual and social life, *Dharma* is highly effective principle. It has remained a problem in communism as to what shall be the regulative force to guide the practical conduct of the individual when he breaks off from his dialectical existence. The State, as the regulative power, was necessary in pre-history. Marx points out that "a power seemingly standing above society became necessary for the purpose of moderating the conflict, for keeping it within the bounds of 'order'."[73] In the transitory phase of communist society, the state would survive as a dictatorship of the working class. This dictatorship lies between the period of the revolutionary transformation of the capitalist into communist society.[74] It is during this period of dictatorship that the conduct will be moulded by the state with a view to prepare man to take final jump into the communist soc ety, which is the realm of freedom.

If we compare the role of *Dharma* and that of this dictatorship in moulding the conduct of man, it will be clear that *Dharma* is more effective force from the socio-ethical point. Not realizing the value of any such principle as this, Marx had to relegate into the realm of politics. The very first question that comes to mind here is, what would be the principle to check the misuse of political power itself when it is being misused. Power has a corruptive influence and if absolute power is handed over to a group of people, what is the guarantee that they will not develop a lust for it and remain clinging to it by hook or by crook. The dictators may turn into a sort of new class of oppressors. The example of Hitler is there with the world. Even if it is assumed for the sake of argument that the power will be used scrupulously and it will be exercised to prepare man ethically to enter the 'Kingdom of Freedom', the role of state-power in regulating the conduct of the people still remains doubtful. The protagonists of man's freedom and opponents of dictatorship, right from Aristotle to now, have been telling us that laws are inefficient when a people is by nature lawless, and when people have become orderly, or wise, the political laws may often be allowed to sink in abeyance. Mackenzie, therefore, rightly suggests that "it is far more important to try to develop good habits of action and of opinion in a people than to furnish it with hard and fast positive enactments."[75] He is right in his judgement, because the political laws have their limited and negative efficacy. They come into operation as a 'sanction' only when a law has been broken. They can serve only as a 'curative device' to cure when pathological symptoms have reached the stage of actual crime, but they have no preventive efficacy. A political enactment may check licentiousness temporarily by repressive techniques, but it fails to bring any improvement.

Unfortunately, Marx could not differentiate between legal order and ethical order of the society. Howsoever efficient the legal institution may be in imparting justice, they cannot promote morality. We may agree with Ginsberg when he says that "those who distinguish between *justice in the law* and *justice according to the law*, assume a crypto-morality of their own."[76] Then what principle will bring law to adjust itself to the public, social morality ? The legal institutions are quite impotent to remedy an unjust law. Prof. Allen rightly brings this lacuna to the fore when he says : "In the application of law, 'justice is an absolute requirement', because the judge is to decide the issue on a principle excluding personal prepossessions and idiosyncracies. But alas, he cannot change the rules as such even if they are unjust."[77] It is at this point of helplessness of the juridical law, that the need of dharma becomes imperative. In this context it is nothing other than what maintains social stability. Dharma is a principle which guarantees that social life should not break down in anarchy and chaos. It is the expression of the rational aspect in man Milne also comes to hold that "rational element in man is co-extensive with moral and social."[78]

It is in the irrational areas of man's conduct where the political and other physical sanctions operate. Notion of dharma implies the idea of social responsibility. Accordingly, a moral man will be he who knows well that such and such action will bring social cohesion, harmony and thereby will avoid social dissipation. If dharma is made the operative social force, then the Marxian principle of "each according to his ability" will be able to work effectively. If the control of dharma is not there, the worker may produce so much as to cause chaos in production, i.e., one commodity may be produced so much that it goes waste. Dharma will also be needed to check the chaos in consumption, so as the artificial shortage of commodities is not created. Dharma, as the social force, i.e., the force of the people, will also put a check on state power, when it goes unbridled. Thus, not the political force but dharma will be more conducive in building the future society even of communism. Realizing the futility of state force in regulating the social affairs, Marx and Engels themselves had to point out that "*public power will lose its political character*"[79] and that having become superfluous the state will wither away. But even then if dharma is not there to regulate life, the whole scheme of things will dissolve into chaos of unmitigated conflicts. Thus the ideal of dharma is a better and more effective force in social engineering than the political authority, whatever its form may be.

References

1. Radhakrishnan, S., *Bhagavadgitā*, p. 190.
2. Marx, Engels, Lenin, *On Historical Materialism*, p. 288.
3. Tucker, Robert C., *The Marxian Revolutionary Idea*, pp. 33-34.
4. Stark, Werner, *The Sociology of Knowledge*, pp. 119, 230.
5. Radhakrishnan, S., *Hindu View of Life*, p. 57.
6. Marx, Engels, Lenin, *On Historical Materialism*, p. 18
7. Afanasyev, V., *Scientific Communism*, pp. 11, 332.
8. Afanasyev, V., Makarova, M. and Minayev, L., *The Fundamentals of Scientific Socialism*, p. 291.
9. Ibid., p. 338.
10. Marx, K., *MEGA*, pp. 85-86.
11. Chesnokov, D., and Karpushin, V., *Man and Society*, p. 219.
12. Gita, XVIII. 34 (*Anāsakti Yoga*).
13. Prabhu, P. H., *Hindu Social Organisation*, p. 79 ff.
14. Gokhale, B.G., *Indian Throught Though the Ages*, p. 24.
15. Vaiśeṣika Sūtra, 1.1.2 in *Kalyāṇa* Hindū Sanskṛti anka (Hindi), p. 370.
16. *Kalyāna* Hindū Sanskṛti anka (Hindi), p. 369.
17. Ibid., p. 161.
18. *Gita*, IV. 7.
19. *Gita*, IV. 8.
20. Westermark, *Moral Ideas*, Vol. I, 1906 (Ed) p. 201.

21. *Mahābhārata* (Karṇaparva) 69. 57 (Gita Press, Gorakhpur, Hindi), prabhavārtham ca bhūtānām dharma pravacanaṁ kṛtam.
22. *Mahābharata* (Sāntiparva) 58 (Gita Press, Hindi Ed). Yas syād ahiṁsāsaṁyuktās sa dharma iti niścayaḥ ; ahiṁsārthaṁ ca bhūtānām dharma pravacanam kṛtam.
23. *Mahābhārata* (Sāntiparva) 59, dhāranād dharma ityāhur dharmo dhārayati prajāḥ ; yas syād dhāraṇa saṁyuktās sa dharma iti niścayaḥ.
24. Radhakrishnan, S., *Bhagavadgītā*, p. 154.
25. Ibid., p. 154.
26. Desai, Mahadeva, *The Gita According to Gandhi*, p. 196.
27. Marx, Engels, Lenin, *On Historical Materialism*, p. 94.
28. *Gita*, III. 35 (*Anāsakti Yoga*).
29. *Gita*, XVIII. 47.
30. *Gita*, II. 33 (tataḥ svadharmam kīrtiṁ ca hitvā pāpamavāpsyasi).
31. Milne, A.J.M., *The Social Philosophy of English Idealism*, p. 35.
32. Sartre, Jean Paul, *Existentialism and Humanism*, pp. 36, 48.
33. Rashdall, H., *Theory of Good and Evil*, Vol. I, p. 278.
34. Russell, B., *A History of Western Philosophy* (1945 Ed), p. 834.
35. Russell, B., *Religion and Science* (Oxford University, 1935 Ed), p. 243.
36. Gokhale, B.G., op. cit., p. 51.
37. Prabhu, op. cit, p. 80.
38. Quoted Radhakrishnan, S., *Religion and Society*, p. 106.
39. *Gita*, I.38.
40. Prabhu, P.H., op. cit., p. 165.
41. Gokhale, B.G., op. cit., pp. 50-51.
42. Kauṭilya's *Arthaśāstra* (Dr. Shamasastry's trans.) Book I, Chap. 3.
43. Rashdall, H., op. cit., Vol. I, p. 259.
44. Marx, K., *MEGA*, p. 83.
45. Marx, K., *MEGA*, pp. 145, 147-48.
46. *Kāmakalā Vilāsa* (Trans. by Arthur Avlon) verse V.
47. *Saundarya Laharī* (Trans. by Norman Brown), p. 3.
48. *Kāmakalā Vilāsa* (Artur Avlon), p. 2.
49. Radhakrishnan, S., *Philosophy of East and West*, Vol. I, p. 416.
50. Dasgupta, S.N., *History of Indian Philosophy*, Vol. V, p. 23.
51. Freud, S., *Beyond The Pleasure Principle*, p. 76,
52. *Gita*, III.37.
53. Desai, Mahadeva, *The Gita According to Gandhi*, p. 246.
54. Lenin, V.I., Quoted by Radhakrishnan, S., *Religion and Society*, pp. 196-97.
55. Maitra, S.K., *The Ethics of the Hindus*, p. 175.
56. Ginsberg, Morris, op. cit., p. 10.
57. Prabhu, P.H., op.cit., p. 256.
58. Maitra, S.K., *Ethics of the Hindus*, p. 253.
59. Ibid., p. 255.
60. *Gita*, VII. 27-28.
61. Marx, K., *Poverty of Philosophy*, p.115 ff.

62. *Gita* XII.10.
63. *Gita*, XVIII.45 (Sve sve Karmaṇyabhirataḥ saṁsiddhiṁ labhate naraḥ).
64. Mackenzie, J.S., *A Manual of Ethics*, p. 165.
65. Radhakrishnan, S., *Hindu View of Life*, p.46.
66. Desai, Mahadeva, *The Gita According to Gandhi*, p. 224.
67. *Gita*, V.23 (*Anāsakti Yoga* bhasya).
68. Tucker, Robert C., *Philosophy and Myth in Karl Marx*, p. 152.
69. Marx, K., *MEGA*, pp. 85-86.
70. Johnson, A.H., *Whitehead's Philosophy of Civilization*, p.5.
71. *Gita*, VI.27.
72. Sorokin, P.A., *Modern Historical and Social Philosophies*, p. 143.
73. Marx, K. and Engels, F., *Selected Works*, Vol.II, p. 290.
74. Ibid., p. 30.
75. Mackenzie, J.S., *A Manual of Ethics*, p. 288.
76. Ginsberg, Morris, op. cit., p. 215.
77. Allen, C.K., *Aspects of Justice*, p. 65.
78. Milne, A.J.M., *The Social Philosophy of English Idealism*, p. 34.
79. Marx, K., *Communist Manifesto* (Trans. Feuer), p. 29.

8

Ethical Basis of Human Progress

Marxists are averse to lay down any abstract criterion of social progress. Lenin, for example, has rejected the very question of discussing the criterion of progress apart from concrete situation of human history. He writes, "To begin by asking what is society and what is progress is to begin at the end. Where will you get a conception of society and progress in general if you have not studied a single social formation in general ?"[1] It means that the question of laying down some *a priori* standard of social progress and then applying that standard to the facts of human history and civilization, is ruled out as a futile effort.

Avoiding all the abstract and theoretical discussions about the concept of 'progress', Marx has started with the descriptive analysis of the history at the formation of capitalist society. The materialistic conception of history has been given by Marx in (i) *Communist Manifesto*, wherein a material explanation of modern legal, political, and philosophical system has been provided ; (ii) *Poverty of philosophy*, wherein the analysis of Proudhan's sociology from materialist point of view has been presented, and (iii) *Das Capital*, wherein Marx has presented a model of the scientific, and materialistic analysis of the formation of the society. In all these explanations, Marx has presented his view that man was in a process of developing a new consciousness, conditioned by his socialized existence.[2] The invincible forces of production, with the inner dynamics of dialectical laws, are directing the course of events for the transformation of the 'alienated' existence into the 'socialized humanity'. The path is predestined from the 'primitive communism' to higher phase of communism. On this path, the humanity has reposed at four clear cut stages, viz., (i) the slave-owning, (ii) the feudal, (iii) the capitalist, and (iv) the transitory stage of the dictatorship of the proletariat, which *ipso facto*, is the first phase of the new society.

The materialist conception of human history is a protest against the view that some Supreme Being guides the destinies of man. It also refuses to recognize human intellect or the 'ideas' as a basic cause of progress. Such theories, according to Marx lacked a scientific character, as they do not give correct knowledge of the regularity, the sequence and the predictability of historical events. He, therefore, started in search of the inexorable laws of the growth of human civilization. In this connection, it is relevant to point out that Marx did not treat the human civilization as the product of the blind unconscious agencies acting on one another. Clarifying the communist standpoint, Engels writes, "In the history of society, the actors are all endowed with consciousness, are men acting with deliberation ; nothing happens without a conscious purpose, without an intended aim."[3] Thus speaking, the individual will act to attain certain objectives. What driving forces, then stand behind these motives ? A true philosophy must, therefore, seek the fundamental dynamic power, which furnishes the individuals with the motive of their action. It must also discover the factors, which are responsible for moulding society and its institutions. These factors are called by Marx as the 'material forces of production'. These forces are not limited to mere technology and the instruments of production, but Marx includes in them the productive power of man also. Marx writes :

> "This productiveness is determined by various circumstances, among others, by the average amount of the skill of the workmen (and the) social organization of production."[4]

These material forces of production, in this way, include the material conditions surrounding man, his own labour force and the organisation of the production with the help of the tools and instruments of production. All these, taken together, are called the economic modes of production, which according to Marx, are the 'basic determinants of history'.[5] The economic foundations, which underlie all historical development, have been characterized by Marx in various ways. He has used such phrases as 'conditions of production', form of production', 'process of production', 'mode of production', 'organisation of production', 'productive forces', 'material forces of production', and 'powers of production'. All these expressions have been used synonymously in the writings of Marx. The underlying idea behind all these expressions is that men depend upon nature for their means of subsistence. To exist, is the first law prior to any other activity of man. Man must live even to think. It means that man must mould the conditions in such a manner as he may wrest from nature the necessities of his life. The structure of the social and political institutions should also be moulded in such a way, as it does not hinder the struggle that man is to wage against nature for his means of subsistence. Thus speaking, the means by which man produces these necessities of life must be the basic driving force in history. These means are not mere modes in which the things are produced, but these include the productive activity of man, and the object or material on which man labours and the instruments that he uses. Marx himself writes : "The elementary factors of the labour process are : first, purposive activity, or the labour itself ; secondly, its subject matter, and thirdly, its instruments."[6] From this analysis, it is evident that when Marx speaks of the modes of production or the productive forces as the ultimate determinant of history, he includes in them all the activity in which these three factors are directly or indirectly engaged in the production of the necessities of life.

Men, in producing the necessities of life must enter into relationship with each other. In this way, the nature of man's productive activities necessarily determines the nature of these social relations. The society will be so structured as it may contribute towards the effective production and distribution according to the modes of production. Marx himself writes :

> "In the social production which men carry on, they enter into definite relations that are indispensable and independent of their will ; these relations of production correspond to a definite stage of development of their material powers of production. The sum total of these relations of production constitutes the economic structure of society—the real foundation."[7]

It is on this real foundation, viz., the mode of production in the material life, that the general character of the social, political, and spiritual process of life is determined. The complicated productive activity gives rise to the more complex structure of society. What Marx wants to convey is that the modes of production determine the nature of social relations, which shall exist between men, and the sum total of these relations is known as society. Thus speaking, it may be said that the nature of society, in any given age, is the direct result of the modes of production, current in that age

According to the description provided by Marx *in Communist Manifesto,* the productive forces repose at various stages of history for the realization of all their hidden potentialities and march ahead when these potentialities are realized. Marx puts his views very clearly on this issue and he says, "no social order could ever disappear before all the productive forces, for which there is room in it, have been developed."[8] In the progressive march towards the next stage, the old society helps by way of creating the conditions for its realization. Accordingly, new higher relations of production never appear before the material conditions of their existence have matured in the womb of the old society. In the progressive development of these forces, a stage of development comes when the material forces of production come in conflict with the existing relations of production and the resultant property relations within which they have been working before. Explaining the process of historical progress, Marx points out, "From forms of development of the forces of production, these relations turn into their fetters. Then comes the period of social revolution."[9] Accordingly, it may be said that any new stage of development is progressive in comparison to the previous one. It is on this account that Marx has commended the progressive role of the bourgeois at a particular stage of human history.[10]

For a correct decision whether a society is progressive or not, it is necessary, therefore, to take into account not only the development of the productive forces but also nature of the production relations prevailing in it. Chesmokov has rightly summarised the position when he says that, "the progressiveness of a social system depends not only on the extent to which man is equipped for the struggle against nature and on the productive forces, but also on his social position and on the opportunities for enjoying the material and cultural wealth created by people on the basis of productive forces."[11] On the basis of this brief discussion, it may be said that according to Marxian account, the human history is a progressive process in which each new phase arises out on the basis of the conditions prepared by the past and it itself constitutes a higher stage of development.

The progress, according to Marx, does not take place as a gradual development but the transition from one stage of historical development to the other is *cataclasmic*. The laws of progress in human social context operate in the form of class struggle. According to the description given by Marx, the whole history moves on the groves of the class antagonism, and revolutions are said to be locomotive of history. Marx conceived that from the very moment when civilization starts, production begins to be based on the antagonism of the order of classes. Marx himself writes : "No antagonism, no progress ; that is the law which civilization has followed down to our own day."[12] Accordingly, the progress takes place when the antagonism of the classes is resolved in a higher synthesis and ultimately in a classless society.

In the light of the above discussion, the position of Marx can be summarized that (i) the progress is a historical fact, (ii) the modes of production determine the type of the socio-economic formation, and (iii) each historical socio-economic formation has a high type of relations of production than the one before it. However, since human society is highly complex, it will not be possible to reach any generalized conclusion, if progress or regress is adjudged on the basis of the separate aspects of life. The communist thinkers uphold that "one is justified to speak of social progress only if there is social advancement in general, in the decisive spheres of social life. The most important is the economic sphere, the development of the mode of production of material values."[13] On this consideration, the progress can be understood scientifically only if it is understood in context of progress in general sociological sense. However, a society will be considered more progressive if it provides more freedom for the improvement of the productive forces including the labour power of man. The more the labour power has the opportunity to participate in the historical action, the more the social system is considered to be advanced. Marx points out to this and says : "With the thoroughness of the historical action, the size of the mass whose action it is, will, therefore, increase."[14] In this way, the growth of the participation of the masses as historical process is also an indicator of the social progress. With the establishment of the dictatorship of the proletariat, the workers will have their full participation in the historical action, and therefore, it will be the highest stage of progress, in so far as the realm of history is concerned.

The laws of progress, which govern the path of history in pre-communist society, will not be applicable to the realm of freedom. The laws of economic determinism and the dialects will be applicable only to the realm of necessity where man is existing as 'unman'. But in the new society, the social progress will not be by contradictions and antagonisms which is typical of the capitalist society. Marx himself confirms this, and says : "When a great social revolution shall have mastered the results of the bourgeois epoch, then only will human progress cease to resemble that hideous pagan idol, who would not drink nectar, but from the skulls of the slain."[15] It means that when the communist society is established, it will have its new laws of social progress and the hideous laws of the pre-history will not be taken over to that society. Although Marx has not laid down any precise and positive conditions of the progress in the communist socio-economic formation, yet negatively it has been pointed out that it will be fundamentally different from the capitalist society. It may be recalled here that Marx has adopted the theme of progressive 'self-creation' of man from Hegel. He himself expressed his view in the *1844 Manuscripts* wherein he upheld that "the whole of what is called world history is nothing but the creation of man by human labour."[16] In this resonant phraseology, Marx wants to convey that through the creative and dynamic interaction between man and nature, the 'man' is successively making himself. In this process, he is trying to realize his real essence. So long a man is at the level of the realm of necessity, he, as Marx tells us "continues the traditional activity in completely changed circumstances and modifies the old circumstances with a completely changed activity.'"[17] But when he leaves the realm of necessity, then instead of history or historical forces determining his path, he becomes free to give direction to history. Then he will not be a creature, but the creator of history. The development of the 'socialized humanity' will be the main content of the communist social order. It is difficult to grasp the laws of the future society and therefore these have not been clearly described. Marx himself says : "But we shall never succeed in understanding them if we rely upon the *parse partout* of a historical-philosophical theory whose chief quality is that of living supra-historical."[18] Thus speaking, we shall have to go beyond the laws of historical necessity to understand the progress in temporalised post-history. That is why, Marx has left them indeterminate. From the negative description, it may, however, be inferred that the factors governing progress in communist society will be unrestricted by any forces, which are alien to the social man, so that they may be conducive to the all-round and unbounded development of the individual.

Detachment (Anasakti) vs. The Philosophy of Attachment Asakti)

Unlike Communism Gita does not elaborate any theory of progress. In India, history has never meant a 'will to power'. This has led some thinkers to conclude that India had no passion for historical progress. Berdyaev, for example, says, "India offers the example of a very ancient and non-historical culture, which has stopped still in the depths of its interior spiritual contemplations without, as yet, venturing to participate directly in the dramatic action of universal history."[19] Oswald Spengler repeats the same charge in another way pointing out that the concept of direction, claim to power, will to effect the distant, are absent in Indian culture.[20] These claims may be true to the extent that the systematic philosophies of world history have arisen only in the modern west. But on this ground, it cannot be said that the notion of process, and idea of progress as such were not known to Indians. The concept of Gita that growth of sin and the decline of righteousness are the recurrent (yadā yadā) historical processes, suggests that the moral codes should be approximated according to the need of the times and according to the requirements of society. In a way, this comes closer to the periodic theory of Marx. However, Gita explicitly suggests that these are the historical phenomena, which give rise to some historic personality, who puts the history to the right path.[21] But, apart from these, the very concept of progress in India is different from the West, and that is why, it does not fit in their notion of progress. As Radhakrishnan says, here in India, "progress does not depend on a mere change of surroundings."[22] Man, as a maker of his own history, cannot be moulded by the material objects and material forces like soft clay. The very tone in which Kṛṣṇa asks Arjuna again and again to rise,[23] is a call for marching ahead towards the realization of goal. If the realization of goal, which in the Anāsakti Yoga of Gita is the gradual realization of human freedom, is the criterion of progress, then Anāsakti Yoga has put forth the guidelines for the progress of mankind.

Moral Basis of Civilization :

The concept of progress may be seen from purely ethical point of view. The civilizations can go to ruins if men do not have any control over their lower passions. We cannot remain indifferent to the chief danger, which may throw back the whole efforts of our proceeding towards our ideal. Mackenzie, therefore, suggests "that we have always to reckon with the Devil."[24] Bradley also suggests that if the progress is to be achieved, man should be taught to control over his baser instinctualities. He says : "The process of evolution is the humanising of the bestial foundation of man's nature by carrying out in it the true ideas of men.[25]

Judging from these standards of moral progress, one can say that Gita has all the passion for moral progress. But Gita has suggested its own criterion also and that is the realization of perfection by feeling oneness with the totality of mankind (Brahma-nirvāṇa). Such a consciousness of oneness with humanity needs altruisation of conduct. Gita's path to self-realization is via non-attachment. The moral strength of a man does not lie in withdrawing from the world but in sacrificing the profit motive and selfish tendencies. Gita, therefore, holds that a man need not go out of this world in search of his moral perfection but he should act without indulging into any sort of attachment. By asking a man to renounce the fruit of all actions (*Sarvakarmaphala tyāgam*) (XII. 11), Gita is, as a matter of fact, asking him to test his moral strength in the face of tempting objects. Thus, Anāsakti Yoga of Gita provides ample scope for moral progress. Altruistic individuals who work for the welfare of humanity (*lokasaṁgraha*) and discharge their duties without any extraneous end or profit motive, can determine the direction of social progress themselves. The immoral ones acting for their personal lust or greed, prevent progress in all spheres. In industrial sphere, these morally depraved will misappropriate the product for their personal ends and monopolize productions, resort to profiteering and hoarding. The workers will also try to neglect their job and leave their job badly done, if they lack moral training. In social field, they will manipulate everything to their own advantage and harm the interests of the institution. Even in the field of science, dishonest intellectuals will propagate many false ideologies instead of scientific theories. Gita therefore lays emphasis that moral factors must be made prior to all progress and that the moral grounds should serve as fundamental, on which the edifice of the civilization and the guideline of progress is to be built.

Material basis of Progress examined :

Communism and Anāsakti Yoga, both have a passion for, and faith in progress. But, which of these two would be more conducive in providing some sound basis for the progress ? In his criticism of classical materialism, Marx himself has made scathing attacks on its neglecting the human activity. In attacking classical materialism, Marx deviated so much from the fundamental postulates of materialism that it is hard to put it in that class. Mannheim points out that " historical materialism was materialism only in name, the economic sphere was in the last analysis, a structural inter-relation of mental attitudes."[26] Eminent economists agree that by his economic determinism, Marx did not mean that religion, metaphysics schools of art, ethical ideas and political volitions were reducible to economic motives. For example, Schumpeter tells us that "Marx only tries to unveil the economic conditions which shape them and which account for their rise and fall."[27] Despite Marx's worry to restore the 'active' side in his materialism *vis-a-vis* the old materialism, he could not detach himself from the idea of material forces of production as the determinant of human history. Marx contradicts himself when on the one hand he thought that the 'objectified world' is the cause of man's alienation ; it appears hostile, and negating his humanity. But on the other hand, he was expecting that the same objects of his production would bring him self-confirmation. He was not aware that so long as the sense of possessiveness is not finished, man will remain defiled. If the material factors dominate in life, it would not make any difference whether the object of gratification is held singly or jointly. Anāsakti Yoga tells that one who is free from attachment (*saṅgavarjitaḥ*) is free from enmity to all fellow-beings (*nirvairaḥ*).[28] But such an idea of curing the tendency of man is unknown to the communism. If the private property is all converted into social ownership, the desire to misuse it will still remain. The individual may, then turn against public property too. He may misappropriate, misuse, and waste it. Therefore, Gita stresses that the very craving to possess is to be given up for making man honest.[29] Even at the communist level, man will be in the snare of possessiveness if the attachment is not given up. Thus, without anāsakti, man will not be able to build a sound civilization. Suggesting that emphasis on economic element in human history is unwarranted, Bonar also says : "In asserting that the economic element is the dominant element in history, the scientific socialists commit the same mistake which they blame in Ricardo and older economists."[30]

Admitting that the economic factors are most important in capitalist stage how can one say that the principal force of one age will also be the principal force in every age ? Marx has not provided any plausible ground for that. Moreover, the emphasis on the materialistic conception of human history leads to an apparent paradox in communist theory. The paradox is that the lust for power is to be cured by a counter lust of power, and greed by a counter greed. That is why he had to posit the dictatorship of the proletariat for the moralisation of the dehumanised man.

Similarly, due to his failure to comprehend the fundamental truth of inner life of man, Marx could not suggest, what dynamics will control the libidinal cravings of man (kāma). If sex is repressed by force, it makes a man neurotic or destructive, as Freud has shown.[31] There will, thus be the society of neurotics if instead of sublimating and channelizing the urges, repressive techniques are used by the dictators. It cannot be avoided as the individual problem but its social manifestations will also be highly catastrophic. What havoc sex rivalry can play in the society is a matter that one daily reads in papers. History has even many instances like that of the Helen of Troy, when sex destroyed an entire society.

Communism has no remedies against such an evil passion. This was due to their obsession with economic factors at the cost of other (decisive) factors in human history. Later on Engels had to admit that Marx and he were partly to blame for the fact that the younger Marxist writers were laying undue stress on the economic factor. He clarified the position and said "Marx had to emphasize that main point in opposition to the idealist adversaries who denied it."[32] It means that the economic factor was brought forth only because the idealists were denying its importance. It obviously was not their intention to make it the sole moving factor of human history. Even if the material modes of production are assumed to be the sole determinants of human history, the problem of human progress is not solved. The relevant consideration in this matter is that the development of economic modes of production need not be ident cal to 'economic progress' or the economic welfare.

Here the Marxist theory will face a dilemma. Either Marxists should recognise the priority of the ethical considerations in building up any civilization, or they should admit that their theory is not able to promote social welfare. They do not see that economic welfare is only a part of social welfare and therefore, it need not promote the general social welfare. That is the reason that many economists suspect that behind the undue emphasis on the economic aspect, there are certain ulterior motives. For example, Eric Roll says: "Economic factors as the sole determinants of social change! what remains in the dialectical materialism except a system suited to the casuitics needs of totalitarian politics."[33]

In criticising the theory of materialist foundations of human history, all these above noted thinkers have assumed the fact that man needs some higher and lofty ideals to inspire him on the path of progress. As a matter of fact, this is the standpoint of anāsakti doctrine of Gita that if ethical basis are lacking, civilization cannot stand on firm grounds. Schwitzer rightly points out that "because of the lack of ethico-philosophical foundation, the western civilization has decayed."[34] If experience of decaying West is to be our guide, this mistake should not be repeated. Therefore, he further tells us that "if the ethical foundation is lacking, the civilization collapses even when in other directions creative and intellectual forces of the strongest nature are at work."[35]

Finding a materialist predominance in some epochs of history and that too in a limited society, Marx should not have made it the sole moving factor of history. Man needs inner regeneration and ethical uplift to give desirable orientation to history. Morally strong personalities in every age and in every society exercise their decisive influence on the history, if the society is to be saved from decadence. Like an insignificant blade of grass, it is very easy to be swayed in the current of the events. But the historic entities would rather change the course of human history towards the higher human ideals. For this purpose, they will need great moral strength, which will come from *anāsakti.* Such historic entities will leave trail of glory behind them to be followed by posterity. The society raises them to the level of '*avatāra*' (divine incarnate).

Commenting on Gita's concept of Avatāra, Radhakrishnan is of the opinion that "the avatāra points out the way by which men can rise from their animal to a spiritual mode of existence by providing us with an example of spiritual life."[36] Thus, the moulding influence of moral forces cannot be denied in human history. Apart from this, the economic abundance of communist society will always stand in need of a principle like 'anāsakti' so that the communists may not also misappropriate and misuse the public wealth. The maxim of Gita that with perfectly disciplined mind and abandoning attachment, one is to do his duty (*yogasthaḥ Kuru Kārmāni Saṅgaṁ tyak-tva dhanañjaya*) is a better principle than the principle of leaving the human destiny in the hands of material forces of production. No doubt the economic factors are necessary in the development of a society, but they are not sufficient to explain the whole history of mankind. Marx could not see this subtle difference between 'necessary' and 'sufficient', and he falsely thought that what is 'necessary', is 'sufficient', also. Oxygen is necessary for human existence, but mere 'oxygen' is not sufficient for man's survival. Other factors may also be equally necessary. That is the reason that Gandhi in modern times has deduced his socialism from the moral premises of anāsakti. Laying down the fundamentals of his socialism, he said, "Truth and ahimsā must incarnate in socialism."[37] Emphasis on these factors shows that the moral factors are equally necessary in building the sound basis of civilization.

Reflecting on all these arguments, we reach a conclusion that although the human happiness and man's dignified existence is the aim of both these great philosophies, yet communism has committed the fallacy of exclusive particularity in laying an undue emphasis on economic factor in human history. Against this emphasis, Anāsakti Yoga wants to say that mankind will not become happy by consuming more economic goods. Its welfare and its progress require the non-economic factors. According to Gita, economic prosperity and progress (Śri and Vijaya) will follow from the principle of honest discharge of every individual's allotted task with a sense of anāsakti, and not *vice-versa.*

Environmentalism and Individual's Self-Improvement

The whole question of human progress converges at the point as to whether the development in the economic sphere will mould the human conduct into desirable channels or the morally progressing individuals exercise their moulding influence on history. Marx starts in his theory of economic interpretation of history with the axiom, which *inter alia* says that, "it is not the consciousness of men that determines their being, but on the contrary their social being that determines their consciousness."[38] Such an assertion does not allow any creative role to the mind. This deterministic attitude leaves no place for the moral progress. Whitehead rightly points out that "if you refuse to admit that mind can have for itself any experiences than those provided for it by the body (senses), then all individual moral responsibility is swept away."[39] If the environment is so tight that it determines man's consciousness, then it puts an embargo on his moral strife. Putting man at the mercy of the material modes of production is, in fact, depriving him of his ethical excellence which requires freedom as one of the fundamental postulates.

Although the concept of the material forces of production determining the consciousness of man plays very important role in Marx's whole theory of economic interpretation of history, yet such propositions as 'their being determines their consciousness' have not been logically tested. If by this statement a causal determinism is meant, then a causal relation will have to be found out between the 'being' and 'consciousness' in such a way that 'being' is the cause and 'consciousness' is the 'effect' and that being is an invariable concomitant antecedent of consciousness. The scientific methodology recognizes the methods of Agreement, Difference, Joint Method of Agreement and Difference, Method of concomitant variation and method of Residue;[40] for establishing the causal relationship between two phenomena. But Marx has nowhere pointed out what method he has used to arrive at this universal general proposition which forms the very basis of his historical materialism. If the very assumption is false then invalid conclusions are bound to follow from it.

We are told that this general proposition has been arrived on the basis of evidence provided by history of human civilization. Marx says that the "relics of bygone instrument of labour possess the same importance for the investigation of the extinct forms of society as also fossil bones for the determination of extinct species of animals."[41] Thus the whole process of arriving at this formula, points to the fact that he arrived at his major premises by method of 'simple enumeration' only. This method can point out a 'conjunction' and co-existence of two phenomena but it cannot tell us whether or not there is any 'connection' between them. Therefore, the propositions based on this method have very high degree of probability and error. This logical defect makes the whole system of economic determinism unsound.

From ethical point of view also, such assumptions are highly vulnerable. Such a principle, as this, does not tell why the ideal of communism ought to be strived for. If consciousness reflects only what 'is' there in the existence, then it can tell only what 'is' ; but it cannot tell 'what ought to be'. The facts reflected into human consciousness do not become 'values' and if the existence determines the consciousness, then it would be a value neutral reflection having no ethical significance. The Marxian theory, therefore. will not be able to serve the purpose because in that case the consciousness of a *better* 'existence' in the form of communist society will never be possible. From where this consciousness will come ? For the value judgements, one will have to transcend the factual level. As James Bo ıar puts it, "we can never find the truth of the present conditions in the present itself."[42] However, if we admit that the consciousness can entertain some ideas, which are not there in the present existential conditions, then it will have to be admitted that ideas are not wholly determined by the environments. If our consciousness can entertain the idea of future existence in such a way that our lives are fashioned according to that idea, then the Marxists will have to agree that some ideas are *a priori* and they exercise moulding effect on our existence. Whitehead also suggests many such other areas and says : "The mathematical ideas are *a priori* and independent of any experience. Mill tried to make them empirical but failed."[43] If consciousness can have the *a priori* mathematical ideas without the corresponding existential conditions, why cannot there be certain other valuational ideas, which consciousness can entertain independant of the existence. If it can, then the role of idea in fashioning the human history will have to be recognised. So long as Arjuna is reflecting the moral crisis, his consciousness is determined by the conditions around him and he is describing them to Kṛṣṇa. Arjuna says : "As I look upon these kinsmen, O Kṛṣṇa, my mouth is parched etc."[44] But from such descriptive statements, man cannot feel the necessity to cancel, to transcend or to transform them. This type of dissatisfaction from the present conditions of existence, comes after the ideal is fully apprehended (*naṣṭo mohaḥ smṛtir labdhā tvatprasādān mayācyuta*).[45] It is this 'Ideal Consciousness' that leads Arjuna to determine in what modes he ought to exist. Thus speaking, it is the consciousness of the 'essential' dignity of man, which is not the actual, but 'ideal' that will determine his future mode of existence, not *vice versa*. Thus, the very expression of the discontent with the present social existence and a desire for a higher social existence disproves that the consciousness is determined by existence. Kautsky has tried to defend the Marxist position. Avoiding the fact that it is the consciousness of the communist ideal which impels man to traverse the path towards the goal, he says that "social impulse is at the basis of all morality,"[46] and that since "this social impulse is being constantly modified, the scope of morality expands."[47] But he does not seem to be aware of the implications of what he is saying. He is conveying the idea that social instinct in order to realize itself is trying to search for higher and higher modes of its expression in the material conditions by discarding the lowers. Thus, all the modes of social existence. social relations are the manifestations of this inherent and immanent principle. In that case, this becomes the Hegelian Absolute, which will appear to be a bitter pill to communism. It does not lead to the inference that we should deduce the social consciousness from the material foundations.

Another Marxist, Baax tries to explain the environmental determinism from the point of view of the individual's conduct. Speaking in Marxian terms, he says that "men are aware that their individual lives are not their sole ends, but they are under some higher compulsion."[43] So far as the consciousness that they are not the sole ends is concerned, it may not be contested. But when he says 'under some higher compulsion', the whole moral fervour is lost. For morality, man should *himself* realize that others are also 'ends' and they are not the sole ends. This should be a matter of inner realization not external imposition. This is the requirement of moral obligation. Sartre puts this idea in all the more clear terms. He says : "I am in contradiction with myself if I *will* these values and at the same time say that these impose themselves upon one."[49] Thus speaking, the fundamental postulate of the economic determinism is logically and ethically indefensible.

Individual Self-Improvement

Anticipating all these difficulties arising out of the implication of the proposition that 'existence' determines consciousness, Gita has taken a balanced view. Man is, no doubt, conditioned by the stimuli producing material conditions (*nibadhnanti māhābāho dehe dehīnamavyayam*).[50] Prakṛti keeps the human consciousness bound to its modes, and by ignorance, puruṣa reflects the modification going in prakṛti. But man has the power to transcend it also and improve his conditions for the realization of his essence. Gita says : "when the embodied one transcends these three guṇas, which are born of his contact with the body, he is released.[51] This released consciousness is the locus of values, and of the assertion of man's creative role over material factor. After knowing that one ought to realize his lost human essences, man moulds the environment to suit him for his ideal-realization. Even at the level of his bondage, the role of *puruṣa* is not merely that of reflecting the modes of environment, but by working for his release from bondage, puruṣa modifies the material process according to his moral needs. Thus, at the level of bondage also, an interaction goes on. This type of interaction has now been supported by various thinkers. Titus, for example, says : "Human behaviour is never the result of environmental factors alone, nor the inborn traits alone, but rather of the interaction of the both."[52] The present day Soviet psychologists have also left the idea of one-way determinism. They now uphold to interaction with the social environment. Protonov points out that, "man is not born with a personality but acquires one. The decisive factor in this process is the fact that individual certainly makes one another physically and mentally."[53] This means that man, while being influenced by the social existence around exercises his own transforming influence on others. If this position is recognised, then we shall have to admit that man's consciousness is not always determined by his existence, but very often his existence is moulded by his value-consciousness. This would give enough moral opportunity to the individual for his self-improvement.

In short, man's progress is multi-dimensional. With the help of science and technology, he has conquered the outer world. But under the capitalist mode of production, the machines overpowered him and he became their appendage. The communist transformation will be a great historical achievement on the path of progress, because then he would have gained victory over those machines. However, it has not given any technique to master the inner cravings, the frailties and the passions for material attachment, which can any time drag the whole of human civilization to catastrophe. Anāsakti Yoga recognises the moral necessity that so long as the attitudes are not changed, and till such time as the cravings for material comforts remain, the material means in our hands may be misused, and the social life may be torn with strife. The ruinous contentions in the field of personal glorification, sex rivalry and the political ambitions may play their perilous role and civilization may become the victim of catastrophic conditions. Therefore, the sound and lasting civilization cannot be built merely on economic foundations. They require ethical foundations. The meanings of man's existence, and of his life are not to be searched in the material world or in the forces of production, but in his own ability to transcend them. This moral ability to transcend the material modes is *anāsakti*. Therefore, anāsakti will provide a more sound foundation for human civilization and his progress than the material principle.

Deterrence vs. Corrective Theory

During the course of the progress of civilization, certain elements may cause impediment and by their evil doings, they may pose danger to it, if the society is to progress, such tendencies will have to be arrested.

But how to deal with the anti-social persons ? How much force is necessary for it ? Due to their over-emphasis on the conditioning of man by creating necessary environment, the communist thinkers assume the necessity of the dictatorship of the proletariat as a preparatory stage to communism. During this transitory period of dictatorship, strict iron laws backed by the state power will be implemented. This unscrupulous strictness will be required to hold back the elements that are enemies of progress. The opponents of socialism and of social progress are supposed to be so incorrigible that they deserve to be dealt with unsparingly. The deterrent methods will be needed to punish these individuals. Engels, accordingly advocated the idea that "so long as the proletariat uses the state, it does not use it in the interest of freedom, but in order to hold down its adversaries."[54] Lenin also justified the deterrent theory. He said, "the revolutionary dictatorship of the proletariat is rule won and maintained by use of violence, rule that is *unrestricted by any laws*.[55] This extreme form of deterrence may be expedient from purely political point of view, but our concern is not to see the political expediency of punishment. The question is whether this type of approach has moral exigency ? The advocates of deterrent theory may say that society has the right to protect itself, and it may do so not only by restraining the criminals, but by deterring others also through the threat of painful consequences.[56] But in advocating the unscrupulousness in dealing with the 'adversaries', Marx and his followers seem to have been misguided by a notion that man is invariably inclined to evil, if he is not subjected to strict control.

Great anthropologists like Ashlay Montague counter this distrust "the co-operative forces in man's nature are biologically even more important than the egoistic and destructive forces."[57] It is the tacit denial of this good element in human nature that leads to subscribe to the deterrent theory. Such an approach is morally untenable. According to Mackenzie, "morality founded simply on force is the negation of morality."[58] McIver also expresses his indignation against deterrence thus : "force alone cannot protect the social order."[59] Force can serve only a limited purpose, but it will not allow the feeling of moral responsibility to grow in the man. That is why, that Rashdall comes with a frontal attack on those, who want to make man moral by the use of State power. He says : "This is a fact that no legislation has succeeded on producing a perfectly moral community."[60] He is right in his assertion, because the authoritative coercion destroys the spontaneity and the individuality of the man and makes him morally destitute.

Gita, therefore, repudiates this deterrent approach. No doubt, at one place, Gita will hold an uncompromising attitude of finishing the evil-doers to the last (vināśāya ca duṣkṛtām) (IV. 8). Here the communist attitude and Gita come to agree on one point that wickedness humbled and subdued, even with iron hand, is a healthier moral condition than wickedness successful and triumphant. But this extremist view has been taken by Gita in the context of those evil forces, who drag the whole humanity to war, putting all human values to ransom. The general attitude towards the sinners is reflected in the law of karma. There are various implications, of this, and briefing them, Dr. Dasgupta rightly remarks : "The law of karma is almost universally regarded as an ethical law by which each person was bound to reap the good and evil effects of his deeds."[61] If man gets reward and punishment, heaven and hell, rebirth etc., according to his own deeds, his own merit and demerit, then it follows from it that Gita subscribed to that principle of jurisprudence which upholds that punishment should be commensurate to the crime committed. This is the principle of 'retribution'. The onus is left on the individual to reform himself and get reward by expropriation. The essence of punishment then is not a threat, but to set a stamp of annulment on what has been done. By his efforts, man can improve his lot and in taking this fact into consideration, punishment is the negation of a bad will by the reaction of the social will for good. It is only when a man has rejected his dharma that he is to be punished.

Bradley also suggests the same criterion. He says : "Punishment is punishment only when it is deserved. We pay the penalty because we owe it."[62] Atonement is implied in the law of karma. For this, the society, through the institutions reflecting the conscience of that society, should convey to the criminal its disapproval of the immoral act. Ewing also suggests this method. He says : "Punishment can be regarded 'as a kind of language intended to express moral disapproval."[63] Accordingly, punishment should above all be expression of the righteous indignation of the society, and the onus on the person concerned to correct and rectify his social conduct himself. This is the principle on which democracy can function well.

Judging the comparative moral worth of both these theories, one can come to the conclusion that retributive theory has greater moral value than deterrence. If the punishment is so regulated and inflicted as to be proportionate to the deed of the individual himself, as the law of karma advocates, it will help man make himself better and induce him to abstain from anti-social acts.

References

1. Marx, Engels, Lenin, *On Historical Materialism*, p. 321.
2. Marx, K. and Engels, F., *German Ideology*, pp. 13-15.
3. Engels, F., *Ludwig Feuerbach and End of German Ideology*, p. 58.
4. Marx, K., *Capital*, Vol. I, p. 47; also pp. 94n, 96, 562.
5. Ibid., p. 94.
6. Marx, K., *Capital* (1930), Vol. I, p. 170.
7. Marx, K., *Contribution to Critique of Political Economy*, p. 11.
8. Marx, K. and Engels, F., *Selected Works*, vol. I p. 357.
9. Marx, K., *Contribution to the Critique of Political Economy*, pp. 11-12.
10. Marx, Engels, Lenin, *Historical Materialism*, p. 86.
11. Chesmokov, D. I., *Historical Materialism*, p. 570.

12. Marx, K., *Poverty of Philosophy*, p. 61.
13. Glazerman G. and Kurasanov, G., *Historical Materialism—Basic Problems*, p. 312.
14. Marx, K. and Engels, F., *The Holy Family*, p. 110.
15. Marx, K. and Engels, F., *On Britain*, pp. 405-6.
16. Marx, K., *Early Writings*, p. 166.
17. Marx, K., and Engels, F., *German Ideology*, p. 60.
18. Marx, K., *Selected Writing in Sociology and Social Philosophy* (Trans. Bottomore, T. B. and Maximillian Rubel), p. 38.
19. Berdyaev, N., *The Meaning of History*, p. 87.
20. Spengler, Oswald, *The Decline of the West*, Vol. I, p. 341.
21. *Gita*, IV. 5-9 (sambhavāmi yuge yuge).
22. Radhakrishnan, S., *Hindu View of Life*, p. 73.
23. *Gita*, II. 3 (kṣudraṁ hṛdayadaurbalyaṁ tyaktvottiṣṭha parantapa) ; and IV. 42 (uttiṣṭha bhārata).
24. Mackenzie, J. S., *A Manual of Ethics*, p. 250 ff.
25. Bradley, F. H., *Ethical Studies*, p. 190.
26. Mannheim, Karl, *Ideology and Utopia*, p. 229.
27. Schumpeter, J. A., *Capitalism, Socialism and Democracy*, pp. 10-11.
28. *Gita*, XI. 55.
29. *Gita*, II.55 (prajahāti yadā kāmān sarvwān pārtha manogatān).
30. Bonar, James, Philosophy and Political Economy, p. 343.
31. Freud, S., *Outlines of Psycho-analysis*, p. 85.
32. Marx, K. and Engels F., *Selected Works*, Vol. I, pp. 381-383.
33. Roll Eric, op. cit., p. 255.
34. Schwitzer, Albert, *Civilization and Ethics*, pp. 9-20.
35. Ibid., p. xii.
36. Radhakrishnan, S., *Bhagavadgita*, p. 156.
37. Gandhi, M.K., *Harijan*, 20-7-1947.
38. Marx, Engels, Lenin, *On Historical Materialism*, p. 137.
39. Whitehead, A. N., *Science and the Modern World*, p. 97.
40. Cohen and Nagel, *Logic and Scientific Method*, p. 249 ff.
41. Marx, K., *Capital*, Vol. I, p. 200.
42. Bonar, James, *Philosophy and Political Economy*, p. 355.
43. Whitehead, A.N., *Modes of Thought*, p. 87.
44. *Gita*, I. 28-30.
45. *Gita*, XVIII. 73.
46. Kautsky, Karl, *Ethics and the Materialist Conception of History*, p. 21.
47. Ibid., p. 123.
48. Baax, E.B., *The Ethics of Socialism*, p. 4.
49. Sartre, J.P., op. cit., p. 51.
50. *Gita*, XIV. 5 (*Anāsakti Yoga*).
51. *Gita*, XIV. 20.
52. Titus, H. H., op. cit., p. 49.
53. Portonov, A.A. and Fedotov, D.D., *Psychiatry*, p. 330.
54. Marx K. and Engels, F., *Selected Correspondence*, p. 337.

55. Lenin, V. I., *Selected Works*, Vol. II, p. 365.
56. Ginsberg, Morris, op. cit., p. 182.
57. Montague, Ashlay, *On Being Human*, p. 97.
58. Mackenzie J.S., *An Outline of Social Philosophy*, p. 139.
59. McIver and Page, *Society*, p. 156.
60. Rashdall, H., op. cit., Vol. I., p. 297.
61. Dasgupta, S.N., Indian Idealism, p. 3.
62. Bradley, F.H., *Ethical Studies*, pp. 24-25.
63. Ewing, A. C., *A Study of Punishment*, p. 23 ff.

9

Means and Ends

Means—End Harmony

Our ideals, howsoever high they may be, they remain mere wishful thinking and unrealisable utopia, without adequate institutionalised means to realize them. Gita has categorically asserted this fact in drawing the conclusions of the whole moral discourse. The working together of a spiritual guide in the form of Kṛṣṇa and practical executor like Arjuna, are essential for success and prosperity.[1] Marx too strikes a similar note in his *VIII Thesis on Feuerbach* that "social life is essentially practical. All mysteries, which mislead theory to mysticism, find their rational solution in human practice."[2] In so emphasizing, both these systems want to make their ideals realisable in practical life. The question of means and ends may be put in another way. Can we adopt any means to realize our ideal ? In this case, the problem becomes very difficult to solve. Some would say that end justifies the means—right or wrong, our ideal must be realized. Titus says, "if the evil of means is such that it outweighs any value gained from the act, as a whole, or alternative better means were available, then the ends will not justify the means."[3] However, the question here is not of the justification but of consistency between them. Milne thinks it clearly impossible to separate means from the ends to which it is means.[4] Many a times, it results in utter failure of efforts if we fail to visualise whether the means that we are adopting would or would not be conducive to the end in view. It is a fundamental condition for building any system that its constitutive elements should not be incompatible with each other. We have already seen that some ideal has been placed before the mankind by communism and by Gita. They have also pointed out the way to achieve it, and in the light of that, it becomes easy to judge and evaluate whether there are any inconsistencies in the system itself. If so, where did these great philosophies falter and what were the main factors leading to create these discrepancies. It will also be possible now to examine critically whether or not the institutions suggested *within* their system are in harmony with their ends. It may help us to make assessment if better alternative ways to accomplish the same goals can also be available.

Deontological vs. Teleological Criterion

Some thinkers argue that Gita preaches a doctrine of 'duty for duty's sake', and therefore, in Gita, the question of harmonising the actions with the end does not arise. They try to drag Gita to fall in line with the Kantian formalism. In support of their stand, they quote certain out of context passages like 'to action alone hast thou a right and never at all to its fruits' (II.47), or that 'hold alike pleasure and pain, gain and loss, victory and defeat, and gird up thy loin for the fight so doing thou shalt not incur sin' (II. 38). But they forget that to interpret Gita in terms of Kantian categorical imperative is to miss its very essence. Of course, in Gita, emphasis has been laid on discharging one's obligation without calculating the consequences. But the moral worth of the conduct is not judged intrinsically. Like Kant, Gita has nowhere said that 'good will' will shine by its light. On the contrary, the goal has always been kept insight, and if the action is not leading to that goal, it would be not a right conduct.

Gita posits the goal as Brahma Nirvāṇa or self-realization. Accordingly, the moral worth of action is to be judged in context with this goal. The statement that "goal (*sthānam*) which is achieved (*prāpyate*) by men of renunciation is also reached (*gamyate*) by yogin,[5] points out clearly that there is a goal towards which various paths are leading. In the light of this, the moral imperative is not 'categorical' in Gita, but it is a *conditional.* 'If this, then this'. If you want the realization of this end, then this is *the* path. Without taking into consideration the antecedent, the consequent cannot be affirmed. Thus, all the institutions are to be evaluated from the point of view of the ideal and the worth of any institutional means is not to be judged apart from, and independent of this ideal.

When Kṛṣṇa asks Arjuna to do his duty (*niyataṁ kurukarmatvam*) (III.8) or (*Yogasthaḥ kuru karmāṇi*) (II.48), he was not talking like a de-ontologist, who holds that such and such kind of action would always be right or wrong, no matter what its consequences might be. He simply says that being finite, one cannot calculate all the permutations and combinations of the events to come. Therefore, he should do it according to his station of life. But whether it is right or not will be judged by its tendency to produce certain consequences (*māphaleṣu kadācana*). This is efficacy to lead to the goal.

Similar confusion also prevails about the theory of communism. Popper has charged Marx of adopting the Hegelian theory of 'moral positivism'.[6] Moral positivism asserted that 'there is no moral standard, but the one which existed'. If the social institutions are adapted to the basic material modes of production of a particular age, then they are justified. It comes to mean that, that which is, is reasonable and good. Such conclusions are drawn on the basis of some of the assertions made by Marx. For example, Marx writes, "In so far as the capitalist is a personified capital, he does play a historic role."[7] Here, Marx wants to say that had not the capitalist been there, the humanity would have remained confined to feudalism, and therefore, the capitalist has also done a great service to human history. Therefore, when capitalism is, it is justified. But from this type of pronouncements, it cannot be inferred that Marx kept no ideal in view as a standard, with reference to which he was condemning the worth of the capitalist institutions. Marx conceived of an 'Ideal form of Social Existence', in which man will be able to realize himself. It was from this teleological point of view that Marx judged all the historical epochs and their institutions and pronounced his judgement that they were imperfect and fit only to be transcended. Consequently, in communism, the means have their value only in so far as they are oriented to it. Otherwise, these are to be condemned and rejected. It was on this ground, i.e., measuring the worth of means in context with the ends that Marx rejected the theories of other socialists as Utopian. Thus Marx was also a teleologist, who evaluated every institution in term of the end. The charge of '*positivism*' against Marxist theory is, therefore, unfounded.

Both Gita and communism uphold teleological ethics, and for both of them, the means have their utility only in so far as they help in the realisation of the end, which for both of them is self-actualization and man-realization.

However, there are certain genuine inconsistencies in the communist system, *vis-a-vis*, the Anāsakti Yoga of Gita.

Penchant for Dictatorship in Marxism

The concept of transitory phase of the 'dictatorship of proletariat' is a stigma on the whole communist theory. Marx started his theory with a quest to find out a 'higher type of society', where conditions may be congenial for full and free development of every individual. Weary of the bondage of dehumanised existence, he had a vision of the 'kingdom of freedom'. He had so much passion for freedom that the whole gamut of the communist society, ultimately signified to him a perfect freedom in the life of production. Disgusted with the tortures of authoritarian management of the capitalists production, Marx visualised that even "within the factory life process of society would be carried on by a 'free association of producers' (when state withers away)."[8] This reflects his zeal for freedom although later on Engels realized the practical difficulty of this dreary conception. Engels wrote in 1872, "wanting to abolish *authority* in large scale industries is tantamount to wanting to abolish industry itself."[9]

A question naturally arises that having so much zeal for freedom, was it not paradoxical that Marx needed 'dictatorship of the proletariat' as the necessary post-revolutionary transitional stage in the historical march of humanity towards freedom ? This paradox is the chief weakness of Marxism. Origin wherefrom the weakness crept into Marxism, can be traced to Hegel whom Marx calls his master. The Hegelian concept of the 'inevitable law of history' led him to weave a 'historico-philosophical myth' in order to lessen the birth pangs of impending political development. "It was under the influence of this Hegelian myth that he posited 'dictatorship' to build a bridge between capitalism and full communism."[10] But Marx apparently did not realize that it was self-contradictory to hold that things should be first made worse, before they are made better.

Dictatorship is apparently the Marxian antidote to the fierce competition in the capitalist economy. He thought that to nullify the competition in the system of capitalist production, the system itself was to be negated. Marx, who was embittered with the corruptive influence of capitalist economy, did not realize that the danger painted by Malthus was imaginary and a *laissez faire* system as conceived by the liberal economists of 19th century existed only in their writings. Instead of exposing the fallacies of that system, and criticising it, Marx took it for granted that conditions depicted therein really existed and he started working out on these *a priori* assumptions to end the vagaries of *laissez faire.* The only refuge, that he could seek, was in Hegelian philosophy of state. Mayo points out "despite its greatness, the philosophy of Hegel will remain always one of the best armouries whence weapons may be drawn by any one, who wishes to launch an attack on liberty, reason, individual freedom."[11] Consequently, Marx invoked the Hegelian law that State represents the social conscience and applied it to crush the dismal effects of the gross individualism which was the product of *laissez faire* economy. He did not realize that the remedy that he was suggesting would be more fatal than the disease.

The concept of dictatorship, thus, is the outcome of the misplaced application of Hegelian theory to unverified and imaginary conditions of the economic life of man. Marx impertinently reacted to the empirically false Malthusian society based on perfect competition. Marx was well aware of the fact that the political implications of Hegelian theory of state lead to fascism, which conceives 'State' as the living embodiment of God on earth. He also expressed his disgust against political absolutism in his idea of the withering away of the state. But still, Marx adopted this Hegelian evil to counteract the other evil of the gross individualism of competitive economy. In counteracting one evil with other evil, this exponent of human freedom, as a matter of fact, lost himself into the mighty political currents of Hegelian Absolutism 'devouring the freedom of the individual'. Mayo decries it thus: "If people can be permanently spoiled by too much bad philosophy in their youth, then Marx was a prime example."[12]

As a matter of fact, putting man under state control for his moral improvement raises serious doubts about the historicity of man, who is the sole denominator of social progress. The managerialism of the socialist stage is nothing but the changed label of totalitarianism, which deprives man of all his moral initiative and reduces him to a mere cog and nut into a vast machinery. The evils of totalitarianism cannot be remedied by substituting tweedledee with tweedledum. Repudiating the evil consequences of totalitarian system, Johnson points out, "when the thought and deed of a man are dictated down to the last detail, the richness of life evaporates in the heart of oppression."[13] Consequently, when oppression dominates society, how it can be hoped that the man, who will emerge out of this transitional period, will be morally so strong as to march ahead in the direction of the communism of Marxian concept. If the individuals remain morally crippled, the dictatorship will go on perpetuating and humanity will never be able to enter the 'kingdom of freedom'.

Dictatorship, a Moral and Social Evil:

Another question about the moral basis of this dictatorship can be raised here. What will this dictatorship do during the transition from capitalism to communism. Does Marx mean to say that unless the economic needs of man, and his biological needs are fully satisfied, man should not be allowed to tread the higher paths of life ? Should man first be freed from the clutches of hunger and other economic necessities by increasing production and by training people to take according to their needs ? The dictatorship will realize this end and afterwards the march to the kingdom of freedom will start. But if this is the assumption, then it means that poor, half-fed people, are all immoral and nothing good can be expected from them. It is only when they are well-fed that they can be expected to be moral. This sort of contempt for the masses is the bane of the fascism and its tacit infiltration into communism will be an apparent contradiction. The difficulty lies in the fact that Marx starting with purely humanitarian problems ends in his concept of dictatorship, a purely political solution. When the faith in the effectiveness of social and moral forces is lost, then only man takes recourse to brute political forces for the improvement. Therefore, it cannot be an ethical approach at all. Actually speaking, totalitarianism is a weapon of those who want to kill mind and thought. When state is given unlimited powers, no matter it is the 'workers' state', it becomes a monster, which devours the dignity and freedom of individual. Collectivism is nothing less than a cloak for tyranny. Popper argues "from the point of view of practical politics, it involves the risk of destroying all prospects of reasonable reform and is likely to bring about another tyranny."[14]

From the Marxian writings, nothing is clearly discerned about the contents of this dictatorship. Marx left the idea vague. Ambitious demagogues merrily prospered on the same. If the State is to wither away ultimately, he should have shown it as something superfluous and redundant. The essence of human freedom required that man should have been given the right to criticise where the state authority was weighing heavily on human dignity and human freedom. Such criticism is possible only when the people are morally strong and are guided by principles, not by temptations or fears. It means that it is possible only when societies are working on 'dharma'. Since Marx had no conception of a socio-ethical principle like dharma, he had to jump into a dangerous concept of organised coercion as the technique to turn the lustful and greedy sinners into free communist man. But this is contradictory to suppose that from organised coercion man will become angelic. Mackenzie rightly observes that "law in general can only provide what is best in general."[15] Law cannot take cognisance of the level of micro-conduct.

How the individual disputes will be removed, how men will feel friendly to each other, and how they will go from egoism to altruism, are such problems, which a dictatorship cannot solve. If man is made totally subordinate to a monstrous authority, where the minor affairs of mutual dealing are also controlled by strong police force it will put an end to his moral zeal.

Marx could not visualize that the dictators, like the guardians of Plato, may also become corrupt. Does not Lenin refer to

Plekhanov as a renegade? If there can be one renegade there can be others too. Excessive power and wealth corrupted Plato's guardians. The same may happen with the dictators of proletarian state also. They may declare each other a renegade, infidel, and fight for administrative power. What is the guarantee that personal pride, sex rivalry, ambition and lust for high posts will not plague the dictators, and also the subsequent communist society ?

Supporters of communism suggest that the dictatorship is necessary in order to end the private ownership of the means of production. But, for social control of means of production, is state control necessary ? By making the means of production as State property, i.e., by their nationalization, the *de jure* ownership will, no doubt, end. But possibly the *de facto* ownership will continue with the bureaucrats perpetuating nepotism, and favouritism. Only a moral force like *Anāsakti* can finish the very sense of ownership.

The concept of dictatorship, as presented by Marx, is negative. It is anti-Darwinian, anti-Malthusian, anti-liberalism, and an attitude, which is anti everything is, as Ortega Y Gasset rightly says, a reaction and nothing else.[16] When the mighty dictatorships in the world were breaking under the burden of their own tyranny and under their own sins against human dignity and freedom, the idea of dictatorship presented by Marx, is a reactionary, a retrogressive idea in human history. Marx should better have left the post-capitalist society to decide what type of socio-political order they would build after freeing themselves from the clutches of the forces of greed.

Freedom and Responsibility in Gita

The ideal that Anāsakti Yoga of Gita has put before mankind is the realization of man's lost unity with humanity. The social order suggested by Gita, is realizable through the democratic institutions. In addition, Gita lays emphasis on *svadharma*, and postulates "there is nothing greater for a man than his loyalty to the obligations of his station." Idealism of Gita does not advocate escapism or renunciation of the world but it wants to prepare man for facing the problems of his actual life-situation.

Unlike the communist path of dictatorship, Gita lays down the path of democracy. This is substantiated by a very illustrative allegory in which the personified social system points out, "I am equally present in all beings ; there is none hateful or dear to Me (IX 20). A successful democracy requires that all the demos should be treated as having an equal capability in them to decide their own welfare and, therefore, they may be granted equal right to make their destiny. A guarantee that there will be no regimentation of thought has been provided in Gita. The whole dialogue of Gita goes on in a climate of intellectual freedom. There is no sign of regimentation or authoritative imposition. The author of Gita, in allowing Arjuna to raise queries after queries with a view to understanding everything before accepting it, suggests that the mind of a man is not a box to be packed ruthlessly by some monolithic ideology. Individual has the right to enquire and to raise doubts wherever he wants to differ. Without such a freedom to raise systematic doubts, the truth cannot be known. There is no tendency in Kṛṣṇa to curb the spirit of free enquiry, which is generally found in highly organised, authoritarian systems in their bid to hammer down the differences. From this style, it can be inferred that the freedom to have difference of opinion has been the tone of Gita. The maxim of democracy is also this : "I may not agree to what you say ; but I shall still defend your right to say it." Gita recognizes not only freedom of expression, but also other kinds of freedoms.

(i) *Freedom to Worship* : Gita says : "Whatever form one desires to worship in faith and devotion in that very form I make that faith of his secure.[17] The same freedom of faith according to one's innate character has been assured in verse 3 of Chapter XVII (*Sattvānurūpā sarvasya śraddhā bhavati bhārata*). These verses bring out the wide catholicity of the Gita. Commenting on the verse, Radhakrishnan says that, "Gita does not speak of this or that form of religion. The same God is worshipped by all. The difference of conception and local colouring are due to social adaptation."[18]

The Indian thinkers rightly uphold that infinite wisdom of God is not exhausted in one path. Nor, the knowledge of God can be limited to this book or that scripture. Therefore, the infinite variety of approaches are possible. Gita does not raise any dispute over it, but it leaves the matter of religion to the free choice of man.

(ii) *Freedom to act according to conscience* : The second kind of freedom that is recognised in Gita is the freedom to act according to one's conscience. In the concluding chapter of discourse, after having suggested various courses and having discussed all pros and cons thereof, the final choice has been left to Arjuna. Gita says : 'having reflected on it fully do as you choose' (*Vimṛśyai tadaśeṣeṇa yathecchasi tathā kuru*).[19] This attitude of Gita shows full faith in human reason and in the fact that 'every man is the end' capable to exercise moral choice. None is to impose his own standards on him. Radhakrishnan calls it the principle of free choice. He says : "We are free at any moment to reject or accept the divine call."[20]

(iii) *Freedom to choose one's vocation* : Another freedom recognized in Gita is the freedom to follow one's vocation according to one's own aptitude. This follows logically from the concept of *Svadharma*. Gita says : "Better one's own duty though uninviting, than another's which may be easily performed (*Śreyān svadharmo viguṇaḥ, paradharmāt svanuṣṭhitāt*)."[21] In preceding two verses, emphasis has also been laid on each man performing his duty (*sve sve karmaṇi*) (XVIII. 45) and *Svakarmaṇā*. Taken together all these verses the author of Gita wants to convey that one is expected to discharge his social work according to his *guṇas* (natural abilities). Four freedoms are logically deducible from these maxims. These are : (i) freedom of thought, including that of discussion and of expression of opinion ; (ii) freedom of worship, according to one's own faith ; (iii) freedom of choice in deciding one's course of action, according to one's reason, and (iv) freedom to select one's vocation. These are the fundamental freedoms on which the democratic institutions can function well.

It becomes evident from this discussion that the means through democratic way of life are more in harmony with the ideal of our realization of man's freedom. It, therefore, becomes imperative that if the realm of freedom is to be reached, then we should equally safeguard the freedom of the individual from being encroached by (i) politically ambitious demagogues, and (ii) economic monopolists. Adequate safeguard against these things is provided in the scheme enunciated by Gita. The individuals, who are morally trained and spiritually disciplined, would put a check on all the exploitations and thereby restore the 'essential equality and dignity of man'. For this purpose, Dharma should be made the root of weal and not *vice versa.*

Freedom and Responsibility

Although Gita makes provision for the fundamental freedoms and Marx has also cherished the dream of human freedom in his vision of communism, yet the unbridled freedom may prove a curse. This implies that freedom should be rationally used. According to communism, the community life is the real sphere of personal freedom. Marx said, "In the real community the individuals obtain their freedom in and through their association."[22] This implies that along with freedom the individuals also carry some responsibility towards whole community. However, the difficulty arises when Marx places the onus of making a man responsible in the workers' state. This was due to his implicit distrust in man's ability to reform himself. Gita on the other hand advocates a society of morally disciplined persons, who will adjust themselves to the need of the system. Accordingly, Gita lays emphasis on making the individual fully responsible for all his deeds, instead of shifting the responsibility on State. A sort of mental equilibrium and impartiality is the pre-condition of the proper and righteous use of one's freedom. If the mind is not free from the prejudices and political bias, it cannot appreciate the rival claims of the alternative doctrines and moral values, and therefore, will not allow others to express any difference of opinion. It is, therefore, necessary that in order to be responsible fully, the onus should be left on the individual himself.

Law of Karma goes very deep to the extent of making men responsible not only for their overt acts but also for their intentions. Man is not only responsible for the consequences of his overt actions, but he should be responsible to bear the consequences of his wrongful and unsocial intentions as well.

After having surveyed broadly, the ideals of both Gita and communism and also the institutions they suggest for the realization of these ideals, it can be very well seen that the Anāsakti Yoga of Gita consistently upholds the individual's freedom as sacred and does not like to infringe on it. There is no inconsistency between the ends and means here. From an extra-systematic consideration, one may either reject or accept the system as a whole. For example, one may reject the system merely on the ground that it belongs to a particular religious community etc. But within the system itself, the institutional means and the ideal of self-realization have been consistently woven together. If *Gita* is understood as having the esoteric meanings, the key to which was provided by *Mahābhārata* (*na mānuṣāt śreṣṭhataram*), then many misconceptions are automatically resolved. In his commentary, *Anāsakti Yoga,* Gandhi has interpreted all the 700 verses from the sociological frame of reference and the metaphysical inconsistencies do not crop up proving beyond doubt that it is a coherent system.

In communism, the apparent contradictions have been introduced by their approach of negating the freedom. Their standpoint seems to be that the freedom will cataclasmically follow from the denial of freedom. From where did this error creep into communism which turned it from a lofty ethical doctrine of self-realisation into a political 'ism', to enthral dictatorship? The maincontradictions and inconsistencies in the system of communism. are :—

(a) *Source of egoistic need* : Throughout the system, Marx has harped upon the corruptive influence of egoistic needs, of profit and money. But he was never clear about the source of this egoistic need. He suggested that money itself is the cause of the greed for money and that competition is responsible for the maniacal, the were-wolf hunger for surplus value. Since the source of this egoism was not clear to him, he could never ask himself what would prevent the inhuman force from rising its ugly head again to estrange man from himself on the yonder side of history. Similarly, in finding out the solution, he could not visualize that the egoistic need can be undone by only individual's own moral efforts and the removal of the sense of attachment. This is anāsakti. Had he deeply thought on this point, the real revolution would have been a social revolution for the change of self and not the political revolution. This could not occur to Marx due to the vagueness about the real source of human need for money.

(b) *Dichotomy of appearance and reality* : Marx was unable to overthrow the Hegelian distinction between 'reality' and 'appearance'. In his materialistic conception of history, he simply substituted the terminology and treated them as 'essentials' and 'accidentals'. This led him to believe that in history the forces of production, which are 'essences', go on growing from stage to stage in order to realize themselves whereas the accidents viz., the superstructure of the society, the political and social institutions, which are the 'appearances' of the modes of production, decay. From this description, it appears that the superstructure is the manifestation through which 'the 'essences'. 'the forces of production' are realising themselves. On this consideration, the question of a political revolution will be mere exchange of persons. Unless the economic foundation, i.e., the reality is changed, what is the use of changing the 'superstructure', by a political revolution.

(c) *Political revolution, no solution of egoism* : Can competitive egoism be eliminated once for all by a political revolution ? The material goods in the world are limited in amount and if one part of them is occupied by one individual, even without owning that, it cannot belong to the other, like the possessions of the bit of public property. This will again introduce a spirit of competition as every one will try to occupy the better part, and then under a fear of deprivation, a sense of permanently owning it, may develop in them.

In order, therefore, that the interests may not clash in an ordered community of human beings, there will be two alternatives : either the planned allotment of material resources will be enforced from above by the State, or the individual will relinquish the tendency of luxurious consumption by sacrificing the surplus share for others. Marx advocated the first and therefore had to seek redress in dictatorship. Marx thereby condemned humanity to remain under the yokes of dictatorship for mutual adjustments of their shares and claims. But if he votes for the second alternative, then he would be voting for anāsakti and thereby recognizing that without anāsakti (non-attachment), higher phase of communism cannot be built. This is the great dilemma of Marxism, because both these suggestions would prove fatal to communism.

(d) *Role of 'mental' factors in production* : The whole history, according to Marx, was moved by the forces of production. But he was not clear about the relative role of physical and mental factors in the productive process. How much of the physical factors constitute the 'forces of production', and how far the productive power of man himself is the determinant of the force of production ? This was never made clear by Marx. Due to this confusion, he asserted repeatedly that whatever man is producing or creating is the externalisation of these productive powers in him. Strangely enough sometimes the forces of production are thought of as coal and iron, steam and water and other things external to man and at other times, without open or conscious transition of meaning, the forces of production are conceived as man's power over coal and iron etc., which he manipulates for his ends. This confusion and his assertion that nature is the externalised form of man himself, reduces Marxian materialism to a mere anthropomorphistic idealism. It has turned out to be an incoherent blend of both idealism and materialism.

(e) *Progress not a historical necessity* : Although Marx shared the belief in the law of progress with the progressive industrialists, yet his naive optimism that progress is a historical necessity is a superstition, because everything is possible in human affairs. Fisher rightly points out that "the fact of progress is written plain and large on the page of history, but progress is not a law of nature."[3] We cannot take progress for granted. Marx ignored that the ground gained by one generation may be lost by the next. The contention then that transition from one historical epoch to the other is necessarily progressive and that with the progressive transformation in the modes of production the social superstructure also changes correspondingly is not justified.

(f) *Deductive Incompleteness* : That there will be transition from the lower stage of communism to the higher one, is not proved on the basis of the fundamental postulates and the rules of deduction available in his system. The laws of historical development will not be applicable to the transitory stage or the lower phase of communism. If the only laws operative in history are: (i) the dialectical law of negation, (ii) class struggle, and (iii) laws of economic determinism. Would these operate in the communist stage also? For their operation, the first requirement is that there should develop contradictions in society. But on Marx's own account, the contradictions in the form of class antagonism will not develop at this stage. Then we are told in *Capital* that "when a society has discovered the natural law that determines its own movement even then it can neither overlap the natural phases of its evolution nor shuffle them out of the world by a stroke of pen. But, this much it can do ; it can shorten and lessen its birth pang.[21] Here he wants to tell us that although man cannot avoid or alter the inevitability yet he can curtail the period by revolutionary means. It means that in order to bring change, revolutions will be necessary. But this law also belongs to the realm of history. At the level of lower phase of communism, 'workers' state' will not be overthrown violently. It was on this point that Marx differed sharply from the anarchists and pleaded that state will not be destroyed but it will 'wither away'. It shows that there are no laws of change from the 'dictatorship of proletariat' to the 'higher phase of communism' deducible from Marxian system of postulates. One has been left simply to believe that there will be transition from this lower level, which he, in earlier writings, called 'raw communism' and in later writings as 'socialism' or 'dictatorship of the proletariat' to the full-fledged communism, the realm of freedom. But logical thinking is not based on mere dogmatic assertions.

(g) *Conservatism* : Once communism is achieved, it will be final achievement and the future generation will have nothing to achieve further. To be content with the past achievement, it not only shows the lack of creative adventure, but it is also to be on the road which leads to death. If change is the law of nature, then we may ask the question, what would be the change at communist level. If communism changes into communism, it is no change ; it is conservatism. If communism changes into something other than communism, then that thing being higher, should have been made our ideal. Marx has left these problems unsolved.

Despite his fervour for relieving man from his bondage, Marxian system lacks deductive completeness. If some new set of postulates and axioms is introduced to explain change in the communist society, then they will be redundant. But if new rules of change and new postulates are not introduced to explain the transition from dictatorship to final communism, then the whole system closes at 'Dictatorship' and Marx becomes the harbinger of a new type of political authoritarianism which subordinates the individual freedom to the demands of totalitarian state having its own defects and dangers.

(h) *Confusion about dialectic* : As a matter of fact, the source of this fallacy lies in Marx's confusion about 'dialectic'. He could not be clear as to whether it is a 'conceptual scheme', or 'methodological device' to understand the history, or it was an ontological principle of nature. This confusion stems from Hegelian philosophy. For Hegel, there was no difference between 'Being' and 'knowing'. Though 'materialist', Marx has sided with the Hegelian position that the structure of reality (the real historical process) is identical to the categories of our thought-scheme, and the dialectical modes of understanding history are operative in ontological sphere also. But Marx does not tell us on what ground (unless he is an idealist) he says that ontological reality is following the laws of human understanding. If he means to say that our modes of understanding history, are the modes followed by the historical process, then he is tacitly assuming that the human mind, the mental modes of understanding, gives law to the course of historical process. But if he thinks that dialectic is only a methodology, then other alternative 'conceptual schemes' cannot be ruled out and then it will have to be admitted that Marxian is not the only scheme to interpret human history.

(i) *Negative Description* : A great lapse in this theory is that first of all Marx conceived communism as 'beyond' historical process, where the history will end. But afterwards he started explaining that meta-historical society in terms of the categories which are operative at this historical level. To explain the ultimate, in terms of determinate categories, is to involve into contradictions. Kant also warned of falling into such antinomies if the categories of phenomena are applied to the realm of noumenon. Better he should have left the final state of human existence, unexplained. In this matter, 'Vedāntins' have saved themselves from such mistaken explanations of the 'ultimate' by calling it '*neti neti*'. When Marx said, it will be beyond economics (i.e. beyond the law of Equi-Marginal substitution, because of its being a society of abundance), and beyond politics (state having been withered away) ; and beyond history (the historical law of dialectical contradictions, negation of negation and class struggle not being operative there) he was saying what was legitimate to say that is, that it is not this, it is not that (*neti neti*). But beyond that he should also have followed Vedānta and have finally said 'it is an indeterminate state of existence which has all the room for human creativity and novelty and therefore unexplainable' (*anirvacanīya*).

(j) *Fallacy of unproved premises* : In arriving at his conclusions, Marx has transferred the unproved postulates of one branch illegitimately to the other fields of knowledge. For example, the Malthusian law of inverse proportion between the growth of population and the means of the subsistence, of Ricardo's theory of surplus value and the pessimist school's law of increasing misery of the labour, were such postulates which were never proved in economics even and were used to serve as rationalisation of their *a priori* assumptions there. Such unproved postulates have become the major premises of Marxian system. Such illegitimate combination of economics with sociology makes communism no different from the romantics of that age both in its 'scholastic barrenness' and its 'political repulsiveness'. Marx arrived at the romantic picture of the future human existence (communism) through *a priori* method of transformational criticism, which he applied to Hegelian philosophy of right. After weaving the fabric of communism by '*a priori* method', he then fused economics and sociology together, with a zeal and a passion to overcome the evils of industrial society. This was the application of *a priori* category on the empirical reality as if the ghost of 'Kant was giving law of nature'. The vision may, therefore, be highly fascinating from romantic point of view, but not provable empirically on his own postulates.

(k) *Confusion about 'need'* : The fundamental principle of communism 'to each according to his need' is also self-contradictory. Marx like Mill seems to anticipate an abundance of goods. But needs is still an unqualified word. Will all Epecurian and hedonistic needs be satisfied ? If the satisfaction will be confined merely to the biological needs, man will be no better than an animal. But if the luxuries are also included in the needs that man will satisfy in communist society, then there will be no limit of needs. Gita calls them unsatisfiable needs (*duspūraṇānalena*). Unless man imposes some control over the satisfaction of these needs by himself, there will be an anarchy of consumption. Marxism makes no reference to the much needed self-control. Besides, if man goes on producing in the society of abundance and takes only as much as 'he needs', then the humanity will suffer from another evil, i.e., the evil of anarchy of producing, leading to the luxurious waste of resources.

On the other hand if it means that every one will get everything to satisfy every need, then if it would mean uncontrolled 'consumption', or the utmost gratification of all needs. The gratification unceased further stimulates the fire of passion for gratification (*na jātu kāmaḥ Kāmānāmupabhogena śāmyati haviṣā Kṛṣṇavartmeva bhūya evābhivardhate*) (Manu. II. 94). For a communist the problem will arise that if every one takes according to his own needs as the formula states, then he will be acting only at the level of private self-satisfaction without caring for the happiness of others. Then he will be following the Benthamite calculus of 'each for himself and not for others'. Marx vehemently rejected this type of psychological egoism. But if he adjusts his needs with other 'communist men' with whom he has direct or indirect relation, then what would be the mechanism to measure the needs of others and their satisfaction. On materialist considerations, no solution to this problem can be found except that some political authority should be there to plan the distribution. This authority Marx wanted to wither away. How then the things will be regulated in communist society?

A natural question may be asked that if the state withers away, but the tendencies of *bhoga* (consumption as much as man likes), *lobhu* (acquisition), *rāga* (attachment) etc. remain, no amount of social disapproval can make man really a communist. Either the very tendency will have to be cured or the communist will again fall into all sorts of vices, which he attributed to capitalist as soon as the fear of political authority relaxes. The question may be put more clearly to Marx. Given his society of abundance, what would be the attitude of the communist towards the wealth created by society in abundance ? It will be either of approach or of avoidance. If it is of approach, then the communist may become a victim of lustful megalomania, satyriasis, and will be trying to appropriate the public goods for his private satisfaction. If the attitude is of avoidance, then he may become an ascetic by observing complete 'aparigraha', which Marx would not like to be attributed to his system. The dilemma is fatal to the communist maxim 'to each according to his need'.

As a matter of fact, the main thing, which Marx missed in formulating his so-called fundamental principle of communism, i.e., 'to each according to his need', was that even in the process of satisfying our needs, we shall have to discover certain values—

a standard whether a particular need is worth satisfying or not. The needs of licentiousness to satisfy the baser element and the needs of a productive type will have to be comparatively evaluated and then regulated in hierarchy. In order to determine the worthlessness of a need itself, some higher standard will have to be made the fundamental principle, which may be like this that 'each according to his contribution to the social good, through the discharge of which he is realizing himself'. Thus speaking, the need-oriented principle will have to be abandoned or sublated to some higher scheme of life. But if they adopt some such standard, then this will be the negation of communism itself. From all these difficulties, it becomes evident that communism will be unachievable through the Marxian methods, because unless we transcend, the limits of our phenomenal nature, which is the source of our individualised existence, and recover a greater consciousness by having a rational apprehension of the social system, we shall always be a prey to the finite fascinations.

Communism will stand in need of introducing some principle through which all temptations are to be avoided and man is prepared for the honest discharge of his social obligations. Searching for the solution of the evils of greed and acquisitive tendencies in the material means and in the formula of 'each according to his needs, is a useless adventure. The temptations for power, for money, for fame are such factors, which may plague the communist society also, and any unscrupulous person may misuse all public property at his disposal to satisfy his ambition for power. That is why that the Indian systems lay emphasis on 'anāsakti' as the regulative force to keep individual within his legitimate limits. What is the alternative to that in communist society ? To overcome all these difficulties, Lenin formulated a subsidiary rule of the pre-communist socialist society. He suggested that "until the higher phase of communism arrives, the socialists demand the 'strictest control' over the measure of labour and the *measure of consumption*."[25] But the formula of 'the control over the measures of consumption' will change the very basic characteristic of communism. In asking the society to control their consumption, Lenin is, as a matter of fact, preaching the lesson of pratyāhāra, which means withdrawal of senses from the objects of consumption, like a tortoise withdrawing its organs.

Lenin did not know that by introducing this measure, he was converting communism into the doctrine of 'anāsakti' i.e., the anāsakti yoga.

From the above discussion, it may, therefore, be concluded that the ethical and philosophical aspects of communism is of great value for humanity but its political and economic solutions crumble under the burden of its own inherent contradictions.

References

1. *Gita*, XVIII.78.
2. Marx, Engels, Lenin, *On Historical Materialism*, p. 13.
3. Titus, H. H., op. cit., p. 72.
4. Milne, A. J. M., op. cit., p. 25.
5. *Gita*, V. 5.
6. Popper, K. R., *The Open Society and Its Enemies*, Vol. II, p. 206.
7. Marx, K., *Capital*, p. 650.
8. Marx, K., *Capital*, p. 54.
9. Marx, K. and Engels, F., *Selected Works*, Vol. II, p. 637.
10. Mayo, H.B., *An Introduction to Marxist Theory*, p. 95.
11. Mayo, H.B., op. cit., p. 5.
12. Ibid., pp. 5-6.
13. Johnson, A.H., *Whitehead's Philosophy of Civilization*, p. 12.
14. Popper, K.R., op. cit., p. 151.
15. Mackenzie, J.S., *Outlines of Social Philosophy*, p. 159.
16. Ortega Y. Gasset, *Treasure of Philosophy*, p. 877.
17. *Gita*, VII. 21 (*Anāsakti Yoga* bhāṣya).
18. Radhakrishnan, S., *Bhagavadgītā*, pp. 158-159.
19. *Gita*, XVIII. 63.
20. Radhakrishnan, S., *Bhagavadgītā*, p. 375.
21. *Gita*, XVIII. 47.
22. Marx, Engels, Lenin, *On Historical Materialism*, p. 62.
23. Fisher, H.A.L., *History of Europe* (1935), Preface to Vol. I, p. vii.
24. Marx, K., *Capital*, p. 864.
25. Marx, Engels, Lenin, *On Historical Materialism*, p. 574.

10

The Confluence and the Divergence

A penetrating eye into the deliberations and the fundamentals of these two systems will see that there are many issues on which both these great philosophies converge to meet.

Jiva Brahman and Prakriti

Gita and communism join hands to the extent that some of the knotty problems of Gita can be well grasped and understood if they are read through the communist viewpoint. One of the foremost problems is that of the relation of Jīva and Brahman. In Gita, Arjuna stands in direct dialogue with Kṛṣṇa and he is told that jīva is the *aṁśa* of Brahman, but following a particular discipline, he can seek communion with Brahman. This problem of relating the Jīva and Brahman was resolved by the Vedāntins by drawing a non-difference between them (*jivo brahmaiva nā paraḥ*). But in order to justify their position, they had to posit a mysterious principle of māyā, which piled more mystery than solving it. In order to end the hellish torment of the alienated existence, this type of the identity was necessary.

Various commentators have tried to put forth various mystifying solutions to resolve the problem of realizing the identity of Jīva and Brahman from various points, but still the mystery remained as it is. This problem would have been solved, had it been resolved through the method of 'transformational criticism', suggested by Feuerbach and used by Marx. In that case, instead of fixing the gaze upon any extra-terrestrial, trans-empirical deity, as the object of realization, man is required to lavish his love upon 'Man'—the love of *other* man—love of humanity in order to establish this relation in practical life. By making Kṛṣṇa a concrete human being, Gita wants to say that real dialogue between man and the Brahman is not a 'monologue in solipsism' but a dialogue between a real 'I' and real 'Thou', both manifestations of humanity. In Vedānta also 'tattvamasi' (you are also that) is the necessary condition for establishing such a real dialogue.

Marx, in accepting the position of Feuerbach, has further resolved the problem. Applying Marxian solution to vedānta, it may be said that the sense of 'otherness' (dvaita) can be resolved if others are also considered as Brahman. How much similarity is there in their views, can be judged from a representative passage of Feuerbach on which the concept of communism was initially founded by Marx. Feuerbach says:

> "The being of man is given only in communion, in unity of man with man. Man for himself is a man in ordinary sense ; man in communion with man, the unity of I and Thou is God."[1]

This principle of I-Thou communion, given by Feuerbach was the concept of 'Communal man', the communist being, as adopted by Marx from him. Gita, in establishing the real dialogue between Arjuna and Kṛṣṇa, wants to convey the same thing that by recovering the lost unity of I-Thou (*yuñjate yogamātmanaḥ*) (VI. 19), one can achieve communion with Brahman (*brahma saṁsparśam*) (VI. 28). This suggests that the realization of a dialogue between I-ness (*aham brahmāsmi*) and Thou-ness (*tattvamasi*) is the process of acquiring the divinity. It also means that if a man asserts 'I am Brahman' he might, in some cases, be expressing the schizophrenic delusion of grandeur and one may doubt his divinity ; but as soon as he asserts that others are also brahman, he becomes divine. Thus the key to understand the knotty problem of divine dialogues, can be found if these passages are read through the binoculars of communism.

Nature and Pṛakṛti :

The dual type of prakṛti is another problem raised in Gita, which brings it very close to communist doctrine. In seventh chapter, Gita speaks of parā (the higher) and aparā (the lower) prakṛti (*apareyami tastvanyāṁ prakṛtiṁ viddhi me parām*).[2] Radhakrishnan calls them the 'unmanifested nature' and 'manifested nature'.[3] But this idea that one prakṛti is created by Brahman while the other is not, does not make the interpretation clear. However, the concept becomes more clear if this problem is seen through the lenses of communism. In explaining the process of self-development of human species, Marx has also used the concept of the two types of *nature*. He conceived man as essentially a producer. Marx pointed out that "in producing the real objects, a man-made 'anthropological nature' or 'nature produced by history', is superimposed over the primeval nature or sensuous external world."[4] How much similarity is there between this view and the concept of 'Parā' and 'Aparā' prakṛti, becomes quite obvious. The only difference is that Gita does not use the concept of superimposition (*adhyāropaṇa*), which is an idea used by the Vedāntins.

Theory and Practice :

Apart from various such similarities on which both these systems show their agreement, they both have a firm conviction in the practical approach to the problems of human alienation. Gita starts with the assertion that dharmakṣetra is kurukṣetra, the battle field of life. The world is dharmakṣetra, the battleground for moral endeavours. The aim of Gita does not appear to be to teach a theory but to enforce practice by bringing the moral agent to the actual life-situation. It wants to convey that we cannot separate in theory what is not separable in life. Otherwise, we shall be committing, in Whitehead's terminology, 'the fallacy of misplaced concreteness'. In the similar voice. Marx in VIII Thesis on Feuerbach says ; 'all social life is practical'. He had a firm belief that all such theoretical questions which make the theoretical schemes mystifying, find their solution in practical life. Similar agreement of views is noticed when Marx says : "the proletariat finds its spiritual weapon in philosophy, the philosophy finds its material weapon in proletariat."[5] Here he is expressing exactly the same idea, which is conveyed in Gita that is that where Kṛṣṇa finds his material weapon in Arjuna and Arjuna finds his spiritual weapon in Kṛṣṇa (*Yatra yogeśvraḥ Kṛṣṇo yatra pārtho dhanurdharaḥ*),[6] the success is guaranteed.

Condemnation of Profit Motive :

However, the most striking similarity is found in their approach to condemn the forces of greed, as the ardent enemy of man. Gita says that lust is the eternal enemy (*nitya vairinā*) of wise man.[7] It says further that craving (*tṛṣṇā*) and attachment (*saṅga*) are great bondage.[8] Explaining the dynamics of human fall, Gita points out that from attachment to material things starts the downfall of man (*saṅgāt saṁjāyate kāmaḥ, kāmāt krodha' bhijāyate*).[9] There are numerous other verses, which condemn the sense of private ownership (*māmakaḥ*), greed (*lobha*) etc. Marx is no less vehement in condemning the forces of greed and private property. He also wants to stress that enemy of human self-realization is egoistic need, the desire to own and possess things. Condemning the evil effects of private ownership, Marx says : "Private property has made us so stupid and one-sided that an object is ours only when we have it, when it exists for us as capital or when we possess it directly."[10] In an elaborate criticism of '*capital*' it has already been seen that for Marx, the only wheel that sets the capitalist economy in motion are greed, the profit motive and war among greedy. It means that both are equally vocal in treating greed and profit motive as the enemies of mankind.

Attitude towards Capitalists :

There is another important point on which Anāsakti Yoga of Gita shows marked similarity with communism. This is in its denunciation of capitalism. Anāsakti Yoga asserts that "these depraved souls of feeble understanding and fierce deeds come forth as the enemies of the world to destroy it" (XVI. 9). Describing the characteristic of these 'enemies of the world', Gita points out that they have insatiable lust (*kāmam āśritya duṣpūram*) (XVI. 10), making indulgence as their sole goal (*kāmopabhogaparamā*) (XVI. 11), and they seek unlawfully to amass wealth for the satisfaction of their appetites (*anyāyenārthasañcayān*) (XVI. 12). In subsequent verses, Gita pronounced their doom, that into foul hell they fall. Similar denunciatory and condemnatory attitude has been expressed by Marx against the capitalists, who possess more or less the same characteristic as given in Gita. The capitalist of Marxian concept is 'personified capital' whose sole motto is acquisitiveness. Marx himself writes : "Capital has but a single life urge, the urge to self-expansion."[11] Throughout his writings, Marx has denounced the capitalist as the embodiment of greed. Marx makes his indignation all the more clear in another passage wherein he says : "Only in so far as the increasing appropriation of abstract wealth is the sole motive of his operations, does he function, as a *capitalist*."[12] Thus, the attitude of indignation towards capitalists reflects the similarity of their views.

Moral Grounds of Revolution :

Yet another similarity is found in their views relating to the moral ground in revolution. Marx thinks that it is when moral norms are flouted that a revolution becomes necessary. He writes : "In its blind unbridled passion, its werewolf hunger for surplus labour, capitalist is not content to overstep the *moral* restrictions upon the length of working day."[13] Calling it a *moral* degeneration of the conditions of the capitalist system of production and then asking the worker to overthrow it, Marx is voicing the feeling that the revolution is a moral necessity to finish immoral conditions of existence. This idea finds its expression in Gita also. It is said therein that whenever there is decline of dharma, the social forces manifest themselves to destroy the evil-minded persons, who drag humanity to degenerative conditions.[14] It means that for both of them, it is the moral decline that needs be cancelled. Thus, the revolution for both of them is to finish moral decline and to establish the human values.

Faith in Ultimate Victory :

At this juncture, it should also be noted that the whole explanation which Marx has furnished in *Capital* and the motto behind the *Communist Manifesto* shows that his paramount task was to make the good forces more fully conscious of the nature and condition of the conflict. He wanted to make them more clearly aware of the total evilness of evil forces of capitalism and to make them cognizant of the hopelessness of any compromise solution in terms of justice. In repudiating the French socialists, who harped upon the idea of distributive justice, he wanted everybody to understand that there is no substitute for the unconditional victory of the good forces and the total defeat of the evil. It was his firm confidence and faith in the victory of goodness over evil, that he ended his manifesto with the assertion that "its (bourgeois) fall and the victory of the proletariat are equally inevitable."[15] It is the main theme presented in Gita also. The War of Mahābhārata was finally declared after leaving all hopes of compromise with the forces of evil. By driving the chariot in between the two forces (*Senayorubhayor madhye*) (I. 24), the purpose of Gita also was the same that it wanted to make the moral agent aware of the total evilness of the evil and also of the conditions of conflict. Gita starts with a hope of victory of the forces of good over the forces of evil. The use of word 'sañjaya' in the opening verse (*kim akurvata sañjaya*) (I. 1) is very significant. It signifies *sam* or 'samyak' and jaya, i.e., rightful victory. Gita also declaims in the end like the *manifesto* '*tatra śrīr vijaya bhūtir dhruvā nītirmatir mama*",[16] meaning thereby that 'fortune', victory, prosperity and morality are sure to be on the side of the forces of good against the forces of evil'. This shows the similarity of the views of both.

Criticism of Profit Motive :

Gita and communism have got another common ground to stand. In the philosophy of Gita, the concept of niṣkāma karma is clearly indicative of the fact that if a man is doing his task without the hedonistic and profit motives, then he will be released from bondage. One who, while living within this world of objects, discharges his duty with devotion, and not under the pressure of ulterior motives (kāmanā) is the ideal man of Gita. The same idea has also been conveyed in the doctrine of communism, which comes to uphold that "man differs from the lower animal in that he is free conscious producer, who could create things even if there were no pressure upon him to produce in order to survive."[17] From this statement, it is evident that compulsion to produce the means of subsistance in order to satisfy the hedonistic ends is an expression of his alienation. But if he produces to express his essence as a 'productive being', a producer, then such production is not the source of alienation, because a carpenter might derive creative satisfaction and a personal sense of fulfilment from the carpentry by which he lives. Gita also says that in so doing his work, a man does not fall into the bondage of karma, his karma will not bind him because he is discharging his work not for profit, but for the sense of fulfilment (saṁsiddhi) that is that with a sense that it is his *svadharma*.

The Proletariat :

We have already seen that while introducing the concept of proletariat with its revolutionary tendency to abolish itself *per se* by the socialisation of private property, Marx saw a mighty manifestation of human self-alienation and the urge to transcend it. His belief was that proletariat is the supreme expression of the alienated man. Consequently, in order to end self-estrangement, communism inspires the dehumanised man to revolt against his dehumanisation. This very idea finds its expression in Gita when Arjuna faces the forces of lust and greed and becomes despondent. Kṛṣṇa calls this condition of recurring predicament of man unsuited to the nobles (*anāryajuṣṭam*) and degenerative (*akīrtikaram*).[18] Calling him to shed his faint-heartedness and his tendency to reconcile with the present state of degenerated existence, Kṛṣṇa also inspires him to revolt against those conditions and fight them to finish.[19] To inspire a man in moral crisis to rise against the dehumanising conditions and thereby converting the dehumanized men into true proletariat is the theme on which they both agree.

Concept of Real Freedom :

Both Marx and Gita agree that it is the freedom from greed that leads to real freedom. Gita tells that those, who are freed from pride and delusion, who have conquered the evil of attachment, go to the eternal state of existence.[20] Marx also joins this voice in his various pronouncements. It may be recalled that the pervasive theme of the doctrine of Marx was the anguish of servitude and the quest for liberation from it. But this servitude was a bondage of man to the forces of acquisitiveness. Summarizing the communist standpoint, Prof. Tucker has suggested that the emancipation of labour meant the release of the creative powers of man from the servitude to greed.[21]

And again the end to be realized by both is also the same, viz., self-realization. Gita names it Brahma-Nirvāṇa and Marx called it man's returning to himself duly socialized. The words may be different but they both express the urge of a man to become one with the totality of mankind. Marx showed the path of ending the dehumanised existence, in his doctrine of world-revolution and Gita called Arjuna to fight against the existing conditions to gain glory (*uttiṣṭha yaśo labhasva*) (XI. 33).

(a) Many other striking similarities of the views are clearly discernible in Gita and communism. The scene in *Das Capital* is that of the conflicts, which make man weary of his present existence and in Gita also the conflict of life has been the opening theme. Both, therefore, recognise that since the present state of existence is full of conflicts and miseries, it must be transcended to gain ideal form of existence in future. For both of them, the discontent with the present existence, is the lever for moral regeneration ; (b) Communism and Gita both emphasize time and again that man becomes dignified by work only. The difference is only of terminology. Marx has called it 'Productive Activity', and Gita calls it *Karma*; (c) Again, both are teleological systems and the means for them have value only if they are conducive to end. Actions not leading to liberation and self-realization are useless; (d) Both are concerned with the problem of human misery and both agree on this important point that behind the apparent crisis, there is real moral *crisis*, the predicament of alienation; (e) Both agree on this point that wars are the outcome of perverse conditions. Gita says: 'war is dear to the evil minded (*durbuddhi*) Duryodhana' and Marx upholds that wars are symptomatic of the perverse capitalist society; (f) Both are the representatives of great cultural traditions. Gita has in its background the whole Indian culture whereas behind the philosophy of communism the great traditions of German culture are clearly discernible.

Probable Impact of Gita on Marx :

Finding out so much similarity of views between the fundamental and major issues, some enthusiastic persons may be tempted to rush to the conclusion that Marx was somehow influenced by the teachings of the Gita. Such inference is sustainable on the basis of some available evidences. Many Indologists in India and in Germany have pointed out several common things in Indian and

German philosophy and it may be said that Marx has incorporated those common elements into his communism. But a more reliable testimony is available to substantiate that Marx might have been influenced by the teachings of the Gita. A learned German Professor of Sanskrit, August Wilheim von Schlegel edited *Gita* in German language in 1823 (5 years after the birth of Marx). This German edition fascinated Prof. Humboldt so much that he exclaimed that "this episode of Mahābhārata was the most beautiful, nay perhaps the only true philosophical poem, which all the literature known to us can show."

As Dr. Radhakrishnan brought out, this is recorded in the proceedings of the Academy of Berlin 1825-26.[22] It is evident from it that when Marx was still a student, Gita was held in German philosophical circles with such high esteem. It is, therefore, natural that Marx would have also come across this 'spiritual treasure of India' (as it was called in the then German philosophical circles). At that time, Marx was facing the problem of putting limits on the extremities of Pan-logism of Hegel, which was the overgrowth of abstract intellectualism. He also wanted to cut the materialism of the Feuerbach to size which had swallowed the creative and active role of man in making the history. It may be pointed out by these enthusiast scholars that solution was already available in Gita, which on the one hand, repudiated such over-intellectualism, which makes man withdraw from the practical life in the ivory towers, and on the other, the Lokāyata materialism, which treats man worse than a consumptive machine. This ready-made solution might have served him as the key to weave the basic theme of communism, which checks the vagaries of both. After finding out this great synthesis, the new theory would have been used as a weapon against the corruptive influences of the industrialised civilization.

We have already seen that Western civilization is inimical to communism and to Indian culture both, and such inferences might be justified on this ground. But one may not agree to such far reaching speculations. Marx has shown his indebtedness to so many thinkers from whom he drew inspiration but, however, surprising it may appear, it is a fact that despite so much reverence shown to Gita in German circles, he has not mentioned to have ever gone across this translated version of Gita. In the light of

Marx's own testimony, we may, therefore, say that Marx did not receive any direct inspiration from Gita. The similarity may be due to the zeal which both these systems had and also due to the common element in German culture from which Marx drew impression for the amelioration of human misery and for relieving him from the vagaries of the dialectical and dehumanised existence.

If the similarities are many, then there are various points on which the systems differ sharply.

(i) First difference comes on the point of determinism of the conscious by existence. Communism subscribes to the theory of double causation. On the one hand, the previous events (the antecedent conditions of the previous historical stage) determine the consequent ones, through the law of transformation of the quality into quantity. On the other hand, man is determined not only by these antecedents causation, but also by the present economic 'Modes of Production'. As Marx said, "Men are the producers of their conceptions, ideas etc.—real active men as they are, conditioned by a definite development of their productive forces."[23] Here comes the point of the divergence of their views because what communism wants to say here is that the human behaviour is determined both at macro as well as micro levels, and by saying so, it does not leave enough ground for making man morally better. In communism, the emphasis is centred on building up a tight type of economic base. It is the conviction of Marxism that by changing the modes of production, man's consciousness will also be changed. But to Gita, all this comes to mean that the dignity of man is dependent on material modes and his destiny is fashioned by the machines as well as by the process as to how these machines are operated. Man definitely has a greater dignity than the machines, and if his dignity is subordinated to machines by saying that the means of production determine his social relations, it will be an unfortunate solution. By asking a man to be *guṇātīta*, i.e., rising above the determinism of the material factors (prakṛti), Gita safeguards the immense dignity of man from being swallowed by the means of production.

(ii) They both differ sharply on the law of Karma also. While emphasizing the fact that man cannot escape the responsibility of his action, Gita does not make the personality of a man merely a chance product of the environment; no does it put any embargo that unless the environmental conditions are suitable, man cannot rise high in life on axiological plane. By shifting the responsibility on history, communism assumes that we can reap where we have not sown, because according to them the ends are already contained in the historical process. Instead of condemning others for our lot, the rational attitude has been adopted by Gita, which emphasizes the supreme responsibility of man for his own actions. Assuring man that his endeavours do not end in mere fiasco, Anāsakti Yoga of Gita tells that: "here no effort undertaken is lost, no disaster befalls. Even a little of this righteous course delivers one from great fear."[24] But communism will say that individual efforts are useless so long as the historical forces are working against his lot. In this way, communism subscribes to a theory of history to which Karl Popper calls 'the conspiracy theory'.[25] According to the implications of this theory whatever happens in the society (including exploitations, misappropriations, etc.) is the result of the direct design by some powerful super-human historical forces.

It appears that Marx has secularised the religious superstition of the Greeks. In Greek mythology, the Homeric gods were believed to have conspired against men, especially in the history of Trojan war. It is on the basis of this conspiracy theory that Marx seems to have entered into a counter-conspiracy against the non-existing conspirators. Anāsakti Yoga, therefore, differs from him and holds that men themselves are responsible for their debased conditions. Thus speaking, Anāsakti Yoga wants to save man from paranoic delusions that all environment and society is hostile to him. Rather it wants to make him so confident that he himself can win his happiness or hellish torment by his own individual or collective efforts.

(iii) Yet there is another point where these two dons do not agree. Marx started negatively and his whole *Capital* is a critical estimate of the miseries and sorrows of man under capitalist economy. But by this negative criticism of the opponent, his own premises is not proved. He seems to have committed the fallacy of '*Ignoratio Elanchi*', because merely by demolishing the opponent's system, one's own is not automatically proved. The communism is said to have risen in opposition to capitalism. But this opposition between the capitalism and the communism may be 'contrary opposition', and in contrary opposition, both the statements may be equally false. When Marx himself upheld that capitalist is 'greed incarnate', then the answer to capitalism, a theory of greed (āsakti) will be anāsakti and the negation of profit-seeking (kāmya karma) would be niṣkāma karma and not communism. Therefore, the alternative of communism, *vis-a-vis*, capitalism need be adequately tested. May it be, that comparatively communism may not prove an alternative better than anāsakti.

As a matter of fact, materialism in whatever form it may be, cannot be an answer to materialism. Definitely, it must be something non-materialism. Thus speaking, communism is not a logical negation of materialism. If it is a substitute for capitalism, it should first allow its own premises to be empirically and scientifically tested. Mises says that "by means of sophistry, it has prevented the scientific treatment of the sociological problems and has poisoned the intellectual atmosphere of our times."[26] Communism protects itself against all unwelcome criticism by unmasking their critic as a 'bourgeois'. Marx and Engels never tried to refute their opponents with plausible and convincing arguments. But hurling of abuses is neither a logical method of proving one's own case, nor of refuting the other. From purely logical point of view, Anāsakti Yoga is the valid logical negation of the philosophy of āsakti

(iv) Out of various other vital issues, Gita does not see eye to eye with communism on the problems of the stratification of the society. Communism is emphatic on a classless society. But this is a vague concept about the community-structure and institutional arrangement of post-historic society. One may pertinently ask, will it be a society of 'jacks of all and masters of none' ? If not, then some professionally specialized groups will always be there. Anāsakti Yoga, therefore, differs in opinion and gives a clear-cut four-fold varṇa vyavasthā, according to which society will need the people excelling in knowledge (Brāhmaṇa), excelling and specialising in productive techniques including managements of distribution (vaiśya), well-trained defence personnel to save the society from aggression (kṣatrīya) and the non-specialised workers (śudras).

(v) 'What type of State administration will be needed by the society ?' is also a point of sharp difference between the two. Marx has started with an assumption that the environment determines the consciousness of man, and therefore, they have led to the conclusion that if environment is perfectly controlled, and moulded, the individuals will also be moulded accordingly. Here Marx is tacitly voicing the Aristotelian view of State as a moral agency and its function is to make man moral. Therefore, he emphasized that the dictatorship of proletariat will prepare man to enter the realm of freedom. Marx also holds that when men start 'working according to their ability and taking according to their needs'. State will not be needed ; it will wither away. Till then, State works for making them into 'communist men'.

Gita does not agree to such argumentation, because putting the responsibility of making men moral, in the workers' State or the dictatorship of the proletariat, will make them moral escapists and moral destitutes. Gita, therefore, starts from the other side, i.e., from making the people, the demos, morally strong and training them in keeping the principles above personalities. Thus, they would themselves decide their own forms of government, as to whether it is parliamentary or presidential or representative or any other form of democracy. Writing the fate of the future generation by prescribing the dictatorship, is to show distrust in the future generation. Anāsakti Yoga advocates that self-discipline comes from a moral training of the individual. But on Marxist account, it is vain to hope that circumstances may be improved by improving man ; communism will again insist that men will be better if the system in which they live is made better.

(vi) On the question of the retaining of State, Gita too differs with Marx. Gita has recognised the freedom (i) of choice, (ii) of worship, and (iii) of acting according to one's conscience, and (iv) select one's vocation. The self-disciplined people of Gita's conception will resist any bid of the state to erode these four fundamental freedoms, and it is immaterial whether the State remains or withers away. If the masses are enlightened, the State will not be able to deprive man of richness of life and his creative freedom. Thus, against the proposed concept of 'dictatorship', Gita places the alternative of tbe 'democracy' of the morally strong people.

(vii) There is another main issue on which the opinion of these two systems differ. Communism upholds that economic emancipation will bring real happiness to men and therefore they emphasize on this aspect only. "Under communism", Afanasyev writes "man will not be burdened with the material worries, which so often take up so much of his time. All his needs will be fully satisfied."[27] By such monistic explanations Marx, as he himself admits it in his own writings, wanted to remain attached to the philosophy of clinging to the material goods. He said, "Lacking any material basis and resting on a purely theoretical foundation, it would be a mere freak and would end in nothing more than a monastic economy."[28] But this assertion does not appear to be correct.

Gita would put the alternative concept of four-fold *puruṣārtha*, including *dharma*, *artha*, and *kāma* in it. This implies that economic prosperity would flow from dharma (if every one discharges his social obligations honestly) and not *vice-versa*. The corollary of Marxian standpoint is that instead of positing a social force like 'dharma', as the basis of human progress, Marx retains the same economic factors, which he himself wanted to transcend. The emphasis on the economic factor seems to be the ramnant of Hegelianism, which recognised the historical beneficence of moral evil. Engels brings forth this point thus, "with Hegel, evil is the form in which the motive force of historical development presents itself."[29] This pronouncement may have two-fold meanings : (i) It may mean that each new advance necessarily appears as a sacrilege against the things hallowed by society in the form of its rituals and customs, and (ii) it may also imply that it is precisely the wicked passion of man, his greed and lust for power, which gives rise to class antagonism and thereby serves as a lever of historical development. Marx makes use of Hegelian aphorism in both its meanings but more explicitly it is the second meaning which has been made use by Marx. It shows that communism tacitly retained the same economic factor as the basis of historical progress, which it considers the source of evil under capitalist economy.

Gita with the idea of *Dharma*, *artha* and *kāma*, comes forward with a more ethical approach that it is not evil but the perpetuation of Dharma, which is the moving force behind the history of human aspirations and human motivations. The difficulty with communism lies in their not discerning the very obvious, that is, that the satisfaction of economic needs may be a necessary factor, but it is not sufficient. Marx could not understand this simple logic that what is '*necessary*' need not be '*sufficient*' also, and therefore, instead of giving a hierarchy of motives, he confined his whole theory to monistic explanation, which reduces his whole system to the philosophy of 'eating'. Accordingly, Gita would point out that by being well-fed, man does not become socially responsible and morally excellent.

In Gita's theory of puruṣārtha, there is a methodology through which relative satisfaction of all the motives is derived. With psycho-biological satisfaction, it also regulates the whole being of man. Therefore, the starting point is the regulative principle of dharma. While communism stops at the determining influence of economic factors, Gita will say that the moral factors exert a far-reaching influence upon the course of human history. In the absence of dharma, it is not clear what principle will save the society of "well-fed persons" from disintegration due to their rivalries in seeking favoured jobs, and satisfying their personal ambitions and passions. It may be admitted that spiritual values can blossom only where the elementary biological values are attained. Admitted also that the creative faculties should not be allowed to be crushed under the burden of economic worries, so that creative section of society may devote itself to the creation of new horizons of human welfare. It is also true that the cultural form of a higher kind can grow only in a soil of prosperity and welfare of certain grade. But this is not the axiological dependence. Hartmann also substantiates this "that the biological are only the ontological pre-supposition of the spiritual—their existence is only a means."[30] Therefore, Gita's standpoint, *vis-a-vis*, communism is that dharma should be at the base of social progress and civilization. Schwitzer echoes similar conviction when he says "the conception of civilization is pre-eminently ethical."[31] It appears that the modern communist thinkers have started realizing this lacuna in their system.

For example, a modern communist thinker Afanasyev, while admitting that the economic abundance is not the ultimate goal, writes : "Not material things and not just riches, but people in all their variety of abilities and requirements are the chief wealth of new society."[32] It is an ethical emphasis rather than emphasizing on the material and technological basis of communism. Gita has always upheld that the material forces and the modes of Prakṛti should not be allowed to determine the direction in which mankind should move ; on the contrary, it should be the man who shall determine as to how the material modes, and material forces including technology and science are to serve him. Whether they should be used for killing or for healing ? Science and technology may tell man merely how to kill and how to heal ; but it will be man who shall decide as to where and when to kill and where to heal. Therefore, Anāsakti Yoga of Gita will not allow the technology to dominate man and his dignity. In forming a sound philosophy of life, the prime need, thus, is to generate a firm conviction that there is a moral order independant of man's changing desires. This moral law is embedded in the nature of man and in the structure of society. This is *dharma* and this should be made the source of weal and prosperity as well as of the civilization.

Conclusion

As far as the fundamentals are concerned communism and Gita agree. The ideal before both of them is to re-establish the lost unity of man with mankind and to realize his essence as 'Man'—as a species being. This is the ideal of self-realization, for which both are trying. They also go hand in hand in discerning the stark enemy of mankind, and they both subscribe to the view that so long as the forces of greed and acquisitive mania are holding sway, man will ever remain dehumanized, exploited, in bondage and therefore 'un-man'. Both want to get humanity rid of this deadly enemy ; communism by abolishing private property and Anāsakti Yoga by curing the very desire to possess. Communism and Gita consider the desire for private ownership and the sense of possession (Parigraha, Saṅgam, rāga) as undesirable. Similarly, both nave discerned that there are two irreconcilable opponents in the arena of the battle-field of life, one of whom is condemned by the 'History' to be destroyed ; the other is to be sustained by history and destined to conquer. They also agree that some practical efforts are invariably needed for working out the salvation of mankind from alienated and bewildered existence.

However, their differences develop only when they start working out the details, the *modus vivendi.* These are, therefore, not the essential but methodological differences. When communism started as a philosophico-ethical doctrine after the transformational criticism of Hegelian philosophy, it started with a mission to fight the forces of acquisitiveness and of ending the alienation of man. Its ideal was to see that man returns to himself as a 'social', i.e., Human Man, after eliminating the enemy of human self-realization, viz., his egoistic needs. It wanted to realize socialized 'humanity'. In this form, it posited a serious challenge to the industrial and mechanistic civilization of the West. Had it consistently followed this mission in the spirit in which Gita advocates '*Svadharme nidhanaṁ śreyaḥ*', it would have given a shattering blow to the dehumanizing and corruptive influences of the civilization of West against which it had raised a banner of crusade in *Das Capital.* But leaving its own sphere of social regeneration of mankind, when it entered into the realm of politics, it itself posited a danger to human freedom. Gita had already warned in this regard that '*para dharmo bhayāvahaḥ*' that to follow another's law is perilous.

Marx himself knew that the realm of politics, the realm of economic and the realm of history are full of contradictions, as in these realms, the law of the 'union of opposites' operates. At the core of things, his own dialectical approach found conflicts, antagonism and clash. Marx realized that at this level, progress and development comes through struggle. In this development, the most important moments were conceived to be those when accumulated tensions and clash go into open struggle, the highest point of all being apocalyptic and eschatological. Therefore, he very sincerely wanted the humanity to transcend this "realm of necessity" and of 'dialectical conflicts'. But this system was the product of the application of inverted Hegelianism to the degenerated conditions of the industrial civilization. In his doctrines, he made battering revolt against the dehumanizing effects of the capitalist modes of production. Consequently, in counteracting those evils and while applying the Hegelian theory of 'planned march of History' to these conditions, it borrowed from these conditions, the tendency to seek all answers of human problems in the material modes of existence and in the baser nature of man. Because of its bid to searching for the remedy of human bondage within the forces of bondage, it entered into the mud of politics and became the victim of all the inconsistencies and contradictions which belong to pre-historic level of dialects. Thus, though starting with a laudable ethical ideal, when it entered into political arena, it spoiled its image. It is the political aspect of communism, now posing a new threat to human freedom. No doubt, the lust for money was dangerous for human progress, and it needed an effective check on it, but communism forgot that still more dangerous is the lust for political aggrandizement. Because, if the economic power goes astray and starts exploiting the mankind, then some strong political sanctions can impose check on it. But if the political power becomes unbridled and lust for political aggrandizement goes on unchecked, it can play havoc for humanity. The history has seen very recently what terror Hitler, Mussolini and such other demagogues have spread on the earth and what global ruins their political ambitions wrought.

Therefore, Gita would tell communism that if the mission of relieving man from his alienation is to be carried consistently, then all attachments will have to be given up ; no matter whether it is an attachment to material goods or it may be an ambition to cling to the political power. In Gita's own language, 'Act You O Dhanañjaya, without attachment, steadfast in yoga' (*yogasthaḥ Kurukarmāṇi saṅgaṁ tyaktvā dhanañjayay* (II. 48). It means that the real mission of removing the bewilderment of man and helping him in realizing his lost unity with mankind will have to be conducted with all sincerity leaving all the temptations. Similarly, Gita started with the problem of finishing the despondency (viṣāda) of man as well as his bewilderment about his duty (*dharmasammūḍhacetāḥ*) (II.7). But some thinkers dragged it into the realm of mythological story-telling. As a consequence to that, it became the victim of the mystifying language and its ethico-philosophical doctrines having been camouflaged in highly devotional religious tone, it came ineffective in the realization of its mission of relieving man from the dehumanizing effects of the actual life-situation. Accordingly, in order to unravel its esoteric meanings and to remove the 'putrescence of the absolute spirit', it needed a formula like the one that was provided by Feuerbach to Marx in the form of his method of 'transformational criticism'. However, this formula was provided by Mahābhārata's aphorism '*na mānuṣāt śreṣṭhataram hi kiñcit*' ; proper object of realization for man is 'Man', his humanity, and nothing beyond that. Moreover, the climate of renaissance in India paved the ground for the humanistic interpretation of the ancient values. Inspired by this, Gandhi did a great service in his commentary to interpret 700 verses of Gita in sociological and humanistic rendering, which, as a matter of fact, brings forth the esoteric meaning of Gita.

Having thus laid down their ideals, they need each others help in fulfilling the mission of fighting the dehumanizing consequences of lust and greed. Communism, in order to avoid all its contradictions and its frightening image, will have to forego its political implications, and Anāsakti Yoga, in order to be more effective, will have to forego its narrative part. Thereafter, a valuational synthesis of these two systems can save the humanity from the aggravating tensions. The economic exploitation and the impending danger of political domination are still creating threat for mankind, and the 'prophets of doom' are blowing their trumpet. Today, the weary world requires that these two great ethical philosophies should work together for the liberation of man from his modern predicament. But the monolithic communism, at this point, will try to assert its uncompromising attitude, and would proclaim that it is *the only* hope of humanity. It will point out in accordance with its 'law of historical inevitability' that a path is already there on which the mankind is destined to walk. But such categorical assertions leave no chance for man's creative endeavours and his moral efforts to evaluate these pronouncements and if necessary make search for alternative paths. When one says that this and this is the final word of wisdom, he closes all the doors for further enquiry, nor he leaves any chance for empirical testing of his doctrine. But when we say that this and this path 'ought' to be traversed, then we are leaving ample room for moral choice.

Anāsakti Yoga, in accordance with the traditions of Indian culture, allows the freedom to choose between the possible alternatives and synthesize them together wherever it may be necessary and possible. We have seen that the goal is the same, viz., the man is to be re-established to exist as 'Man'. But communism and Gita have described it in their own terminology, and tried to lay down in their own way, the path to reach it. This variety of the explanation is allowed in Indian traditions, which say that the truth is one, although the wise men of the world state and restate it according to the needs of their respective times and social milieu (*ekaṁ sud viprā bahudhā vudanti*). The prophets, the avatāras and the great historic entities have been placing the ideal of transforming man's dehumanized existence in every age. and in almost every society. Humanity encompasses all these efforts, if there is sincerity in them. Social integration is not complete so far. Nor there will be any perfect integration till man has overcome all his frailties as man, i.e., till man is man and he does not become an angel. This does not mean that we should leave all efforts for marching ahead *in the direction of the* progressive realization of this ideal. Gita has, therefore, put forth the principle of '*yadā yadā dharmasya glāni*', which shows that endeavour should continue from age to age. It is the recognition of the fact that in every age the forces of evil will play their devilish game to create the crisis beyond the tolerable limits. If the society is not dead, then the self-corrective process of society will manifest itself in the form of some historic person, who would restore the lost equilibrium. This process will continue in every age. The great men will continue to come again and again, and the creative and corrective wisdom of mankind will never be exhausted. Gita does not talk of any finality or any ultimate end of human history where the process will come to final close and man will become free from all the problems. The ideal of a classless, stateless and structureless society, as conceived by communism, leads to the utopians flight of imagination. The passage to the 'Realm of Freedom' sounds like the secularised version of the Christian idea of the pilgrim's progress from 'Paradise Lost' to 'Paradise Regained'. This reduces the communist ideal of the higher phase of communist society to a historical myth of this century. These dreams of Paradise are nothing but the nocturnal hallucinations. The Christian dictum that 'blessed are those who are poor, for theirs is the kingdom of heaven' 'was a bid to keep man contented with his poverty with a hope to enter 'heaven'. Now the bid of communism is that "blessed are those who are oppressed under the yoke of an unscrupulous dictatorship" for their is the kingdom of freedom. Gita does not want to take man to Paradise but to rehabilitate and to confirm him on this very earth with variety of his individual differences (guṇa karma) and variety of the tastes for various levels of enjoyment (Dharma Artha, Kāma). Let, therefore, the efforts to bring complete social integration continue and go on from various directions. But this type of approach is the teaching of Gita. According to the teachings of Gita, in whatever way one works for that integration, humanity admits all these varied efforts and variegated solutions. Gita says : "In whatever way men resort to Me even so I do render to them. In every way, the path, men follow, is mine."[33]

This liberalism and catholicity to allow every sincere efforts to work for the welfare of mankind, not in discord with each other, but in unison with each other, is the unique characteristic of Gita. Here the question of my or mine is not there, but the question is that humanity must be saved from bewilderment. This catholicity shows the greatness of Gita that whosoever works for salvation of mankind, let him work it out sincerely and with all integrity and not with a lust for political conquest. Therefore, Gita would always be ready to shake hand with communism and bring out a workable synthesis of all whatever is lofty and noble in this philosophy. If the synthesis is really sought for, it can be seen that their disputes are minor and question of difference is only of priorities. Communism throughout has emphasized that moral regeneration of man is not possible without economic abundance, whereas Anāsakti Yoga will say that without moral regeneration (*dharma saṁsthāpanā*) the dream of economic prosperity will be a fiction. If men are not sincere in their job, if they are not honest in the discharge of their allotted task, then all economic planning would collapse. The present day communist thinkers have come to realize this fact. For example, Afanasyev says that "communism presupposes also a new type of man, a man who combines in himself spiritual richness, moral purity and physical perfection."[34] Therefore, communism can find a nitch in the ethico-social doctrines of Anāsakti Yoga.

It is the property of a 'deductive system' that it need not lay down specifically all its theorems but it should contain a set of basic postulates and axioms, such as that all the theorems should be deducible from these postulates, which the system wants to prove within itself. The basic postulates and the axioms, from which communism deduced all the other theorems within its system are already found contained in the system of the postulates of Anāsakti Yoga. The fundamental of all these axioms is "from each according to his ability". This means that each person will contribute to the social productive process according to his skill, his intelligence, his taste and temperament. Anāsakti Yoga also lays emphasis that each man by complete absorption in the performance of his duty, wins perfection,[35] meaning thereby that in order to seek perfection, people will contribute their share by discharging their allotted social obligation. Similarly, the other axiom of communism is "to each according to his need". In taking his share from society, each will take as much as he needs, keeping in v ew the needs of others. Provision for th s also exists in Anāsakti Yoga of Gita, which says that "man is to take as much from the society as is residual, i.e., what remains after discharging all the social obligations" (III. 12). As a corollary to this, those, who try to appropriate the surplus value for their personal benefit, are condemned as capitalist, the evil, by communism. Similarly, he, who takes everything for himself and devours without caring for the share of others, is declared a sinner by Gita (III.13). This increased production will be "achieved through the growth of productivity, i.e., the higher productivity of labour",[36] as Afanasyev tells us. On the basis of this, it was concluded that "Communism will be the society of abundance."[37] But if all these basic postulates and axioms of communism are already found in the Anásakti Yoga of Gita, then in this synthesis, communism will lose its separate identity and will be left with nothing but 'political adventurism'. However, this system would not make any difference to Gita except that some of its verses will have to be re-arranged. Such a state of affairs, as deducible from the fundamental postulates of communism, is also, according to the axioms of Gita, achievable by the honest, disciplined persons, who have excelled themselves in the performance of their job (*yogaḥ karmasu kauśalam*) (II. 50). When these fundamental postulates and axioms are arranged into a postulational system from which all the theorems may be proveable within the system, then it may come to be read as this :

sve-sve karmaṇyabhirataḥ saṁsiddhiṁ labhate naraḥ (XVIII.45) : *yajñasi stāśinaḥ santo mucyante sarvakilbiṣaiḥ* (III. 13) ; *yogasthaḥ kuru karmāṇi saṅgaṁ tyakvā dhanañjāya* (II.48) ; *tasmād yogāya yujyasvo yogaḥ karmasu kauśalam* (II.50), and therefore, *tatra śrīr vijayo bhūtirdhruva nītir matir mama* (XVIII. 78).

In English these would mean : (i) for seeking his self-actualization, every one is absorbed in his own job, according to his guṇa and karma ; (ii) every one takes from the society as much as is residual after his contribution in the social productive process; (iii) every one discharges his social role in the productive process, leaving all sorts of profit motive and without the desire to appropriate it for private ownership ; (iv) every one disciplines himself into social discipline and this social discipline is the increased efficiency of the social production ; and therefore, there will be economic prosperity, social progress and dignified existence of man. Thus speaking, if *Anāsakti Yoga of Gita* is synthesized with communism, then all the postulates and doctrines of communism will be merged into and therefore deducible from Gita. This synthesized form may be disowned by the communism, because by adding a specific axiom of the renunciation of desire for private ownership, it becomes a doctrine of *anāsakti*. This shows that whereas the 'deductive completeness' of communism will be exhausted by Gita, the communism will be lacking many fundamental postulates to exhaust the ethico-philosophic system of anāsakti yoga, specially because it has no substitute for the anāsakti, although it is to prove within its own system also that the profit motive and lust for appropriating the surplus value and for private property is to be finished. It is because of the absence of this great axiom of 'anāsakti' in the system of communism that it had to seek help from the unscrupulous political authority. The statement that 'dictatorship of the proletariat is needed to turn man into communist man', is a theorem, which is incompatible within the whole communist system itself. Thus, there is a need for some other principle to counteract the forces of greed and the acquisitiveness. This sure weapon of detachment (*asaṅgaśastreṇa*) (XV. 4), has been provided by Gita. Gandhi, in his commentary, emphasizes the need of this principle and he writes : "unless man is determined to cut himself off from the temptations of the world of senses, he will go deeper into its mire every day."[38] Thus, without anāsakti, the concept of communist man will remain a representative fiction. Accordingly, in order to make man fit for entering the realm of freedom, communism will always stand in need of 'anāsakti'.

Here comes a great dilemma for communism. If it confines itself to the realm of necessity and the realm of history, it becomes full of contradictions, and if it enters the realm of freedom, it becomes only a historical myth. But if it limits itself to its basic postulates and axioms, then the whole of its postulational system will be exhausted by the postulational system of the Gita (as rendered in the present commentary, Anāsakti Yoga). This shows the infinite richness of Gita ; its impregnable and indomitable spirit, which has shown the path down the ages at the time of all crises.

Taking inspiration from this lofty philosophy, Indians have overcome various crises, which threatened the survival of society. When country was under the yoke of a colonial power, the exploitative imperialism, boasted that sun never sets in British Empire, then Gita gave inspiration to the national leaders in their political fight. Tilak, Aurobindo, Gandhi, and many other fighters for freedom made Gita as their source of inspiration to fight the alien power and the political servitude. Not only this, but as Manmathnath Gupta has shown, even the revolutionaries sought inspiration from Gita's aphorism '*vināś-āye ca duṣkṛtām*' in their fight against the imperialist power.[39] An eminent communist leader, Prof. Hiren Mukherjee admits that "perhaps, Gandhi's greatest contribution to Indian life was *abhaya* or fearlessness rather than the more celebrated notion of ahiṁsā or non-violence."[40] And, this fearlessness came to Gandhi from Gita's call where Kṛṣṇa is exhorting the demoralized Arjuna to cast off his petty faint-heartedness and to arise to fight back the foes (*Kṣudraṁ hṛdayadaurbalyaṁ tyaktvottiṣṭha paraṁtapa*) (II. 3).

When a political crisis came, Gita was there to help the Indian society to overcome that. Similarly, when the cultural onslaught was going on, the scholars like Aurobindo and Vivekanand sought inspiration from the invincible philosophy of Gita to win the cultural battle in India's favour. Now in the present day crisis, when the society seems to have fallen the victim of a sort of bewilderment, in which we have lost the goal, Gita may serve as a source and provide sound social philosophy to the society. India does not lack man-power, nor does she lack the natural resources. What it lacks, is a sound social philosophy arising out of her own soil and befitting her socio-cultural conditions. Gita can fill this gap. But for this, the veil of sanctity will have to be torn, which the pious hands have woven around it, to hide the ugly aspect of our socio-cultural institutions. These institutions have fossilized our thinking pattern and now they will have to be discarded. Gita itself suggests that if they were born at some time, their death now is inevitable (*Jātasya hi dhruvo mṛtyuḥ*) (II.27). As Gita asks why mourn for them whom we should not mourn (II. 11). After discarding these obsolete institutions, which have outlived their utility, new institutions will have to be worked out on the basis of the essential principles laid down in our own ancient value-system. Gita tells us to know the imperishable (*avināśi*). No one can destroy that immutable essence (II. 17). Who will sift this accidental and superficial dogmatism and ritualism of our culture from the essential ? This work cannot be accomplished by those who have wrapped Gita into a cloth, just as a dead body is wrapped in coffin and have made a fetish of it. But by those social philosophers and the philosophers of culture, who *understand* it and who can discern what is essential and what is not. The commentary by Gandhi, the Anāsakti Yoga is an attempt in this direction, to restore the glory of Gita in solving the social problems of our society, and to remove the present day bewilderment.

Have not the British idealists like Green and Bonsanquet and German idealists like Hegel worked out their whole social, political and educational institutions on thebasis of the fundamental postulates provided by their idealism? Why not then all these institutions can be worked out from the basic postulates laid down in Gita and interpreted in Anāsakti Yoga? If the socio-political implications of the basic postulates and axioms laid down in the Anāsakti Yoga of Gita are worked out by the scholars, then it can serve as the firm and sound social philosophy for building a prosperous and strong social order in which the man will be free to express his creative talent and to realize his capacities. This is self-realization. The harmony of social order is an essential aim of the spiritually enlightened man. This does not leave any gap between spiritual freedom of man and his socio-economic progress, because the realization of one's essence is the real spiritual achievement. It is on the basis of Gita that the society can be firmly established with the social ownership of material means and with the democratic order in which each man will have full freedom to decide his own fate and to realize dharma, artha, kāma. Gita has always stood by this society in every crisis, and it is now once again that in the form of Anāsakti Yoga, it may help in overcoming the present social crisis. Gita is undoubtedly one of the greatest books produced by mankind. We can close our discussion with Bahm's prophecy : "As the world's three historically great civilizations, the Hindu, the Chinese and the European, intermingle and merge in a world super-culture enjoying the riches of all three, the Gita becomes one of the world's greatest classics."[41] It can now be safely said that even when the communist culture intermingles, Gita will still remain a great ethico-philosophical treatise.

References

1. Kleine Philosophische Schriften (p. 169), quoted by Tucker, Robert C., *Philosophy and Myth in Karl Marx*, p. 91.
2. *Gita*, VII. 5.
3. Radhakrishnan, S., *Bhagavadgītā*, p. 214.
4. Marx, K., *Early Writings*, p. 164.
5. Marx, K., *Towards the Critique of Hegel's Philosophy of Right*, p. 265 of *MEGA*.
6. *Gita*, XVIII.78.
7. *Gita*, III.39.
8. *Gita*, XIV.7.
9. *Gita*, II.62.
10. Marx, K., *Early Writings*, p. 159.
11. Marx, K., *Capital*, p. 138.
12. Ibid.
13. Ibid., p. 268.
14. *Gita*, IV.8 (vināśāya ca duṣkṛtām).
15. Marx, K. and Engels, F., *Manifesto of the Communist Party*, p. 60.
16. *Gita*, XVIII.78 ; Also XI.34 (Fight, Victory is thine).
17. Tucker, Robert C., *Philosophy and Myth in Karl Marx*, p. 136.
18. *Gita*, II.2.
19. *Gita*, II.3 (Kudraṁ hṛdayadaurbalyaṁ tyak tvottiṣṭha paraṁtapa.)

20 *Gita*, XV.5.
21. Tucker, Robert C., *Philosophy and Myth in Karl Marx*, p. 242.f
22. Radhakrishnan, S., *Eastern Religion and Western Thought*, p. 247.
23. Marx, K. and Engels, F., *German Ideology*, p. 14.
24. *Gita*, II.40 (*Anāsakti Yoga*).
25. Popper, K.R., op. cit., p. 95.
26. Mises, Ludwig Von, *Socialism*, p. 28.
27. Afanasyev, V., *Socialism and Communism*, p. 179.
28. Marx, Engels, Lenin, *On Historical Materialism*, p. 60.
29. Marx, K. and Engels, F., *Selected Works*, Vol. II, pp.345-46.
30. Hartmann, N., *Ethics*, Vol. II, p. 26.
31. Schwitzer, Albert., op. cit., pp. 22-23.
32. Afanasyev, V., *Socialism and Communism*, p. 123.
33. *Gita*, IV.11 (ye yathā mām prapadyante).
34. Afanasyev, V., *Socialism and Communism*, p. 132.
35. *Gita*, XVIII. 45.
36. Afanasyev, V., *Socialism and Communism*, p. 125.
37. Ibid., p. 123.
38. Desai, Mahadeva, *The Gita According to Gandhi*, p. 339.
39. Rao, M.B. (Ed.), *The Mahatma—A Marxist Symposium*, pp. 95-99.
40. Ibid., p. 80.
41. Bahm, A.J., *The Bhagavad Gita or The Wisdom of Krishna*, pp. 2-3.

BIBLIOGRAPHY

I. ANĀSAKTI YOGA OF GITA

1. Aurobindo, *Essay On The Gita.* First Series, Arya Publishing House, Calcutta, Fifth Edition, 1949.
2. Bahm, Archie J., *Bhagavadgītā Or The Wisdom of Krishna* (Bombay, Somaiya Publications, 1970).
3. Betai, Ramesh S., *Gita & Gandhiji* : (Ahmedabad, Gujarat Vidyapith, 1970).
4. Bhandarkar, R.G., *Vaishnavism, Shaivism and Minor Religious Systems* (Varanasi, Indological Books House).
5. *Bṛhadāraṇyaka Upaniṣad* (Hindi). Gorakhpur, Gita Press, 1955.
6. *Chandogya Upaniṣad* (Hindi), Gorakhpur, Gita Press, 1955.
7. Das Gupta, S.N., *History of Indian Philosophy,* Vol. II, Second Impression : (Cambridge University Press, 1952).
8. ——— , *Indian Idealism.* (Cambridge, Cambridge University Press, 1962).
9. Desai, Mahadev, *The Gita According to Gandhi.* (Ahmedabad, Navjivan Publishing House, 1970).
10. Gambhirananda, Swami, *Eight Upaniṣads* Vol., I. (Calcutta, Advaita Ashrama, 1965).
11. ——— , *Eight Upaniṣads,* Vol. II. (Calcutta, Advaita Ashrama 1965).
12. Gandhi, M.K., *Anāsakti Yoga* (Hindi). (Ahmedabad, Navjivan Prakashan Mandir, 1969).
13. ——— , *Ethical Religion.* (Ahmedabad, Navjivan Publishing House, 1968).
14. ——— , *In Search of the Supreme,* Vol. I. (Ahmedabad, Navjivan Publishing House, 1961).

15. Gandhi, M.K., *In Search of the Supreme*, Vol. II. (Ahmedabad, Navjivan Publishing House, 1961).
16. ———, *In Search of the Supreme*, Vol. III. (Ahmedabad, Navjivan Publishing House, 1961).
17. ———, *My Religion*. (Ahmedabad, Navjivan, Publishing House, 1955).
18. ———, *My Socialism*. (Ahmedabad Navjivan Publishing House, 1959).
19. *Iśhādi Nava Upaniṣads*. (Translation, H.R. Goyandka) (Hindi). Gorakhpur, Gita Press, 1959.
20. *Kaṭha Upaniṣad*. Gorakhpur, Gita Press, 1955.
21. *Mahābhārata*. (Kalyana Visesanka) (Hindi). Gorakhpur, Gita Press, 1958.
22. Maitra, S.K., *Ethics of the Hindus*. (Calcutta, University Press, 1925).
23. Radhakrishnan, S., *Bhagavadgītā*. (London, Allen & Unwin, 1967).
24. ———, *Hindu View of life*. (London, Allen & Unwin, 1960).
25. ———, *Indian Philosophy*, Vol. I. (London, Allen & Unwin 1958).
26. Ranadey, R.D., *A Constructive Survey of Upanishadic Philosophy*. (Poona, Oriental Book Agency, 1926).
27. Ray, Benoy Gopal, *Gandhian Ethics*. (Ahmedabad, Navjivan Publishing House, 1958).
28. *Śrimadbhagavadgītā Saṁkara Bhāṣya* (Hindi). Gorakhpur, Gita Press, S. 2017).
29. Śrinivasacharya, P.N., *Ethical Philosophy of Gita*. (Madras, Srikrishna Library Chitrakulan, 1948).
30. Subrahmanyam, S. & Srinivasa, T.R., *Saundarya Laharī* (Madras, Theosophical, 1948).
31. *Taittirīya Upaniṣad* (Hindi). (Gorakhpur, Gita Press, 1955).
32. Thibaut, George, (Trans). *Vedānta Sūtra of Bādarāyaṇa* with commentary by Śaṁkara (Part I). (New York, Dover Pub. 1962).
33. Tilak, Bal Ganga Dhar, *Srimadbhagavadgītā Rahasya*, Vol. I. (Poona, Tilak Bros. 1935).
34. ———, *Srimadbhagavadgītā Rahasya*, Vol. II. (Poona, Tilak Bros. 1936).

II. COMMUNISM

1. Adoratsky, V., *Dialectical Materialism.* (London, M. Lawrence, 1934).
2. Afanasyev, V., *Scientific Communism.* (Moscow, Progress Publishers, 1967).
3. ———, *Socialism & Communism.* (Moscow, Progress Publishers, 1972).
4. Afanasyev, V., Makarova, M. and Minayev, L., *Fundamentals of Scientific Socialism.* (Moscow, Progress Publishers, 1969).
5. Avineri, S., *Social and Political Thought of Karl Marx.* (Cambridge, Cambridge University Press, 1968).
6. Bober, M., *Karl Marx's Interpretation of History.* (Cambridge Harvard University Press, 1927).
7. Bottomore, T.B. and Maximillan Ruber. *Karl Marx: Selected Writings in Sociology and Social Philosophy.* (New York, McGraw Hill Book Co.).

7A. Brij Narain, *Marxism is Dead* (Minerva Book-shop, Lahore, 1939).

8. Chang, S., *The Marxian Theory of the State.* (Philadelphia, University of Pennsylvania Press,,1931).
9. Chesnokov, D., *Historical Materialism.* (Moscow, Progress Publishers, 1969).
10. Clezerman, G. and Kursanov, G., *Historical Materialism.* (Moscow, Progress Publishers, 1968).
11. Cole, G.D.H., *Socialist Thought : Marxism and Anarchism, 1850-1890.* (London, Macmillan, 1953-54).
12. ———, *Socialist Thought : The Forerunners 1789-1850.* (London, Macmillan, 1953-54).
13. Conquest, Robert, *Where Marx Went Wrong ?* (New Delhi, Pee Kay Publications).
14. Cooper, R., *The Logical Influence of Hegel on Marx.* (Seattle, Washington University Press, 1925).
15. Cornforth, Maurice, *Communism and Human Values.* (Bombay, PPH Bookstall, 1973).
16. Dahrendorf, Ralf, *Class and Class Conflict in Industrial Society.* (Stanford, 1965).
17. Djilas, Milovan, *New Class.* (London, Unwin Books).
18. Easton, Lloyd D. and Guddat, Kurt H., *Writings of Young*

Marx on Philosophy and Society. (New York, Easton and K.H. Guddat, 1967).

19. Engels, F., *Ludwig Feuerbach and the End of Classical German Ideology*. (Moscow, Progress Publishers, 1969).
20. ———, *Anti-Duhring*. (Moscow, Progress Publishers, 1969).
21. ———, *Dialectics of Nature*. (Moscow, Progress Publishers, 5th print, 1972).
22. Feuerbach, Ludwig, *The Essence of Christianity*. (New York, Torch Harper & Row, 1957).
23. Fromm, E., *ed. Marx's Concept of Man*. (New York, Frederick Ungar, 1961).
24. Giddens, Anthony, *Capitalism and Modern Social Theory*. (Cambridge University Press, 1971).
25. Hook, Sidney, *From Hegel to Marx*. (Ann Arbor, University of Michigan Press, 2nd edition, 1962).
26. ———, *Towards an Understanding of Karl Marx*. (New York, John Day Co. 1933).
27. Kamenka, Eugene, *Ethical Foundation of Marxism*. (London, Routledge, 1962).
28. Kautsky, K., *Ethics and the Materialist Conception of History*. (Chicago, Charles H. Kerr, 1907).
29. Kosolapov, R., *Communism and Freedom*. (Moscow, Progress Publishers, 1970).
30. Lenin, V.I., *Collected Works*, Vol. 24-25. (Moscow, Foreign Language Publishing House).
31. ———, *Foundation of the Communist International*. (New York, International Publishers, 1934).
32. ———, *Marx Engels Marxism* (8th revised edition). (Moscow, Progress Publishers, 1968).
33. ———, *Materialism and Empirio-Criticism*. (Moscow, Foreign Language Publishing House, 1952).
34. ———, *On Culture and Cultural Revolution*. (Moscow, Progress Publishers, 1970).
35. ———, *On Utopian and Scientific Socialism*. (Moscow, Progress Publishers, 1965).
36. ———, *Selected Works*, Vol. 2. (Moscow, Foreign Language Publishing House, 1947).
37. Lindsay, A.D., *Karl Marx's Capital : An Introductory Essay*. (London, Geoffrey Cumberlege, 1947).

38. Lobkowicz, Nicholas, *Marx and the Western World*. (Notre Dame, 1967).

39. Mac Murray, J., *The Philosophy of the Communism*. (London, Faber and Faber, 1933).

40. Marx, Karl, *Poverty of Philosophy*. (Chicago, Charles H. Kerr).

41. ———, *Capital* trans. by Eden and Cedov Paul. (London, J.M. Dent & Sons, 1933).

42. ———, *Communist Manifesto* trans. by L.S. Feuer. (New York, Anchor Dks 1959).

43. ———, *Contribution to the Critique of Political Economy*. (Chicago, Charles H. Kerr & Company, 1904).

44. ———, *Das Capital*, Vol. I (Moscow, Foreign Language Publishing House, 1954).

45. ———, *Das Capital*, Vol. II (Moscow, Progress Publishers, 1967).

46. ———, *Das Capital*, Vol. III (Moscow, Progress Publishers, 1967).

47. ———, *Economic and Philosophic Manuscripts of 1844*. (Moscow, Foreign Language Publishing House, 1961).

48. ———, *Early Writings* trans. by Bottomore, T.B. (New York, Mc Graw Hill Pub., 1964).

49. ———, *Eighteenth Brumaire of Louis Bonapart*. (New York, International Pub.).

50. Marx, Karl and Engels, Frederick. *On Britain*. (Moscow, Progress Publishers, 1962).

51. ———, *Feuerbach: Opposition of the Materialistic & Idealistic Outlook*. (Moscow, Progress Publishers, 1972).

52. ———, *German Ideology*. (Moscow, Progress Publishers, 1968).

53. ———, *Manifesto of the Communist Party*. (Moscow, Progress Publishers, 1969).

54. ———, *Selected Correspondence*. (Moscow, Foreign Language Publishing House).

55. ———, *Selected Works*, Vol. I (Moscow, Progress Publishers, 1969).

56. ———, *Selected Works*, Vol. II (Moscow, Progress Publishers, 1969).

57. ———, *Selected Works*, Vol. III (Moscow, Progress

Publishers, 1969).

58. Marx, Karl and Engles., *The Holy Family Or Critique of Critical Critique* (Moscow, 1956).

58A. ———, *MEGA*. (Historisch-Kritische Gesamtausgabe). Ed. by D. Rjazanov.

59. Marx, Karl., Engels, F., and Lenin, V. I. (*Anarchism and Anarcho-Syndicalism*. (Moscow, Progress Publishers, 1970).

60. ———, *On Historical Materialism*. (Moscow, Progress Publishers).

61. McFadden, Charles J., *The Philosophy of Communism*. (New York, Boston, Cincinnati, Chicago, San Francisco, Benziger Brothers, Inc.).

62. McLellan, Devid, *The Young Hegelians and Karl Marx*. (London, 1970).

63. Ossowski, Stanislan, *Class and Class Structure in the Social Consciousness*. (London, 1963).

64. Petersen, William *ed.*, *Realities of World Communism*. (New York, Prentice Hall Inc., 1963).

65. Russell, B., *Bolshevism : Practice and Theory*. (New York, Bruce and Howe, 1920).

66. Sheed, F., *Communism and Man*. (London, Sheed and Ward, 1938).

67. Surovtsev, Y. *ed.*, *Socialism and Culture*. (Moscow, Progress Publishers).

68. Tucker, Robert C., *Marxian Revolutionary Idea*. (New York, W.W. Norton and Co. Inc. 1969).

69. ———, *Philosophy and Myth in Karl Marx*. (Cambridge University Press, 1961).

70. Ulam, Adam, *An Essay on the Sources of Influence of Marxism and Communism*. (New York, Random House, 1960).

71. Wolfe, Bertram D., *Marxism : One Hundred Years in the Life of a Doctrine*. (New York, Dell Publishing Co. 1965).

72. Zeitlin, Irving M., *Marxism : A Re-examination*. (Princeton, New Jersy : Van Nostrand 1967).

III. GENERALIA

1. Allen, C.K., *Aspects of Justice*. (London, Stevens & Sons, 1958).

2. Ashley, Montague, *On Being Human.* (New York, Hawthorn).
3. Bedan, Hugo A., *Justice and Equality.* (New Jersy, Prentice Hall Inc., 1971).
4. Bernard, Bosanquet, *Some Suggestions in Ethics.* (New York, Kraus Repr. 1968).
5. Bogardus, Emory S., *Development of Social Thought.* (Bombay, Vakils, Feffer & Simons Pvt. Ltd. 2nd Indian Print, 1969).
6. Bonar, James, *Philosophy and Political Economy.* (London, Allen and Unwin, 3rd ed., 1922).
7. Bradley, F.H., *Ethical Studies*, 2nd Ed. (Oxford, Clarendon Press, 1927).
8. Broad, C.D., *Five Types of Ethical Theory.* (London, Routledge & Kegan Paul, 1956).
9. Chesnokov, D. and Karpushin, V., *Man and Society.* (Moscow, Progress Publishers, 1966).
10. Cohen, Morris R. and Nagel, Earnest, *Introduction To Logic and Scientific Method.* (New Delhi, Allied Publishers, 1968).
11. Copi, Irving M., *Symbolic Logic*, 3rd ed. (London, Macmillan, 1971).
12. Damodaran, K., *Indian Thought : A Critical Survey*, (Bombay, Asia Publishing House, 1967).
13. ——— , *Man and Society in Indian Philosophy.* (New Delhi, People's Publishing House, 1970).
14. Danial, J. Bronstein, Yervant H. Krikorian, Phillip P. Wiener (eds.), *Basic Problems of Philosophy.* (New York, Prentice Hall Inc., 1964).
15. De Bary, W.M. Theodore, *Sources of Indian Traditions.* (New York, Columbia University Press, 1958).
16. Devaraja, N.K., *Philosophy of Culture.* (Allahabad, Kitab Mahal, 1963).
17. Durkheim, Emile, *Division of Labour in Society.* (New York, Simpson, 1937).
18. Faurot, Jean, H., *Problems of Political Philosophy.* (Pennsylavania, Chandler Publishing Co., 1970).
19. Feuerbach, Ludwig, *Essence of Christianity.* (Torch, Harper & Row).

20. Fisher, H.A., *History of Europe.* (London, Arnold, 1936).
21. Freud, S., *Beyond the Pleasure Principle.* Trans. by Strachey James. (New York, Liveright, 1970).
22. Freud, S., *Civilization and Its Discontents* trans. by James Strachey. (New York, Norton C. Norton, 1962).
23. ——— , *General Introduction to Psycho-Analysis.* Rev. ed. 1969. (Clarion S & S Black & Gold Lib., 1969).
24. ——— , *Outlines of Psycho-Analysis.* Rev. ed. (New York, Norton C. Norton, 1970).
25. Gasset, Ortega Y., *Treasury of Philosophy.* (London, Commonwealth Edition, 1964).
26. Gide, Charles and Rist Charles, *History of Economic Doctrine.* (London, George G. Harrap & Co., 1945).
27. Ginsberg, Morris, *On Justice in Society.* (London, Heinemann, 1965).
28. Green, T.H., *Prolegomena to Ethics,* Fifth Edition (Oxford, Clarendon Press, 1906).
29. Harding, D.W., *Social Psychology and Individual Values.* (London, Hutchinson's University Library, 1953).
30. Hare, R.M., *Language of Morals.* (London, Oxford University Press, 1952).
31. Hartmann, Nicolai, *Ethics, Vol. II—Moral Values.* Trans, by S. Coit. (London, Allen & Unwin, 1951).
32. Hartshorne, C., *Reality as Social Process.* (Illinois, Free Press, 1953).
33. Hegel, G.W.F., *Logic of Hegel.* (London, Geoffrey Cumberlege, 1950).
34. ——— , *Philosophy of History.* (New York, Dover Publications, 1956).
35. ———, *Philosophy of Right.* (Oxford, Clarendon Press, 1953).
36. ——— , *Science of Logic,* Vol. I (London, George Allen & Unwin, 1951).
37. Heinemann, F.H., *Existentialism and Modern Predicament.* (Torch, Harper & Row).
38. Herbert, Marcuse, *Reason and Revolution : Hegel and Rise of Social Theory,* 2nd ed. (New York, Humanities, 1963).
39. Hill, T.E., *Contemporary Ethical Theories.* (New York, The Macmillan Co., 1950).

40. Hook, Sidney, *Reason, Social Myths and Democracy*. (New York, The John Day Company, 1940).
41. Horney, Karen, *Neuroses and Human Growth*. (New York, Norton Lib. Norton, 1970).
42. Huxley, T.H., *Brave New World*, Rev. ed. (London, Harper, 1958).
43. Jayaswal, K.P., *Hindu Polity*. (Calcutta, Butterworth, 1963).
44. Johnson, A.H., *Whitehead's Philosophy of Civilization*. (New York, Dover Publication, 1962).
45. Johnson, H.M., *Sociology : A Systematic Introduction*. (London, Routledge & Kegan Paul, 1960).
46. Jung, C.G., *Modern Man in Search of a Soul*. (London, Routledge & Kegan Paul, 1961).
47. Kant, Immanuel, *Fundamental Principles of the Metaphysics of Ethics*. Trans. by Manthey Zorn Ott. (New York, Appleton).
48. Kolarz, Walter, *Religion in the Soviet Union*. (London, Macmillan, 1961).
49. Kosminsky, Y., *Professor Toynbee's Philosophy of History*. (Moscow, Progress Publishers).
50. Laird, John, *An Inquiry Into Moral Notions*. (New York, AMS, 1936).
51. Laski, Harold J., *Grammar of Politics*, 4th ed. (New York, Humanities, 1964).
52. Leontyev, A. *ed. Psychological Research in the USSR*. (Moscow, Progress Publishers).
53. Lillie, William, *An Introduction to Ethics*. (London, University Paperback, Methuen, 3rd ed. 1966).
54. Mackenzie, J.S., *Mannual of Ethics*. (London, University Tutorial Press, 6th ed., 1957).
55. ———, *Outline of Social Philosophy*. (London, Allen & Unwin, 1963).
56. Mannheim, Karl, *Ideology and Utopia : An Introduction to the Sociology of Knowledge*. (New York, Harv. Harbacc J.)
57. Marcuse, Herbert, *Reason and Revolution*, 2nd ed. (Boston, Beacon Press, 1954).
58. Marshall, Alfred, *Principles of Economics*. (New York, Macmillan, 1961).

59. Martin, Buber, *Paths in Utopia.* (New York, Beacon Press, 1958).
60. Marx, Karl, *Future Results of British Rule in India.* (Moscow, Progress Publishers, n. 9).
61. McIver, R.M. and Page, C.H., *Society.* (London, Macmillan, Paper Mac, 1962).
62. Meir, G.M. and Baldwin, R.E., *Economic Development.* (Bombay, Asia Publishing House, 1962).
63. Mill, J.S., *System of Logic.* (Canada, U. of Toronto Press).
64. ———, *Utilitarianism.* (London, Lib. Bobbs, 1957).
65. Milne, A.J.M., *Social Philosophy of English Idealism.* (London, Allen and Unwin, 1962).
66. Mises, Ludwig Von, *Socialism.* (London, Jonathan Cape, 1951).
67. Muirhead, J.H., *Elements of Ethics.* (London, John Murray, A Street Third Ed. 1912).
68. Murphy, Gardner, *Historical Introduction To Modern Psychology,* Rev. ed. (London, Routledge & Kegan Paul).
69. Northrop, F.C.S., *Meeting of The East and West.* (Collier, Macmillan, 1960).
70. Page, James D., *Abnormal Psychology.* (Bombay, Tata Mcgraw Hill Pub. 1947).
71. Passmore, John, *A Hundred Years of Philosophy.* (London, Gerald Duckworth and Co. Ltd., 1957).
72. Plamentaz, John, *Man and Society,* Vol. II. (New York, McGraw Hill, 1963).
73. Popper, K.R., *Open Society and its Enemies,* Vol. II. (London, Routledge and Kegan Paul, 3rd ed., 1957).
74. Portonov, A.A. and Fedotov, D.D., *Psychiatry.* (Moscow, Mir. 69).
75. Prabhu, P.H., *Hindu Social Organisation,* 3rd Ed. (Bombay, Popular Prakashan, 1963).
76. Radhakrishnan, S., *Eastern Religions and Western Thought,* 2nd ed. (London, Oxford University Press, 1924).
77. ———, *Religion and Society.* (London, Allen and Unwin, 1969).
78. Radhakrishnan, and Raju P.T., *Concept of Man,* 2nd ed. (Lincoln, Johnson, 1966).

79. Raju, P.T., *Indian Idealism and Modern Challenges.* (Chandigarh, University Publication Bureau, 1961).
80. Rao, M.B. *ed. Mahatma : A Marxist Symposium.* (Delhi, People's Publishing House, 1969).
81. Rashdall, Hastings, *Theory of Good and Evil*, Vol. I (London, Oxford University Press, 1948).
82. ———, *Theory of Good and Evil*, Vol. II, 2nd ed. (London, Oxford University Press, 1948).
83. Renon, L., *Religions of Ancient India.* (New York, Schocken, 1968).
84. Roll, Eric, *History of Economic Thought.* (London, Faber and Faber).
85. Rose, A.M., *Human Behaviour and Social Process.* (London, Routledge and Kegan Paul, 1962).
86. Russell, B., *Freedom Versus Organization.* (New York, Norton and Co., 1934).
87. ———, *History of Western Philosophy.* (New York, S and S 1945).
88. ———, *Human Society in Ethics and Politics.* (London, Ment. Nal, 1962).
89. ——— , *Religion and Science.* (London, Oxford University Press, 1961).
90. ——— , *Road to Freedom.* (New York, Barnes & Noble, 1965).
91. ——— , *Wisdom of the West.* (New York, Faweett World Lib.).
92. Sabine, George H., *History of Political Philosophy*, 3rd ed. (Calcutta, Oxford and IBH Publishing Co., 1961).
93. Sarma, D.S., *Renaissance of Hinduism.* (Madras, Law Journal Press, 1944).
94. Sàrtre, Jean Paul, *Existentialism and Humanism.* Trans. by Philip Mairet. (London, Methuen, 1957).
95. Schmlhausen, S.D., *New Road to Progress.* (New York, Falcon Press Inc., 1934).
96. Schumpeter, Josheph A., *Capitalism, Socialism and Democracy*, 2nd ed. (New York, Harper & Row, 1941).
97. Schweitzer, Albert, *Civilization and Ethics.* (London, Black, 1955).
98. ——— , *Philosophy of Civilization.* (New York, Adam &

Charles Black, 1949).
99. Smelser, Neil J., *Sociology of Economic Life*. (New Delhi, Prentice Hale of India, 1965).
100. Sorokin, Pitirim A., *Modern Historical and Social Philosophies*. (New York, Dover Publications, 1963).
101. Spengler, Oswald, *Decline of the West*. (New York, Knopf, 1942).
102. Stace, W.T., *Concept of Morals*. (London, Macmillan, 1937).
103. Stebbing, L.S, *Modern Introduction to Logic*. (London, Methuen & Co., 1947).
104. Tagore, Rabinder Nath, *Religion of Man*. (London, Allen & Unwin, 1953).
105. Thilly, F., *A History of Philosophy*. Revised by Wood, (London, George Allen & Unwin, 1962).
106. Titarenko, A., *Morality and Politics*. (Moscow, Progress Publishers, 1972).
107. Titus, H.H., *Ethics for Today*. (New Delhi, Eurasia Publication House, 1966).
108. Titus, H.H. and Keeton, M.T., *Range of Ethics*. (New Delhi, Affiliated East-West Press, 1972).
109. Toynbee, Arnold J., *Study of History*, Vol. I. (New York, Dell)
110. Trotsky, L., *The History of the Russian Revolution*. (New York, Simon and Schustov, 1936).
111. Urban, W.M., *Fundamentals of Ethics*. (New York, H. Holt and Co., 1930).
112. Varma, V.P., *Political Philosophy*. (Agra, Lakshmi Narain Aggarwal, 1970).
113. Wayper, C.L., *Political Thought*. (London, Teach Yourself Eng. University Press, 1954).
114. Weber, M., *Religion of India*. (New York, Macmillan).
115. Werner, Stark, *Sociology of Knowledge*: *An Essay in aid of a deeper Understanding of the History of Idea*. (New York, Humanities, 1958).
116. Whitehead, A.N., *Adventures of Ideas*. (Cambridge, Cambridge University Press, 1961).
117 ——, *Modes of Thought*. (London, Free Press, 1968).
118 ——, *Science and the Modern World*. (Cambridge, Camb-

ridge University Press, 1953).

119. Wolfe, Bertram D., *Marxism : One Hundred Years in the Life of Doctrine*. (New York, Dial, 1965).

120. Wolfson, Murray, *Reappraisal of Marxian Economics*. (Calcutta, Scientific Bk. Agency, 1968).

121. Woodroffe, John, *Introduction To Tantra Sastra*. (Hollywood, Vedanta Press).

122. Zietlin, Irving M., *Ideology and the Development of Sociological Theory*. (New Delhi, Prentice Hall, 1969).

IV. JOURNALS AND PERIODICALS

Aryan Path, XL, No. 2, 12, Bombay, Theosophy Hall, 1969.

Darshan International, X, No. 1, 2. Moradabad, 1970.

Darshnik Traimasik, Vol. 9, No. 3, Varanasi, July, 1963. Vol. 10, No. 4, Jaipur, October, 1964.

History of Religions, Vol. 12, No. 2. The University Chicago Press, November, 1972.

Journal of the American Oriental Society, Vol. 88, No. 3, 4. New Haven (U.S.A.), September, 1968.

Journal of Ganga Nath Jha Research Institute, Vol. XXII, Parts 1-2, Vol. XXIV, Pts. 1-4. Vol. XXVI, Pts. 1-3. Allahabad, 1965-70.

Kalyana, Hindu Sanskriti Visheshanka, Vol. 24, No. 1. (Gorakhpur, Gita Press, 1950).

Modern Review, CXXVII, No. 4. Calcutta, 1970.

Mysore Orientalist, Vol. II, No.2. Mysore, 1969.

Philosophical Quarterly, Andrews University Andrews, October, 1960.

Philosophy, London, Macmillan, July, 1960.

Philosophy : East and West, Vol. XIX, No. 2. Hawaii, April, 1969.

Philosophy : East and West, Vol. XX, No. 1. Hawaii, January, 1970.

Problems of Communism, Vol. XVII, No. 3, 5, Vol. XVIII, No. 4-5. Vol.XIX, No. 5, 6. Vol. XXI, No. 5, Vol, XXII, No. 2. Washington, March-April, 1968-73.

Purana, XI, No. 2, Varanasi, 1969.

Sharda Pitha Pradipa X, No. 1. Dwarka, 1970.

Sodha Patrika, XX, No. 2. Udaipur, 1969.

Soviet Research, No. 2. Summer, 1954.

Soviet Survey, No. 33. July-September, 1960.

Vishveshvaranand Indo'ogical Journal Vol. II, Part 1. Vol. VII, Pts. 1-2. Hoshiarpur, 1964, 1969.

Wiener Zeitschrift fur die Kunde Sudund Ostasieus and Archiv fur Indische Philosophia, Vol. XII-XIII, 1968. West Germany, 1969.

World Buddhism, XIX, No. 5. Colombo (Ceylon), 1970.

INDEX

Academy of Berlin 1825-26, Proceedings, 252
Afanasyev, V., 3, 4, 118, 147, 257, 258, 264
Against Religion and Mammon, 12-15
A Heuristic Ideal, 196-7
A life-affirming Philosophy, 71-3
Allen, C.K., 198
An Essay on the Principles of Population, 90
Anāsakti a Remedy for Modern Problems, 44-5
Anāsakti Yoga, Social Philosophy, 43-5
Argentina, 10
Aristotle, 82, 149
Arnold, Edwin, 102
Artha, 186-8
Attitude towards Capitalists, 247-8

Baax, 217
Bahm, A.J., 39, 41
Beard, 81
Bentham, 64, 92, 145
Berdyaev, 208
Besant, Annie, 40
Betai, Ramesh, 44, 102
Bhagavadgītā, 95
Bid to Perfection, 192-4
Bonar, James, 81, 211, 216
Borodulina, T., 19
Bradley, F.H., 68, 209, 221
Brahma Nirvan, Meaning, 46-58
Brahma Sūtras, 38
British idealists, 268
British Rule, 99
Buber, Martin, 20

Carlyle, 7
Carr, E.H., 139
Cassirer, F., 41
Chesnokov, D., 19, 163, 206
Classes and Division of Labour, 165-6
Classless Society under Communism, 163-75
Cohen, M.R., 82
Communism, a Society of Abundance, 180
Communism, Ethics, 19-32
Communism, Sovietization, 5-6
Communist ideal as Economic Emancipation, 181
Communist Menifesto, 184, 202, 205, 206, 248
Communist Social Order, 106-19
Communist Society, Inner Dynamics, 117-18
Communist theoreticians, 164
Comte, 40, 123
Concept of Real Freedom, 250-51
Concept of Social Justice, 136-52
Conclusion, 259-69
Condemnation of Profit Motive, 247
Confluence and the Divergence, 244-70
Confusion about dialectic, 238-43
Conservatism, 238
Cooper, R., 84
Criticism of Profit Motive, 249-50
Critique of Gotha Programme, 143
Critique of Political Economy, 85
Cultural Influences on Gandhi's commentary, 96-7

Dange, S.A., 97
Darwin, Laws, 92
Das Capital, 4, 203, 251
Dasgupta, S.N., 39, 220
Deductive Incompleteness, 237-8
Democracy, Moral Basis, 126-8
Democracy of the Enlightened, 125-33
Deontological vs. Teleological Criterion, 225-7
Detachment vs. The Philosophy of Attachment Asākti, 208-14
Deterrence vs. Corrective Theory, 219-21
Dharma, 182-6

Dharma, Concept, 73-5
Dharma as Regulative Principle, 197-9
Dichotomy of appearance and reality, 235-6
Dictatorship, a Moral and Social Evil, 229-31
Disgust with Machines, 169-71
Dissatisfaction with the Present Form of Existence, 20
Distribution of Happiness, 145-7
Distributive Justice and Communism, 138-41
Durkheim, 74, 124, 155

Economic and Philosophic Manuscript of 1844, 14
Economic Equality, Myth, 144-5
Economic foundations, 204
Economic Interpretation, Meaning, 15-19
End of Private Property, 116-7
England, 89, 99, 101
English Political Economy, Influence, 89-93
Engels, F., 6-7, 15, 18, 21, 30. 83-86, 91, 92, 109, 111-12, 114, 139-42, 146-4, 163, 166, 168, 173, 174, 181, 199, 203, 212, 219, 227, 255, 257
Environmentalism and Individual's Self-improvement, 214-19
Equality is Spiritual, 147
Essay on Demography, 92
Essence of Christainity, 40, 86, 120
Europe, 2
Evil, Nature, 21
Ewing, 221

Faith in Ultimate Victory, 248-9
Fallacy of Unproved premises, 240
Feuerbach, Ludwig, 40, 43, 48, 82, 86, 89, 120, 245, 252
Fedo, 160
Fedotov, 157
Finishing the Division of Labour, 166-7
Fisher, 237
Fourier, St. Simon, 82, 140
France, 84
Freedom and Responsibility, 231-43
French Socialists, 249
Freud, 39, 63-4, 189

Gandhi, M.K., 38, 40, 41-4, 47, 54, 60, 65, 70, 73, 75, 95, 100, 101-2, 131, 156, 184, 189
Gandhian Anāsakti Yoga, 44
Social Philosophy, 44
Gasset, Ortega, 231
German Classical Philosophy, 82, 85
German Classical Idealists, 268
German Ideology, 29, 65, 174
Germany, 251
Greek mythologies, 12
Giddens, Anthony, 164, 167-8
Ginsberg, Morris, 129, 137-8, 190, 198
Gita of Our Times, 41-2
Gita, Philosophical Doctrines, 45-6
Symbolic Meaning, 42-3
Gita's Anāsakti Yoga, Ethical Doctrines, 58-73
Glezerman, G., 19
Gokhale, B.G., 182, 186
Gopi, 41
Gotha Programme, 112, 113
Greed Dehumanizing Effects, 8-12
Greek Mythology, 254
Green, 33

Hartmann, 258
Hartshom, 84, 122, 161
Hearnshaw, 147
Hedonism, Critism, 63
Hegel, G.W.F., 16, 18, 31, 53, 57-8, 82, 93, 107, 109, 113, 120, 171, 175, 227, 239, 252, 257
Hegal and Feuerbach, 84-9
Hegelian Philosophy, 93
Hegel's Philosophy of Right, 171
Heidegger, Martin, 22, 48
Hindu ethics, 126, 187
Historical Materialism, 19
Hook, Sidney, 20, 84, 139
Horney, Karen, 2, 22, 23, 53
Human Bondage and Release, Nature, 25-8
Human Fall, Dynamics, 62-3
Human Life, Ideals, 178-201
Human Progress, Ethical Basis, 202-23
Humboldt, 252
Hume, 122
Huxley, Aldous, 154

Ideal More Significant than Actual, 178-81
Ideal Social Order accorting to Gita, 119-24
Ideal Society, 156
Ideals of Human Life in Gita, 182-97
India, 1, 93, 97, 120, 208, 251
India, Cultural Life, 40, 43, 100, 182
Indian ethics, 148
Indian Mythologies, 12
Indian Philosophy, 2, 39, 53, 72, 83, 95, 182, 189, 191
Indian Renaissance, 98-101
Indian Social Thought, 154
Society, 38, 39
Thinkers, 232
Individual Self-Improvement, 217-9

Indo-Gangetic Plane, 146
Influences of Classical Materialism, 82-4
Influence of Gita on Gandhi, 44
Isopaniṣad, 131

Jibran, Khalil, 40
Jīva Brahman and Prākriti, 244-59
Jīva, Nature, 55-8
Johnson, A.M., 196, 229
Justice and Dharma, 137-8
Justice and Svadharma, 149-51

Kama, 188-90
Kant, Immanuel, 47, 52, 56, 60, 67, 109, 118, 147,185, 225, 239
Karma, Doctrine, 68-70
Karma; Law, 70
Kautilya, 187
Kautskf, 179, 216
Kierkegaard, 53, 58
Kinds of freedoms, 232-4
Kolarz, Walter, 19
Kṛṣṇa, 151, 183
Kursanov, G., 19

Laski, 139
Lenin, V. I., 6, 82, 84, 92, 97, 111, 165, 179, 190, 202, 219, 242
Lewis, 69
Liberation from Alienated Existence, 28-32
Life Affirming Scheme, 190-1
Lindsay, A.G., 139
Locke, 82
Lowith, Karl, 8
Luther, 9

Macaulay, 98
Machiavelli, 82, 110
Mackenzie, J.S., 33, 122, 149, 193, 198, 209, 220, 230
Madhavacarya, 95
Madis, James, 82
Mahābhārata, 48, 119, 120, 129, 183, 235
Maitra, 191
Malthus, 90
Man and Divine, Identity, 52-5
Man, Concept, 23-5
Man, Socialization, 115-6
Mangles, 98
Manuscripts, 1844, 207
Marcuse, Herbert, 15
Marx, K., 2, 3, 4, 7-34, 42, 59, 64, 68, 72, 75, 82-4, 86, 88-9, 91, 97, 99, 107-11, 113, 115-9, 130-1, 139, 141-4, 146-7, 163, 164-74, 179-81, 188, 192, 195, 197, 199, 202-5, 206-8, 214-5, 224, 231, 234, 239, 245, 247, 248, 250, 255-6
Marxian Concept of Wealth, 147
Marxism, impact, 97
Marxist view of Society, 123
Material Basis of Progress examined, 210-4
Materialism and Empirio-Criticism, 6
Mayo, 228-9
McIver, 41, 123, 156, 158, 163, 220
Means-End Harmoney, 224-5
Mill, 54, 64, 92, 114, 115, 145, 216
Milne, A.J.M., 74, 123, 124, 159, 185, 198, 225
Minute on Education, 98
Mises, 255
Modern Psychotherapy, 192
Mokṣa, 191-7
Montague, Ashlay, 220
Moral Basis of Civilization, 209-10
Moral Freedom, Concept, 70-1
Moral Grounds of Revolution, 248
Moral Positivism, 141-2
Muirhead, 125

Nature and Prakṛti, 246
Need for Ethical Approach, 1-3
Negative Description, 239
New Look at Communism, 1-37
No Communist Influence, 97-8
Northrop, F.C.S., 5
Not merely Economics, 6-8

On Jewish Question, 11
Organic Theory, 122-4
Other Influences on Ghandhi, 101-3
Owen, Robert, 140

Penchant for Dictatorship in Marlism, 227-31
Petersen, 81
Phenomenology of Mind, 85
Philosophical and Cultural Influences, 80-105
Political revolution, no solution of egoism, 236
Pope, Alexander, 128
Popper, Karl, 118, 173, 226, 230, 254
Poverty of Philosophy, 202
Prabhu, 156, 186, 191
Private Property, 130-3
Probable Impact of Gita on Marx, 251-9
Process of historical Progress, 205
Progress not a historical necessity, 237
Proletariat class, 171-2
Proletariat, Dictatorship, 111-13
Proudhan, 148
Psycho-Social Efficacy of Varṇa, 156-8

Radhakrishnan, S., 43, 50, 53, 59, 60, 63, 66, 74, 121, 125, 131, 150, 155, 157, 179, 180, 183-4, 189, 193, 209, 213, 252
Ramanuja, 94
Rashdall, H., 33, 67, 68, 145, 146, 158, 160, 186, 188, 220
Ricardo, 90
Role of Mental Factors in production, 236-7
Roll, Eric, 84, 212
Role of Specialization, 167-9
Royal Enquiry Commission, 10
Ruskin, 101, 102
Russell, 136, 186
Russia, 6
Russian ideology, 97

Sabine, 6
Saint-Simon, 140
Salmond, 132
Saṁkara, 40, 52, 57, 94
Sanyal, Sachindranath, 102
Sardesai, 98
Sarma, 100
Saraswati, Madhusudan, 94
Sartre, J.P., 48, 52, 56, 58, 60, 71, 185, 217
Saundarya Lahari, 189
Schlegel, August Wilhelm Von, 252
Schumpetr, 81, 210
Schwitzer, 213, 258
Self-Realization Theory, 32-4
Sidgwick, 67, 69, 115
Smith, Adam, 8, 11, 28, 89, 90
Social Justice and Equality in Gita, 147-51
Social Philosophers, 196
Society, Divine Nature, 124
Socio-Cultural Influences on the Modern Committee of Gita, 93-103
Socio-Political Institutions, 118-9
Son of Man, 40
Sorokin, P.A., 1, 100, 121
Source of egoistic need, 235
Soviet Scholar, 143
Spengler, Oswald, 5, 208
Sri Aurobindo, 95, 96, 99
Stalin, 146
Standard in Ethics, 33
Stark, Werner, 179
State Authority, Nature, 128
Svadharma and Varṇas, 158-9
Swami Daya Nand, 99

Tagore, Rabindra Nath, 48, 99
Tantric, Sāktism, 43
The Brave New World, 154
The Cambridge History of India, 98
The Class Struggle in France, 111
The Critique of Political Economy, 6
The Elementary Forms of Religious Life, 124
The French Working Class, 84
The Holy Family, 32
The Ideal Social Order, 106-35
The Logical Influence of Hegal on Marx, 84
The Origin of Species, 92
The Proletariat, 250
The Teleological Approach, 179-80
Theory and Practice, 246-7
The rapists of Freudian/Jungian School, 22
Tilak, 40, 95
Timons, of Athens, 27
Titus, H.H., 125, 126
Toynee, Arnold, 81, 99
Tucker, Robert, 9, 13, 14, 16, 25, 34, 42, 45, 53, 85, 123, 144, 175, 179, 195, 250

Uddalaka, 49
Uniformity not tenable. 154-6
Unity with Mankind, 180-1
Upaniṣad, Bṛahadāraṇyaka, 47, 50, 121
  Chāndogya, 42, 121
  Kaṭha, 55
  Māṇdūkya, 121
  Muṇdaka, 55
  'Svetāṣvatara, 55
  Taittirīya, 49

Vaiśeṣika Sutra, 182
Vallabha, 94
Various commentaries on Gita, 93-6
Various Interpretation of Gita, 93-6
Varna 160-1
Varṇa and Caste, 156
Varṇa and Division of Powers, 161
Varṇa Vyavasthā, 153-63
Varṇa, Vyavastha and Classless Society, 172-75
Visāvasāra tantra, 43
Vivekanand, 99
Vulgar Marxists, 26

Way to Release, 65-8
Wealth of Nation, 89
Wester mark, 183
Western Materialistic philosophy, 82
Western Psychologists, 157
Western thinkers, 2, 53
Weydemeyer, 164
Wealth of Nations, 28
What is a Class, 164-5
What is a Communism, 3-19
What is State, 113-4
Whitehead, A.N., 154, 214, 216, 246
Yamunācārya, 95